Popular Mechanics
WORKSHOP

Outdoor Woodworking

Popular Mechanics WORKSHOP

Outdoor Woodworking

Hearst Books
A Division of Sterling Publishing Co., Inc.
New York

POPULAR MECHANICS WORKSHOP
OUTDOOR WOODWORKING

Produced by Spooky Cheetah Press • www.spookycheetah.com
Design: Art Gecko Studios! • www.artgeckostudios.com

Library of Congress Cataloging-in-Publication Data
Popular Mechanics Workshop: Outdoor Woodworking.
p. cm.
Includes index.
ISBN 1-58816-284-2
1. Outdoor furniture. 2. Furniture making. 3. Garden ornaments and furniture—Design and construction.
I. Title: Outdoor woodworking. II. Popular mechanics (Chicago, Ill.: 1959)

TT197.5.o9P665 2003
749'.8--dc22
2003057108

10 9 8 7 6 5 4 3 2 1

Published by Hearst Books,
A Division of Sterling Publishing Co., Inc.
387 Park Avenue South, New York, N.Y. 10016

Popular Mechanics is a trademark owned by Hearst Magazines Property, Inc., in USA, and Hearst Communications, Inc., in Canada. Hearst Books is a trademark owned by Hearst Communications, Inc.

www.popularmechanics.com

Distributed in Canada by Sterling Publishing
c/o Canadian Manda Group, One Atlantic Avenue, Suite 105
Toronto, Ontario, Canada M6K 3E7

Distributed in Australia by Capricorn Link (Australia) Pty. Ltd.
P.O. Box 704, Windsor, NSW 2756 Australia

Manufactured in China

ISBN 1-58816-284-2

Contents

Foreword

Improving outdoor space is easy when you complement it with the beauty of wood structures built by your own hand. Whether it's a sturdy two-tier deck that adds a whole new aspect to a bare backyard, or a classic redwood recliner that makes sunbathing even more pleasurable, woodworking projects bring something special and lasting to your yard, garden, and home exterior. To provide you with the most options, we've selected projects ranging from small—a simple porch planter—to large—a "backyard barn." But regardless of size, all of these projects share the ability to increase your enjoyment of the outdoor space around your home, and they all offer ways to expand your woodworking skills and experience. As is the case with all outdoor projects, preparation is key. You'll want to make sure your skill level matches that required for the project. Few things are as frustrating as realizing—too late—that you're in over your head. And when we suggest one or two helpers, we mean it. Going it alone increases the time a project takes, but more importantly, it increases the risk of injury associated with lifting heavy lumber or working with power tools on unwieldy structures. Enlist as much help as you can and the work will not only go faster, it will be more fun as well. Finally, remember: A little rain can make for a messy worksite and ruin tools and equipment. So check the forecast and always have a small, dry staging area set aside in case of a surprise shower. With a little nice weather and the help of *Popular Mechanics*, you'll ensure that the outside of your house is every bit as beautiful as the inside!

Joe Oldham
Editor-in-Chief
Popular Mechanics

Decks and Structures

Garden Hideaway

This trellis with seating is the perfect garden escape from the pressures of the outside world.

What makes your backyard special? If you're lucky, you already have a luscious lawn and a few well-placed shrubs and trees—and the garden gets better every year. However, if you really want to add a touch of luxury and distinction to your backyard landscape, accent your grounds with an elegant wooden trellis. Our version is built of clear red cedar and features lattice side panels that are perfect for supporting vines or flowers. Unlike a deck, our structure is freestanding—you can reposition it as inspiration dictates, or easily remove it if your backyard plans change.

*Key*POINTS

TIME

Prep Time	7 hours
Shop Time	20 hours
Assembly Time	20 hours

EFFORT

Skill Level	intermediate
Maintenance	none
Assistance	none

COST / BENEFITS

Expense: moderate
- Great garden structure that **can support climbing plants**.
- **Moveable** yard or garden feature that can go with you if you change residences.

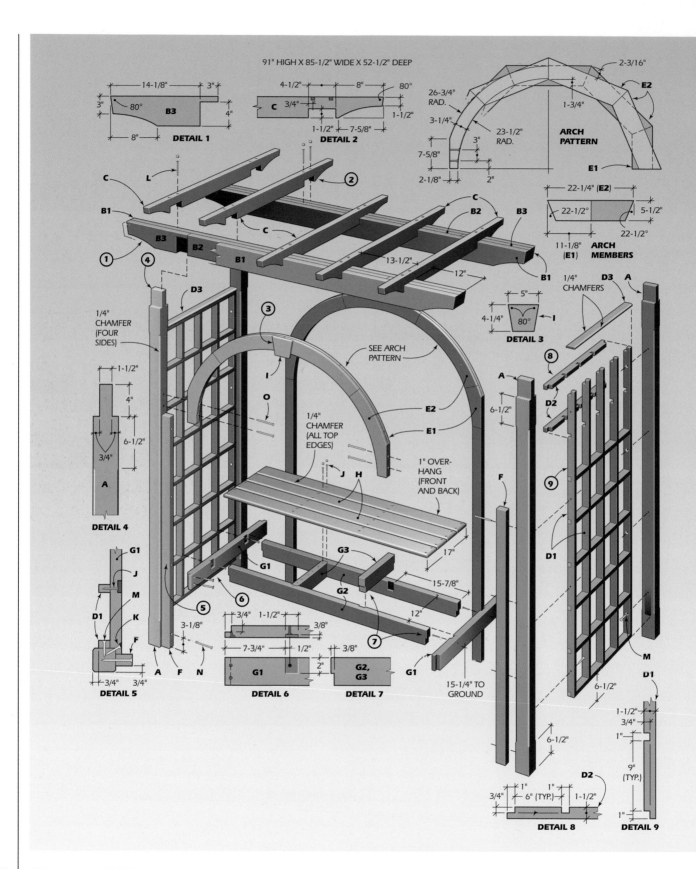

91" HIGH X 85-1/2" WIDE X 52-1/2" DEEP

DETAIL 1
14-1/8"   3"
3"   80°   B3   4"
8"

DETAIL 2
4-1/2"   8"   80°
C   3/4"   1-1/2"
1-1/2"   7-5/8"

ARCH PATTERN
26-3/4" RAD.
3-1/4"
23-1/2" RAD.
7-5/8"
3"
2-1/8"   2"
2-3/16"
E2
1-3/4"
E1

ARCH MEMBERS
22-1/4" (E2)
22-1/2°
22-1/2°
5-1/2"
11-1/8" (E1)

C   L
B1
B3   B2
B1
①   ④   B3   B2
②
B1
C
C
B2   B3
13-1/2"
12"
B1

DETAIL 3
5"
4-1/4"   80°
I

1/4" CHAMFERS
D3   A
⑧
D2
A
6-1/2"
F
⑨
D1

1/4" CHAMFER (FOUR SIDES)
D3
③
I
O
SEE ARCH PATTERN
1/4" CHAMFER (ALL TOP EDGES)
E2
E1
1" OVERHANG (FRONT AND BACK)

DETAIL 4
1-1/2"
4"
6-1/2"
3/4"
A

J   H
⑤   ⑥
G1
G2
G3
15-7/8"
12"
G1
17"
15-1/4" TO GROUND

DETAIL 5
G1
J
M
D1
K
F
A   F   N
3/4"   3/4"

DETAIL 6
3/4"   1-1/2"   3/8"
7-3/4"   1/2"   3/8"
2"
G1

DETAIL 7
G2, G3

⑦

D1
6-1/2"

M
6-1/2"

DETAIL 8
3/4"   1"   1"   1-1/2"
6" (TYP.)

DETAIL 9
D1
1-1/2"
3/4"
1"
9" (TYP.)
1"
D2

We've equipped our trellis with a bench, making it a great place to relax and enjoy a warm summer afternoon. If you decide to do without the bench, the trellis becomes an elegant arched gateway to your garden.

For good glue joints, it's important that you start with lumber that's not too wet. To avoid problems, buy your wood at least a few weeks before starting the project. Stack the lumber in your garage or basement, with spacers between layers, and aim a fan at the pile. For the best durability, be sure to use water-resistant exterior glue for assembly.

Posts and Top Frame

Reduce the 4x4 cedar posts to 3 in. square with either a thickness planer or by ripping with a band saw. Crosscut them to length and use a dado blade in your table saw to cut the tenon at the end of each post (**Fig. 1**). Mark the ends of the stopped chamfers on the posts and rout the chamfers (**Fig. 2**).

Make each of the two top beams by gluing up three layers of 1½ x 5-in. stock. To avoid cutting traditional mortises for the post tenons, make each center layer from three separate pieces as shown in the drawing. Precisely cut a notch in each inner end-beam segment to form the mortises in the assembled beams.

Apply glue to the mating faces for one beam, then place the center layer on one of the outer boards. Use screws to keep the pieces from shifting (**Fig. 3**). Place the third layer into position and clamp it (**Fig. 4**). Then assemble the second beam in the same way.

Make a template for the end shape of the top beams and trace the shape onto the beams. Use a band saw to cut the beam ends. Follow the same procedure for the stretcher ends.

Lay out the notches along the bottom edges of the

Fig. 1 *Use a dado blade to cut the post tenons. Clamp a stop block to the saw table to ensure consistent shoulder cuts.*

Fig. 2 *Mark the stopped-chamfer end points on the cedar posts, and then rout the corners using a chamfer bit in the router.*

Materials List

Key	No.	Size and description (use)
A	4	3 x 3 x 88" cedar (post)
B1	4	1½ x 5 x 85½" cedar (outer beam)
B2	2	1½ x 5 x 51¼" cedar (inner beam)
B3	4	1½ x 5 x 17⅛" cedar (inner end beam)
C	5	1½ x 3½ x 52½" cedar (stretcher)
D1	10	1 x 1½ x 71" cedar (vertical lattice)
D2	16	1 x 1½ x 29" cedar (horizontal lattice)
D3	2	½ x 2 x 29" cedar (lattice cap)
E1	4	¾ x 5½ x 11⅛" cedar (arch segment)
E2	14	¾ x 5½ x 22¼" cedar (arch segment)
F	4	1½ x 2⅛ x 57¼" cedar (arch support)
G1	2	1½ x 3½ x 30½" cedar (bench cleat)
G2	2	1½ x 3½ x 50½" cedar (bench apron)
G3	2	1½ x 3½ x 12¾" cedar (bench rail)
H	4	¾ x 4 x 52¾" cedar (slat)
I	2	¾ x 4¼ x 5" cedar (keystone)
J	36	1½" No. 8 fh deck screw and plug
K	16	2½" No. 10 fh deck screw
L	20	3" No. 10 fh deck screw and plug
M	16	2" No. 10 fh brass screw
N	16	3½" No. 10 fh brass screw
O	8	4" No. 10 fh brass screw

Misc.: Exterior glue; clear decking stain.

stretchers and use a dado blade to make the cuts. Bore screw pilot holes and plug counterbores in one operation with a combination bit. Then fasten the stretchers to the beams with screws (**Fig. 5**).

Use a plug cutter in the drill press to make plugs and install them over the screws. When the glue dries on the plugs, cut them off and pare them flush with a sharp chisel.

Lattice Construction

Rip and crosscut the lattice frame parts to finished size. Clamp together like-size pieces for each frame and lay out the half-lap joints. Use a dado blade in the table saw to make the cuts (**Fig. 6**). Bore and countersink the screw holes on the outside vertical pieces.

Lay out all parts for one of the lattice sections and spread glue on the joints. Assemble the frame and apply spring clamps to each half-lap joint (**Fig. 7**).

Fig. 3 *Cut notches from the end inner pieces to form the mortises. Apply exterior glue and use screws to hold the parts in place.*

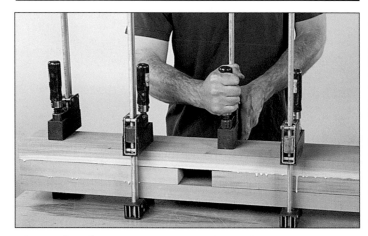

Fig. 4 *Glue the remaining outer beam layer to the center pieces. After you're done, leave the clamps in place for at least 1 hour.*

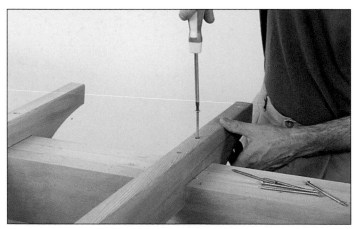

Fig. 5 *After you're finished cutting the notches in the stretchers, bore the screw holes. Then secure the stretchers to the beams.*

Fig. 6 *Cut the lattice parts to size and clamp the pieces that are the same size together. Then cut the notches with a dado blade.*

Fig. 7 *Apply exterior glue to the lattice joints and assemble the grid. Spring clamps are ideal for holding the joints until the glue sets.*

Fig. 8 *Spread glue on both the cap and top end of the lattice grid, and then clamp the cap in place. The cap overhang is ¼ in.*

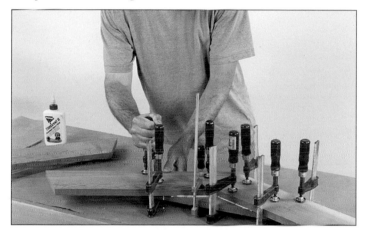

Fig. 9 *Carefully glue together the staggered layers that make up each arch blank. Assemble each of these blanks in stages.*

Fig. 10 *Make a simple beam compass to precisely lay out the arch shape on panel stock. Then cut to the line with a sabre saw.*

When you're done, compare opposite diagonal measurements on this grid to make sure that the assembly is truly square.

With both frames built, cut the caps to size and chamfer the top edges. Spread glue on the top end of each lattice and on its cap, then clamp the parts together (**Fig. 8**).

Place a post on the worktable and position one of the frames on it. Mark and bore screw pilot holes into the post. Fasten the lattice to the post with brass screws. Screw the opposite post to the frame and repeat the procedure for the other side of the trellis.

Building the Arches

Each arch is constructed of two overlapping layers of mitered segments. The joints of each layer fall on the centerlines of the segments on the adjacent layer. Begin by cutting 1x6 stock to length with 22½°-angled ends. Note that

Fig. 11 *Clamp the arch pattern to a glued-up blank and trace the shape. Next, mark the straight cuts on the arch ends.*

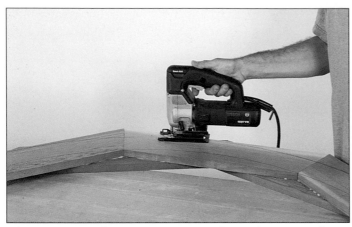

Fig. 12 *Use a sabre saw to cut out the arch. Cut on the waste side of the line and smooth the arch with 100-grit sandpaper.*

Fig. 13 *Dry assemble the trellis upside down. After inserting the posts in the top frame, bore screw holes and attach the arches.*

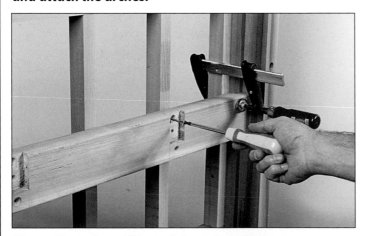

Fig. 14 *Turn the trellis upright to install the seat frame parts. Then disassemble the trellis and take it to the site for installation.*

the end segments of one layer are half the length of the regular segments, and these have one square end.

Mark the centerline on one segment, and then place two segments over it, allowing the spacing indicated in the drawing. Mark the outline of the top pieces on the segment below. Then spread glue on the mating surfaces, reposition the parts, and clamp them together (**Fig. 9**). When the glue has set, add the next two segments, and continue in this manner until the arch is complete.

With both arches assembled, create a template for the arch shape. First make a beam compass from a roughly 32-in.-long board and a dowel.

Bore a hole for the dowel at one end of the board, and bore a matching hole in the template panel that defines the center of the arch. Next, measure the inner and outer arch radii from the dowel hole on the board, and bore holes for a pencil at those marks. Use the beam compass to scribe the arch on the template stock (**Fig. 10**) and then cut to the lines with a sabre saw to finish the template.

Clamp the template to one of the arch blanks and trace the outline (**Fig. 11**). Lay out the straight cuts where the arches join the posts. Cut out each arch with a sabre saw (**Fig. 12**), and sand the sawn surfaces.

Cut the arch supports to size. Lay out the screw holes for both the arches and the supports, then bore and countersink the holes.

Assembly and Finishing

Preassemble the trellis in the shop. Begin by laying the top assembly upside down. Slide the post-and-lattice assemblies into place and check their fit. Next, position the arches and

TECH *Tips*

Out of the Windup
Boards are sometimes warped so subtly that the warp can be hard to see. But even a minor warp can put a workpiece out of square or throw the spacing of other pieces out of whack. Experienced woodworkers check their boards with "winding sticks." These basic but handy measuring devices are simply two thin boards usually twice as long as the piece being checked. Set the board across a pair of sawhorses or a flat surface you are sure is square, and set the winding sticks at either end of the board, perpendicular to it. Now sight across the sticks—if the edges do not align, the board you are checking is warped.

MATERIAL*Matters*

Dealing with Defects

Imperfections are a part of the process when you're working with wood. Some are critical and need to be corrected or removed to make the wood usable; other imperfections can be carefully incorporated into a project, increasing its beauty without destroying structural integrity. When in doubt, you should remove the imperfection. Here are a few of the defects you might come across, and guidelines for dealing with them:

Wormholes: *These small holes in the wood are caused, obviously, by worms. Generally, you'll want to remove the affected portions of the wood. In some cases, though, this defect can provide an interesting visual effect—given that you ensure that the insects are dead and the wood has been completely dried.*

Knots: *You'll encounter two types of knots, those that are still integral to the piece of wood (their pattern is seamlessly integrated with the grain swirl of the surface), and loose knots in which there is a small or large physical separation between the knot and the surrounding wood (you'll often be able to move them or see through the board). Sections of wood with loose knots should be removed entirely, but integral knots are another story. Experienced woodworkers can incorporate certain knots into the workpiece, creating beautiful surface patterns. If you're sure that the knot is stable and you like the pattern, consider using it. If, however, you have any doubts about it's stability, remove the section of wood.*

Crooking: *This is warping along the edge of a board. If it's subtle, it's hard to detect ... until you incorporate it into your project alongside other boards, where it will stick out like a sore thumb. If the crook isn't severe, cut off the high points with a saw, jointer, or plane. If it's fairly pronounced, cut the board down to smaller stock. Be sure to age the newly cut boards though, because crooking is generally a result of the location in the tree from which the board was cut. Unless cured correctly, the smaller board may crook as well.*

Twisting: *Sometimes torsional forces within the board conspire to pull alternate corners up toward each other. This effect makes it extremely difficult to work with the board. You can cut it into shorter and thinner boards, or remove the high spots where the effect is modest. But if the twist is severe, you shouldn't use the board at all.*

Bowing: *Like crooking, only the deformity is end to end rather than side to side. This is fairly easy to detect. In serious cases, you have no choice but to cut the board into smaller boards. Where the effect is light, you can joint or plane the board level.*

Splitting: *These cracks along the end of the board are the result of drying too quickly, and should be cut off to avoid further splitting up the board.*

Sap: *This is sticky resin left over from a trauma to the tree. This substance can bleed through just about any finish, and should be scraped off or removed prior to working with the board.*

---

bore pilot holes into the posts. Fasten the arches with screws (**Fig. 13**) and then attach the vertical supports.

Cut the bench parts to size. Use your table saw and a dado blade to cut the notches in the ends of the aprons and rails, and readjust the blade to cut the notches on the bench-support cleats. Lay out the stopped dadoes in the cleats and aprons and use a Forstner bit to bore out most of the waste. Finish the joints with a sharp chisel.

Turn the trellis upright, screw the bench cleats to the lattice assemblies (**Fig. 14**), and test fit the bench frame. Cut the seat slats to size and rout the chamfer on the top edges of the slats.

With the dry run complete, disassemble the trellis and take the parts to the site. Reassemble the trellis using glue at the top mortise-and-tenon joints. Make sure that the posts are square to the beams while the glue sets.

Reattach the bench cleats with screws. Then glue the bench frame to the cleats. Lay out the bench slats and bore the holes for screws and plugs. Screw the slats to the frame and plug the holes. Cut the keystone blocks then glue and clamp them to the arches. Finally, apply one coat of clear decking stain.

Super Shed

This shed provides a dedicated space that won't detract from the beauty of your plants.

Not everyone needs a garden shed. But if you've got no more space on your garage wall for that new leaf rake, or you can't find the potting trowel because it fell behind the kids' bikes, it's time to face the undeniable truth—your gardening tools and supplies need a place of their own. The design of your garden shed can take any form, from a simple lean-to, to a large, detailed, freestanding building. Our shed occupies a very modest 6 x 8 ft. area—enough for a variety of tools, bags of peat moss, and seed trays, but not so much that the structure becomes an eyesore.

*Key*POINTS

TIME
Prep Time	4 hours
Shop Time	8 hours
Assembly Time	24 hours

EFFORT
Skill Level	intermediate
Maintenance	none
Assistance	one

COST / BENEFITS
Expense: moderate
• Handy shed that **blends** with other garden features.
• Durable outbuilding that **will age well**.

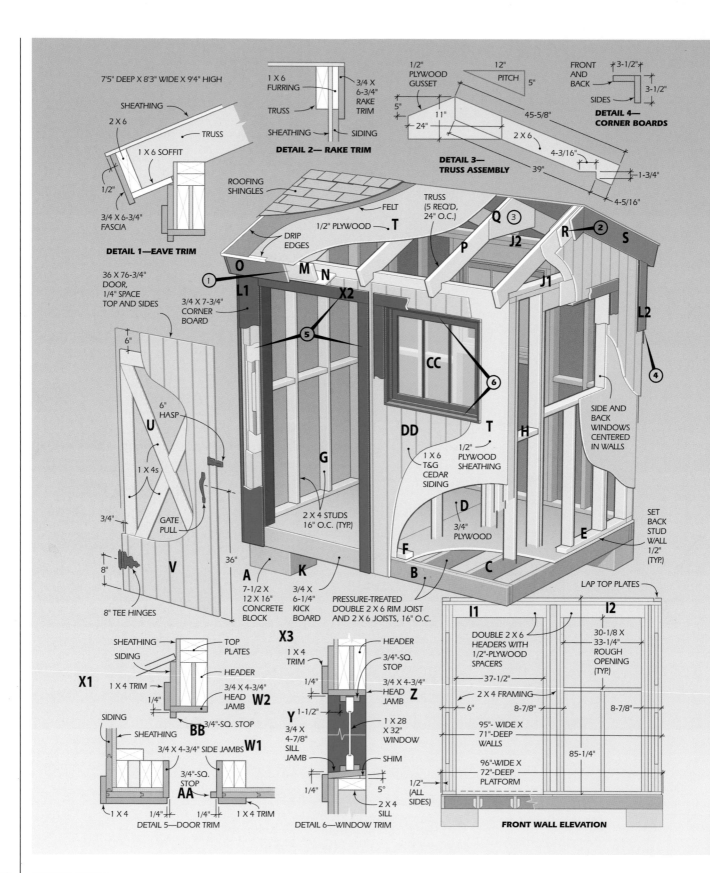

7'5" DEEP X 8'3" WIDE X 9'4" HIGH

SHEATHING
2 X 6
TRUSS
1 X 6 SOFFIT
1/2"
3/4 X 6-3/4"
FASCIA

DETAIL 1—EAVE TRIM

1 X 6 FURRING
TRUSS
SHEATHING
3/4 X 6-3/4" RAKE TRIM
SIDING

DETAIL 2— RAKE TRIM

1/2" PLYWOOD GUSSET
PITCH 12" 5"
5"
11"
24"
45-5/8"
2 X 6
4-3/16"
39"
1-3/4"
4-5/16"

DETAIL 3— TRUSS ASSEMBLY

FRONT AND BACK
SIDES
3-1/2"
3-1/2"

DETAIL 4— CORNER BOARDS

ROOFING SHINGLES
FELT
1/2" PLYWOOD
DRIP EDGES
TRUSS (5 REQ'D, 24" O.C.)

O
M
N
L1
3/4 X 7-3/4" CORNER BOARD
X2
5
P
Q
3
J2
R
2
S
J1
T
L2
4

36 X 76-3/4" DOOR, 1/4" SPACE TOP AND SIDES

6"
6" HASP
1 X 4s
GATE PULL
3/4"
U
V
8"

8" TEE HINGES

36"

A
K
B
C
E

7-1/2 X 12 X 16" CONCRETE BLOCK
3/4 X 6-1/4" KICK BOARD
PRESSURE-TREATED DOUBLE 2 X 6 RIM JOIST AND 2 X 6 JOISTS, 16" O.C.

CC
DD
T
H
G
F
D
2 X 4 STUDS 16" O.C. (TYP.)
1 X 6 T&G CEDAR SIDING
1/2" PLYWOOD SHEATHING
3/4" PLYWOOD

SIDE AND BACK WINDOWS CENTERED IN WALLS

SET BACK STUD WALL 1/2" (TYP.)

LAP TOP PLATES

X1
SHEATHING
SIDING
1 X 4 TRIM
1/4"
SIDING
SHEATHING
1 X 4
1/4"
3/4 X 4-3/4" SIDE JAMBS
3/4"-SQ. STOP
1/4"
1 X 4 TRIM

TOP PLATES
HEADER
3/4 X 4-3/4" HEAD JAMB
W2
3/4"-SQ. STOP
BB
W1
AA

DETAIL 5—DOOR TRIM

X3
1 X 4 TRIM
1/4"
Y
1-1/2"
3/4 X 4-7/8" SILL JAMB
1/4"
HEADER
3/4"-SQ. STOP
3/4 X 4-3/4" HEAD JAMB
Z
1 X 28 X 32" WINDOW
SHIM
5°
2 X 4 SILL

DETAIL 6—WINDOW TRIM

I1
I2
DOUBLE 2 X 6 HEADERS WITH 1/2"-PLYWOOD SPACERS
30-1/8 X 33-1/4" ROUGH OPENING (TYP.)
37-1/2"
2 X 4 FRAMING
6"
8-7/8"
8-7/8"
95"- WIDE X 71"-DEEP WALLS
85-1/4"
96"-WIDE X 72"-DEEP PLATFORM
1/2" (ALL SIDES)

FRONT WALL ELEVATION

This straightforward design is easy to expand—up to about 8 x 12 ft.—to suit your gardening needs. Before you begin work, contact your local building department and find out about any necessary permits or other requirements for this type of building. Our shed uses standard framing techniques and materials. It's sheathed with ½-in. C/D plywood and sided with 1x6 tongue-and-groove cedar boards. The exterior trim is rough-sawn cedar. In most cases, a shed of this size will not require an elaborate foundation—it's fine to simply rest the structure on four corner blocks that sit on the ground. Some excavation is inevitable to provide a level and firm base, but there is really no need to dig below the frost line. If the building settles unevenly, simply jack up a low corner and place cedar shims between the corner block and floor framing. We used 7½ x 12 x 16-in. solid concrete blocks at the corners.

To bring light into our shed, we installed 24 x 32-in. barn-sash windows. If you can't find these stocked at your local home center or lumberyard, you can order them over the Internet.

Site Work

Begin by marking out the building's location in your yard. For a structure of this size, it's simplest to build a lightweight frame that's the exact size of the shed, then use the frame to mark the site.

Use ¾-in.-thick pine to build your frame. Cut the sides to the exact dimensions of the floor, and use one screw in each corner to fasten the sides into a rectangle. Screw a diagonal brace between two sides of the frame to hold it square.

Clear the building site and level any obvious high spots. Place the frame in the site and adjust its position until you're happy with the location of the shed. Drive stakes into the ground to mark each corner, stretch string between them (**Fig. 1**), and then remove the frame.

Find the highest corner of the site and excavate for the first foundation corner block. Plan on having 3 to 4 in. of block exposed above grade. Dig out an area several inches wider than the block. Spread 2 or 3 in. of crushed stone or gravel in the hole to form a stable base for the block.

Now you're ready to position the first block, aligning its edges with the layout string. Check that the block is level across its length and width (**Fig. 2**), and adjust the crushed

Materials List

Key	No.	Size and description (use)
A	4	7½ x 12 x 16" concrete block (foundation blocks)
B	4	2 x 6 x 99" pressure-treated pine (double joist)
C	5	2 x 6 x 81" pressure-treated pine (floor joist)
D	2	¾ x 49½ x 89" plywood (floor)
E	2	2 x 4 x 98½" pine (side sole plate)
F	2	2 x 4 x 80½" pine (sole plate)
G*	35	2 x 4 x 79¼" pine (wall studs)
H	10	2 x 4 x 14" pine (blocking)
I1	2	2 x 6 x 41½" pine (door header)
I2	6	2 x 6 x 37¼" pine (window header)
J1**	4	2 x 4 x 95" pine (top and cap plate)
J2**	4	2 x 4 x 71" pine (top and cap plate)
K	1	¾ x 6¼ x 37½" pressure-treated pine (kick board)
L1	1	¾ x 7¾ x 91¼" cedar (front corner board)
L2	7	¾ x 3½ x 91¼" cedar (corner board)
M	2	2 x 6 x 99" pine (roof ledger)
N	2	1 x 6 x 99" pine (soffit)
O	2	¾ x 6¾ x 99" cedar (fascia)
P	10	2 x 6 x 45⅝" pine (rafter)
Q***	1	½ x 8 x 4" plywood sheet (gusset)
R	4	1 x 6 x 45⅝" pine (rafter)
S	4	¾ x 6¾ x 45⅝" cedar (rake trim)
T***	12	½ x 8 x 4" plywood sheet (roof and wall sheathing)
U***	5	1 x 4 x 64¾" pine (door brace and rail)
V	8	1 x 6 x 76¾" cedar (door panel)
W1	2	¾ x 4¾ x 75¼" pine (side jamb)
W2	1	¾ x 4¾ x 37½" pine (head jamb)
X1	1	1 x 4 x 75¼" cedar (door trim)
X2***	7	1 x 4 x 41½" cedar (trim)
X3	6	1 x 4 x 30⅛" cedar (window trim)
Y	3	¾ x 4⅞ x 33¼" cedar (sill jamb)
Z	3	¾ x 4¾ x 33¼" cedar (window head jamb)
AA	1	¾"-sq. x 75¼" pine (stop)
BB	1	¾"-sq. x 37½" pine (stop)
CC	3	24 x 32" barn sash window
DD*	68	1 x 6 x 112" cedar (siding)

Misc.: Aluminum drip edge; 2-8" tee hinges; shims; gate pull; 6" hasp; roofing felt; shingles; 10 joist hangers; 1½" joist hanger nails; 16d common nails; 8d common nails; 6d common nails.

*Cut to trim windows and door. Use waste pieces as corner spacers.

**Cut alternating pieces to lap.

***Cut to suit.

Fig. 1 *Use a wooden frame to find the best spot for your shed. Drive a stake at each corner and use string to delineate the site.*

Fig. 2 *Dig a hole for the first block at the highest point in the grade. Add gravel, install the block , align it with string, and level it.*

Fig. 3 *Use a straight 2x4 and a 4-ft. level to check that the corner blocks are installed at the same height all the way around.*

Fig. 4 *After marking the joist locations on the long front and rear rim joists, install metal hangers with 1½-in. joist hanger nails.*

stone as required. Use a long, straight 2x4 and level to check the relative height of the second corner, then excavate the site for the block. Check that the second block is level with first (**Fig. 3**) and add the remaining corner blocks in the same way.

Building the Floor

It's a good idea to use pressure-treated lumber for the floor joists. Cut 2x6 stock to length for the front and back rim joists, and then lay out the locations of the floor joists on 16-in. centers. Nail joist hangers to the inside surface of each inner joist using 1½-in. joist hanger nails (**Fig. 4**). Next, place the inner front and back joists between the corner blocks and cut and position the floor joists (**Fig. 5**). Nail the floor joists in place, then attach the outer rim joists to the front and back of the floor frame. Compare opposite diagonal measurements of the floor assembly to check that it's square. Nail ¾-in.-thick plywood to the joists for the shed floor (**Fig. 6**).

Wall Construction

Cut 2x6 stock to size for the door and window headers. Use pieces of ½-in. plywood as spacers between the 2x6s to bring the header assemblies to 3½ in. thick. Nail together the header pieces with 16d common nails.

Cut 2x4 stock to length for the window, wall studs, and door jack studs. Nail each jack stud to a wall stud with 8d common nails. Build the four corner posts by nailing three 2x4 spacers between two studs.

Begin framing the back wall by laying out the stud locations on the top and bottom plates. Then lay out the framing members on the deck (**Fig. 7**). Nail through the top plate and into the wall members, then secure the bottom plate. Frame the window opening, and nail the second top plate to the wall, keeping its ends back 3½ in. from each end of the wall.

Now compare the opposite diagonal measurements of the

Fig. 5 Lay the front and rear joists on the corner blocks. Then cut the joists, position them in the joist hangers, and secure them with nails.

Fig. 6 After doubling the front and rear joists, add the ¾-in. plywood floor. Nail it in place with 8d nails spaced about 6 in. apart.

Fig. 7 With the back wall framing members cut to length and headers assembled, lay out the pieces on the shed floor and join them with nails.

Fig. 8 Install ½-in. plywood wall sheathing on the framed back wall. Then raise the assembly and secure it in place with diagonal braces.

Fig. 9 Frame and raise the remaining walls without sheathing. After nailing together the corner studs, add the top and cap plates.

Fig. 10 When the framing is in place and the assembly is square and plumb, add the remaining plywood sheathing.

Fig. 11 *To find the rafter cutting angle, align the 5- and 12-in. marks on the framing square's legs with the edge of the rafter stock.*

Fig. 12 *Set up a worktable with the outline of the rafter assembly marked. Then join each pair of rafters with a plywood gusset.*

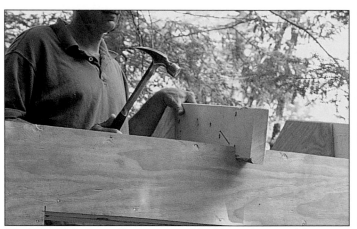

Fig. 13 *With the rafters assembled in pairs, position each pair on the wall cap plates and secure them by toenailing.*

Fig. 14 *Use 1/2-in. plywood for the roof deck and cover it with roofing felt. Install shingles following the manufacturer's instructions.*

wall and adjust the assembly until it's square. Then apply ½-in. plywood sheathing, using 6d common nails spaced about 6 in. apart. Stand the rear wall, bracing it with 2x4s nailed between the wall and the outside floor joists (**Fig. 8**). Nail the bottom plate to the deck so that the plywood sheathing is flush with the edge of the deck.

Frame the front wall, but don't apply the sheathing yet. Instead, stand the framed wall and brace it. Position the wall ½ in. from the deck edges to allow for the thickness of the sheathing. Then frame the side walls, one at a time, and stand them. Leave the cap plate off the side walls until they are raised. Nail the walls together at the corners, and then cut and install the side wall plates (**Fig. 9**).

Use the level to check that the corners of the building are plumb, and nail temporary diagonal braces to the inside surface of each wall.

Apply the remaining plywood sheathing (**Fig. 10**). At the side walls, keep the plywood 1½ in. down from the top to provide room to nail the gable-end sheathing.

Framing the Roof

Use a framing square to lay out the 5-in. pitch on the first roof rafter (**Fig. 11**). Cut out the rafter and use it as a pattern to make the second rafter. Test the first two for proper fit, then trace and cut the remaining rafters.

Cut a gusset for each truss from ½-in.-thick plywood as shown in the plans. Use a sheet of ¾-in plywood as an assembly table, and draw the outline of the roof truss directly on the plywood surface. Align two rafters over the pattern and nail the gusset to the rafters with 1½-in. roofing nails (**Fig. 12**).

Toenail the trusses to the front and rear walls with 8d common nails (**Fig. 13**). At the gable ends, keep the gussets on the inside faces of the trusses.

Cut 2x6 stock to length for the subfascia, and nail the boards to the rafter ends with 16d common nails. Cut and install the gable-end sheathing, and then nail 1x6 pine furring over the gable rafters.

Rip cedar stock to width for the front and back soffits and cut it to length. Use 6d galvanized finishing nails to fasten the soffit boards to the rafters and subfascia. Then install the cedar fascia and rake trim. Install the plywood roof deck, allowing it to overhang the fascia by ½ in. along the eaves. Nail aluminum drip edge to the eaves, and apply roofing felt. Then install the drip edge along the rake edges.

Roofing and Siding

Follow the manufacturer's directions for installing the roof shingles (**Fig. 14**). Because the tongue-and-groove siding is installed vertically, add 2x4 nailing blocks between the studs, about halfway up the wall. Cut and install these nailers by toenailing them between adjacent studs. If you plan to stain or paint the trim a different color than the shed siding, it's a good idea to finish the roof trim before applying the siding. Cut siding boards to length and begin installing them at a corner of the building. Use galvanized finishing nails to fasten the boards—8d nails for fastening the 2x4 framing and 6d nails for the plywood sheathing (**Fig. 15**). Face nail the first board, but fasten succeeding boards with nails driven diagonally through the tongue so that the heads will be hidden. Set the nailheads slightly below the wood surface.

Windows and Doors

After staining or painting the siding, install the door and window jambs (**Fig. 16**). Nail the jambs directly to the framing, with the outside edge of each jamb flush to the face of the siding. At the windows, slope the sill pieces about 5° toward the outside of the building, add the top jambs, and then cut the side jambs to fit.

Cut stops for the windows from 1x cedar stock, and install the outer stops with 6d galvanized finishing nails. Then place a window in each opening and add the inner stops. Rip door and window trim and shed corner boards from rough sawn cedar. Cut each piece to length and nail in place.

Cut siding boards to length for the shed door. Use clamps to pull the boards together, but don't use glue on the joints. Cut the battens for the door, and screw them to the inside surface of the boards.

Hold the door hinges in place and mark the mounting-hole locations. Bore pilot holes and fasten the hinges to the shed. Position the door with a ½-in. space on the sides and top, and mark the hinge holes. Bore pilot holes and mount the hinges (**Fig. 17**). Install the door pull and hasp. Cut the doorstops and nail them in place on the top and open side jamb. Then stain or paint the windows, door, and remaining trim.

We built a ramp from pressure-treated stock to make it easier to wheel a mower or wheelbarrow into the shed. To build a ramp, use 2x6 material spaced about ½ in. apart for the ramp deck, and 2x4 stock for battens underneath.

Fig. 15 *Nail 1x6 tongue-and-groove cedar siding in place. Use 8d nails over wall framing and 6d nails when nailing into plywood alone.*

Fig. 16 *Cut the stock for the doorjambs and nail it in place. At a window, install the angled sill piece first, then the top jamb, then side jambs.*

Fig. 17 *Position the door in its opening with a ½-in. space at the top and sides. Bore pilot holes for the hinge screws and secure the hinges.*

Planter Place

This welcome-home deck provides a place for plants, and adds a lush new face to your home.

The entrances to some homes are very grand and stylish, while others are more functional than impressive. In either case, a home's entrance serves as a bridge from the outdoors to the indoors. It provides a place to greet friends, send children off to school, collect the occasional pizza delivery, and even watch the world go by. But the common tract home or split-level ranch-style structures aren't known for their powerful entryways. This lovely planter deck can change all that with uncommon beauty and style. With the addition of planter boxes, a lovely deck becomes a blooming entryway statement.

*Key*POINTS

TIME
Prep Time	5 hours
Shop Time	10 hours
Assembly Time	30 hours

EFFORT
Skill Level	intermediate
Maintenance	light
Assistance	one-two

COST / BENEFITS
Expense: expensive
- A stunning addition that **adds real value** to your home.
- Create a **front garden** that takes little work and time.

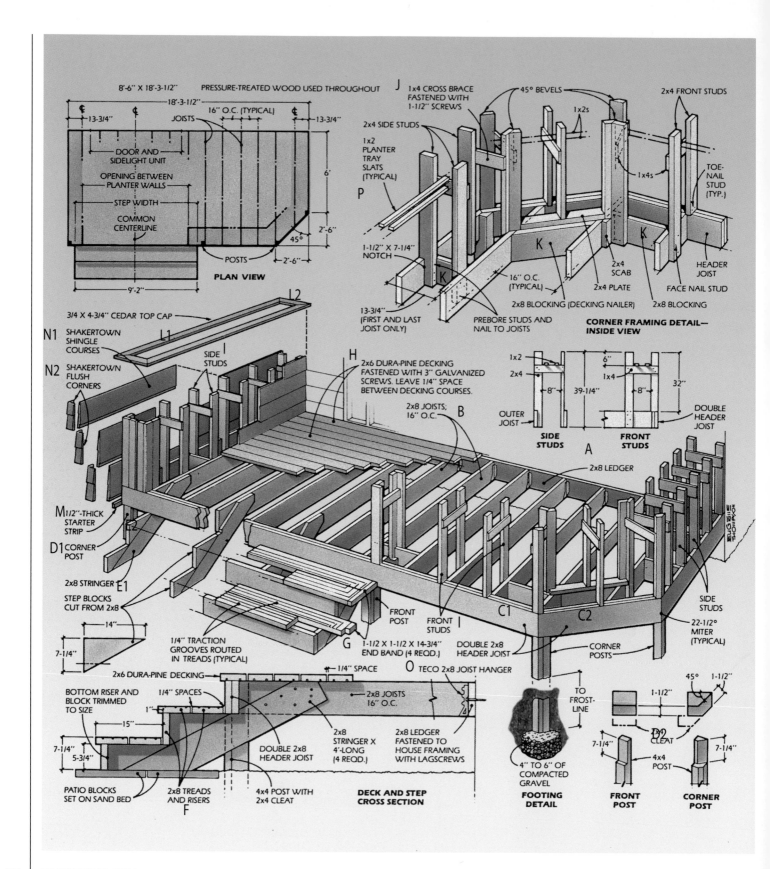

8'-6" X 18'-3-1/2"   PRESSURE-TREATED WOOD USED THROUGHOUT

18'-3-1/2"
13-3/4"   16" O.C. (TYPICAL)   13-3/4"
JOISTS
DOOR AND SIDELIGHT UNIT
OPENING BETWEEN PLANTER WALLS
STEP WIDTH
COMMON CENTERLINE
6'
45°
2'-6"
POSTS
2'-6"
9'-2"

PLAN VIEW

J 1x4 CROSS BRACE FASTENED WITH 1-1/2" SCREWS
45° BEVELS
2x4 FRONT STUDS
2x4 SIDE STUDS
1x2s
1x2 PLANTER TRAY SLATS (TYPICAL)
P
1x4s
TOE-NAIL STUD (TYP.)
1-1/2" X 7-1/4" NOTCH
K
K
13-3/4" (FIRST AND LAST JOIST ONLY)
16" O.C. (TYPICAL)
2x4 SCAB
2x4 PLATE
PREBORE STUDS AND NAIL TO JOISTS
2x8 BLOCKING (DECKING NAILER)
2x8 BLOCKING
HEADER JOIST
FACE NAIL STUD

CORNER FRAMING DETAIL— INSIDE VIEW

3/4 X 4-3/4" CEDAR TOP CAP
L2
N1 SHAKERTOWN SHINGLE COURSES
L1
SIDE STUDS
I
N2 SHAKERTOWN FLUSH CORNERS
H 2x6 DURA-PINE DECKING FASTENED WITH 3" GALVANIZED SCREWS. LEAVE 1/4" SPACE BETWEEN DECKING COURSES.
2x8 JOISTS; 16" O.C.
B

1x2
2x4
OUTER JOIST
8"
SIDE STUDS
39-1/4"
6"
1x4
8"
FRONT STUDS
32"
DOUBLE HEADER JOIST
A

2x8 LEDGER

M 1/2"-THICK STARTER STRIP
L2
D1 CORNER POST
2x8 STRINGER
E1
STEP BLOCKS CUT FROM 2x8
SIDE STUDS
22-1/2° MITER (TYPICAL)
C1
C2

14"
7-1/4"
1/4" TRACTION GROOVES ROUTED IN TREADS (TYPICAL)
FRONT POST
FRONT STUDS
I
G
1-1/2 X 1-1/2 X 14-3/4" END BAND (4 REQD.)
DOUBLE 2x8 HEADER JOIST
CORNER POSTS

2x6 DURA-PINE DECKING
1/4" SPACE
O TECO 2x8 JOIST HANGER
BOTTOM RISER AND BLOCK TRIMMED TO SIZE
1/4" SPACES
1"
15"
2x8 JOISTS 16" O.C.
7-1/4"
5-3/4"
DOUBLE 2x8 HEADER JOIST
2x8 STRINGER X 4'-LONG (4 REQD.)
2x8 LEDGER FASTENED TO HOUSE FRAMING WITH LAGSCREWS
PATIO BLOCKS SET ON SAND BED
2x8 TREADS AND RISERS
F
4x4 POST WITH 2x4 CLEAT

DECK AND STEP CROSS SECTION

TO FROST-LINE
4" TO 6" OF COMPACTED GRAVEL
FOOTING DETAIL

45°   1-1/2"
1-1/2"
2x4 CLEAT
7-1/4"
4x4 POST
FRONT POST
7-1/4"
4x4 POST
CORNER POST

The house shown was originally equipped with a concrete stoop—hardly a design feature worth preserving. Later, a rather plain wooden deck, one that was more functional than attractive, was added over the concrete. So, when the house-remodeling plans were being developed, a lot of time was spent designing the entrance. The idea was to build something that looked like it was part of the house—not simply tacked on the front. Plus, we wanted to show off rather than hide the attractive new door and sidelight. The entrance had to be large enough to be functional, but if too large, it would distort the house's scale. And finally, the entrance had to be stylish without being grandiose. With these design considerations as guidelines, our entrance deck was born.

The 8½ x 18-ft.-long deck features walls that are covered with the same cedar-shingle siding as the house. The tops of the walls have an 8-in.-wide trough that accepts flower pots and planter trays. Expansive 9-ft.-wide steps, which are centered on the doorway, welcome you to the home. A small brick walk connects the driveway to the deck and helps soften the transition from the black asphalt to the stained wood deck.

The deck is built entirely of Wolmanized pressure-treated wood. The understructure framing and steps are made of 2x8s.

The planter walls are framed with 2x4s with 1x4 crossbraces. For the deck's surface, we used 2x6 DuraPine pressure-treated decking.

DuraPine is a special type of pressure-treated wood, featuring rounded top edges and kerfs cut in the bottom surface to prevent cupping. These decking boards are specially made to ensure that the wear and tear a deck endures—and the extremes of exposure—don't leave a mark on the deck surface. Expect to pay more, but the durability and finished look are unequaled by any other decking lumber.

The deck was stained with deck stain and preservative. It contains hard resins that resist wear and stand up to heavy traffic. It's worth mentioning that we stained all the decking before installing it. This not only saved time, but it made for a neater, more effective staining job. However, this goes against the recommended procedure that says to wait 8 to 12 weeks

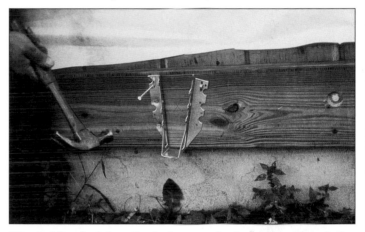

Fig. 1 *After bolting the ledger to the house, nail metal 2x8 joist hangers 16 in. on center. Nail only one side of the metal joist hangers.*

Materials List

Key	No.	Size and description (use)
A	1	2 x 8 x 219½" pressure-treated pine (ledger)
B	14	2 x 8 x 66" pressure-treated pine (joists)
C1	2	2 x 8 x 189½" pressure-treated pine (header joists)
C2	2	2 x 8 x 72" pressure-treated pine (header joists)
D1*	4	4 x 4 x 48" pressure-treated pine (corner post)
D2*	4	2 x 4 x 48" pressure-treated pine (corner post cleat)
E1	4	2 x 8 x 48" pressure-treated pine (stair stringer)
E2*	2	2 x 8 x 48" pressure-treated pine (stair blocks)
F*	6	2 x 8 x 110" pressure-treated pine (treads and risers)
G	4	½ x ½ x 14¾" pressure-treated pine (stair end band)
H*	18	2 x 6 x 192" DuraPine (decking)
I	44	2 x 4 x 39¼" pressure-treated pine (planter stud)
J	17	1 x 4 x 14" pressure-treated pine (planter cross brace)
K	8	2 x 8 x 14" pressure-treated pine (planter blocking)
L1	2	¾ x 4¾ x 13¾" cedar (top cap side)
L2	2	¾ x 4¾ x 102" cedar (top cap end)
M*	8	½ x 1 x 102" pressure-treated pine (starter strip)
N1*	18	12 x 108" cedar (shingle courses)
N2	12	12" cedar (flush prefab shingle corners)
O	12	2 x 8" metal joist hangers
P	6	1 x 2 x 102" pressure-treated pine (planter tray slats)

Misc.: 1½" wood screws; 3" galvanized screws; lagscrews; gravel; patio blocks; sand; metal corner brackets; aluminum drip cap; 16d nails; deck stain and preservative.

*Cut to size as required.

Fig. 2 *Nail the first and last joists to the end of the ledger and then install a metal corner bracket to strengthen the joint.*

(longer if the wood gets wet) after construction before applying stain to pressure-treated wood. It was not practical for us to wait this long and the deck has shown no ill effects so far.

Deck Construction

Before starting construction, check the local building codes and obtain any permits that are required. This is especially important because if your deck violates any codes, such as rules about setback distance, a single crabby neighbor can bring down a cease-and-desist order that will stop your construction in its tracks.

Once you get working, there are four basic steps to building the deck: construct the understructure framing and steps; frame the planter walls; apply the decking; and install the siding to both sides of the walls.

Begin by fastening a 2x8 ledger to the house with lagscrews. Be sure to screw securely into the house framing. Nail an aluminum drip cap so that it overhangs the top edge of the ledger.

Next, construct the 2x8 header joist that forms the perimeter of the deck. Use concrete blocks or bricks to support the header until the posts are installed.

The floor joists are joined to the ledger with metal hangers. Nail the hangers to the ledger 16 in. on center (**Fig. 1**). The exceptions to this are the first and last joists, which are located 13¾ in. from the outside edge of the deck's perimeter to their center (see illustration detail). This is necessary to form the 8-in.-wide trough in the planter walls. To alter the width of the trough for larger or smaller plants, simply reposition these two joists. Use metal corner brackets with these joists to ensure a strong, lasting joint (**Fig. 2**).

Next, dig the four post holes and level the header joist (**Fig. 3 and 4**). Fill the holes with 4 to 5 in. of gravel. Then cut the 4x4 posts to length.

Note that the tops of the posts are notched to fit under the

Fig. 3 *A post-hole digger makes quick work of post holes. Dig down about 6 in. below the frost line and add 4 in. to 5 in. of fine gravel.*

Fig. 4 *With the header joist temporarily supported by concrete blocks, shim the header level. Then take the measurements for the posts.*

Fig. 5 *Nail each 4x4 post to the header joist with 16d galvanized nails. Note how the post is notched to form a shoulder to support the joist.*

Fig. 6 Drop the joist into the hanger and nail the hanger to the ledger first. Then nail the hanger to the joist with the nails provided.

Fig. 7 Fasten the other end of the joist by simply nailing through the galvanized header and into the joist end. Use three 16d nails per joist.

TECH *Tips*

Saving Sanding Time
Sometimes it's more efficient to sand parts together, rather than one at a time. One of the easiest ways to do this is to simply bar clamp all pieces of equal thickness. Light pressure is all that's necessary to hold the parts in place. If you apply too much pressure, the parts will arch upward from the clamping force. For paint-grade work, you may find it easier to sand the lumber smooth before cutting and shaping it. All that's necessary after cutting and shaping may be some touch-up.

Fig. 8 After installing all the joists, nail a second 2x8 to the header. Add 2x4 cleats to the posts to support the double 2x8 header.

header joist. Nail a 2x4 cleat to each post to extend the notch and provide a shoulder for the second 2x8 that will be nailed to the header joist later. Nail the posts in place (**Fig. 5**) and then thoroughly backfill around each post with compacted soil.

Then cut the joists to length and drop them into the hangers. Nail the hanger to the ledger first, and then to the joist (**Fig. 6**). Secure the other end of each joist by nailing through the header (**Fig. 7**).

Once all the joists have been installed, nail a second 2x8 to the header joist (**Fig. 8**). The double 2x8 header is needed only across the front of the deck and on the short, angled wall adjoining the short side.

Next, construct the steps. Make the four stringers from 2x8s. Triangular blocks, cut from 2x8 stock, are nailed to the stringers to support the treads and risers. Use concrete patio

Fig. 9 Prebore the 2x4 studs and then nail them to the joist 16 in. on center. Note that the stud is notched to fit onto the 2x8 joist.

Fig. 10 *Clamp opposite studs in place and level across their tops. Inside studs aren't notched, but instead, nailed flat against the 2x8 joist.*

Fig. 11 *Screw 1x4 crossbraces to the outside studs. Then plumb the inside stud and clamp the brace to it. Now screw the brace to the inside stud.*

Fig. 12 *Front studs positioned on the double 2x8 header must be toenailed in place. Nail the studs flush with the outside edge of header.*

Fig. 13 *Add a piece of 2x8 solid blocking between the joists in front of the angled wall. The blocking provides a nailing surface for the decking.*

blocks as the foundation under each stringer. Each tread is made of two 2x8s. For additional traction, rout ¼ x ¼-in. grooves in the treads.

Planter Walls

The planter walls consist of pairs of 2x4 studs connected by 1x4 cross braces. Two 1x2 slats run across the 1x4 braces to support planter trays and flower pots.

The studs on the outside of the walls are notched to extend down alongside the joist and are then nailed in place (**Fig. 9**). The exception is along the double 2x8 header joist where the studs are toenailed in place. The studs that frame the inside of the walls aren't notched. They are simply nailed flat against a joist (**Fig. 10**).

When nailing each pair of the studs in place, be sure that the two studs align so that you can attach the 1x4 crossbraces. Before screwing the crossbraces in place, plumb the studs with a level (**Fig. 11**). The front studs that are positioned over the double 2x8 joists in front must be toenailed into place, flush with the outside of the header (**Fig. 12**).

Along with the block between the bottom of the regular studs, you'll need to add a blocking piece between the angled joists (**Fig. 13**).

Next, install the decking. Cut each board so that its end falls on a joist and stagger the joints from one course to the next. Instead of nails, we fastened the 2x6 decking with 3-in. galvanized screws. The screws hold better and look neater than nails. Counterbore screw pilot holes and then drive the screws with an electric screwdriver or drill (**Fig. 14**).

Siding the Walls

Applying siding to the planter walls is similar to siding the house. Start by nailing a ½-in.-thick starter strip around the deck perimeter (**Fig. 15**). Next, establish a level line and nail the first siding course to the deck wall. Run the siding across the deck wall and onto the house. This helps to visually blend the deck into the house and make it look less like an add-on. Crosscut the siding at 22½° for the angled section of the wall.

Use prefabricated corners at the ends of the walls. Nail the corners up first and then butt the siding to the corners. Note that additional 2x4 blocking must be added to the wall ends to provide solid nailing for the siding.

Continue the siding around to the inside of the walls. Making tight-fitting joints at the inside corners of the angled-wall section can be tricky.

First, crosscut the siding to 22½° and then use a block plane to trim the siding to fit.

The last few pieces of siding butt against the house siding at a right angle (**Fig. 16**). Notch the planter-wall siding, as needed, to fit tightly against the house.

Now nail ¾ x 4¾-in.-wide, rough-sawn cedar trim to the tops of the walls (**Fig. 17**). Completely sand the cedar trim lightly to eliminate any splintering, and then stain it to match the siding.

TECH *Tips*

Magic Mallet
Sometimes, with a little ingenuity, one tool can become two. Increase a hammer's usefulness by padding its handle end with a disc of rubber or leather, secured with electrician's tape. Thus modified, the handle end makes a handy mallet for tapping small boards into place without marring the finish or denting their surface.

Fig. 14 *Counterbore pilot holes and fasten the decking with 3-in. galvanized screws. A 16d nail is used as a spacer between the boards.*

Fig. 15 *Before installing the siding, nail a ½-in.-thick starter strip along the bottom of the header joist. Continue the strip onto the house.*

Fig. 16 *Install cedar siding across the deck walls and onto the house. Cut the siding panels so that all butt joints fall on a stud.*

Fig. 17 *Finish the top of the walls with ¾ x 4¾-in.-wide rough-sawn cedar. Fasten the cedar trim with 6d galvanized finishing nails.*

Shady Shelter

This handsome, spacious arbor has operable louvers, built-in seating, and an easy-to-build privacy screen.

This arbor features something you probably haven't seen in any other outdoor woodworking project: operable overhead louvers. Essentially, they work like horizontal venetian blinds. And the clever adjusting mechanism is simple and surprisingly inexpensive to build. These louvers allow you to effectively block out—or let pass through—just the amount of sunlight you want. On warm summer days when the sun is beating down, you may well elect to bounce back a good deal of heat and light. Yet on cooler days in the spring and fall, you may want to feel the full effect of the sun's warmth.

*Key*POINTS

TIME
Prep Time . . . . 15 hours
Shop Time . . . . 15 hours
Assembly Time . . . . 20 hours

EFFORT
Skill Level . . . . advanced
Maintenance . . . . light
Assistance . . . . one-two

COST / BENEFITS
Expense: expensive
• Entire outdoor seating area allows you to **control light** for dining, sunbathing, or outdoor social events.

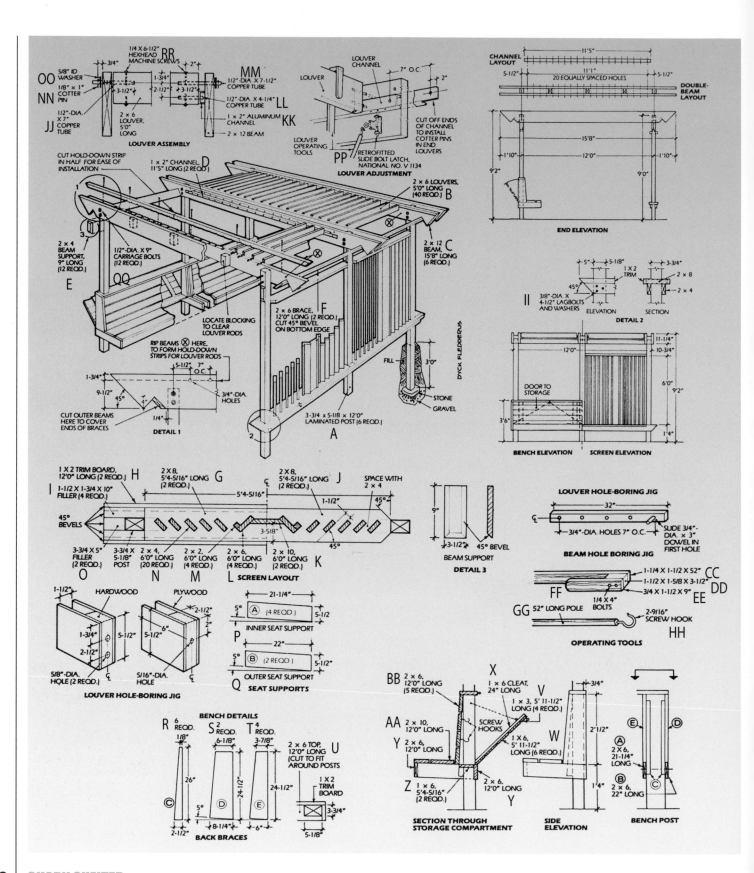

Materials List

Key	No.	Size and description (use)
A	6	3³/₄ x 5¹/₈ x 144" pressure-treated pine (laminated post)
B	40	2 x 6 x 60" pressure-treated pine (louvers)
C	6	2 x 12 x 188" pressure-treated pine (beam)
D	2	1 x 2 x 137" pressure-treated pine (channel)
E	12	2 x 4 x 108" pressure-treated pine (beam support)
F	2	2 x 6 x 144" pressure-treated pine (brace)
G	2	2 x 8 x 64⁵/₁₆" pressure-treated pine (screen header)
H	2	1 x 2 x 144" pressure-treated pine (screen trim board)
I	4	1¹/₂ x 1³/₄ x 120" pressure-treated pine (filler board)
J	2	2 x 8 x 64⁵/₁₆" pressure-treated pine (screen header)
K	2	2 x 10 x 72" pressure-treated pine (screen post)
L	4	2 x 6 x 72" pressure-treated pine (post support)
M	4	2 x 2 x 72" pressure-treated pine (post trim)
N	20	2 x 4 x 72" pressure-treated pine (screen partition)
O	2	3³/₄ x 5 x 72" pressure-treated pine (filler board)
P	4	2 x 6 x 21¹/₄" pressure-treated pine (inner seat support)
Q	2	2 x 6 x 22" pressure-treated pine (outer seat support)
R	6	2¹/₂ x 26 x 22" pressure-treated pine (seat back brace)
S	2	8¹/₄ x 24¹/₂ x 22" pressure-treated pine (seat back brace)
T	4	6 x 24¹/₂ x 22" pressure-treated pine (seat back brace)
U	2	2 x 6 x 144" redwood (seat top)
V	4	1 x 3 x 71¹/₂" pressure-treated pine (seat back cleat)
W	6	1 x 6 x 71¹/₂" pressure-treated pine (seat back cleat)
X	2	1 x 6 x 24" pressure-treated pine (seat back cleat)
Y	2	2 x 6 x 144" redwood (seat base back/front trim)
Z	2	1 x 6 x 64⁵/₁₆" pressure-treated pine (seat base cleat)
AA	2	2 x 10 x 144" redwood (seat base board)
BB	5	2 x 6 x 144" redwood (seat back)
CC	1	1¹/₄ x 1¹/₂ x 52" pine (louver operator handle)
DD	1	1¹/₂ x 1⁵/₈ x 3¹/₂" pine (louver operator handle block)
EE	1	³/₄ x 1¹/₂ x 9" pine (louver operator leg)
FF	2	¹/₄ x 4" louver operator bolts
GG	1	52" hook pole
HH	1	2⁹/₁₆" screw hook for louver operator
II	36	³/₈"-dia. x 4¹/₂" lagbolts and washers
JJ	40	¹/₂"-dia. x 7" copper tube for louver
KK	2	1 x 2 x 188" aluminum channel
LL	40	¹/₂"-dia. x 4¹/₄" copper tube for louver
MM	40	¹/₂"-dia. x 7¹/₂" copper tube for louver
NN	80	¹/₂" x 1" cotter pin for louver tubes
OO	80	⁵/₈" ID washer
PP	2	slide bolt latch
QQ	12	¹/₂"-dia x 9" carriage bolts
RR	80	¹/₄ x 6¹/₂" hexhead machine screws

Misc.: 2 chains and eyehooks; gravel; galvanized hinges; 10d galvanized nails.

As unique as they are, the louvers in this project aren't the whole story. Also designed into the structure is a substantial privacy screen. It mimics the configuration of the louvers, while shielding your neighbor's view and letting the cool breezes pass through. Add to this the built-in seating benches—which include storage for garden hose, small lawn care equipment, and the tools to operate the louvers—and it's easy to see what this innovative structure can bring to just about any yard.

As unique and useful as the features are on this arbor, they are also complex. Accurate measurements are essential to the success of this project. Also, it's not a good idea to tackle this project by yourself. The work is painstaking and an extra pair of hands (or two) will not only make all the work go quicker, it will also ensure that another person is there to check your work as you go. Finally, take the extra time to plan and be sure that you have all the right tools and materials for the project before you start. This will head off a lot of frustration that comes from having to stop in the middle of a big project to make a run to the home center.

Arbor Layout

Begin by determining the position for the six posts. Follow the dimensions given in the drawing carefully. Because all the other parts in this structure are attached to the posts, if you make layout errors, you will have to change all the parts' dimensions to fit. We used factory-laminated posts, for their extra strength.

Fig. 1 *After the posts are set in their holes, plumb and brace them in place. Then begin the benches by nailing the back braces to the post sides.*

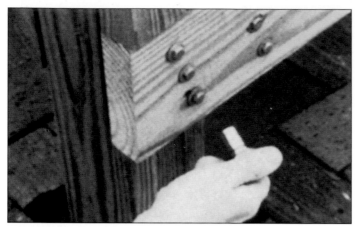

Fig. 2 *Prebore clearance holes, then attach the seat supports using lagbolts and washers. Tighten until the washers begin to depress the wood.*

Fig. 3 *Cut the seat supports to size, then tack-nail them to the post sides directly under the back braces. Maintain a 5° angle for best seating comfort.*

Fig. 4 *Join the boards and cleats with screws to form the storage compartment doors. Use ½-in.-thick spacers to maintain alignment.*

These posts measure 3¾ in. x 5⅛ in. and were positioned with the longer side aligned front to back. If you plan to use 4x4 or 6x6 posts, alter the layout to accommodate this change. Take your time with the posts, because they are the most important elements in the layout. It's always a wise idea to have someone double check your measurements on a project like this.

Set up batterboards and mason's string at the four corners of your layout and check where the strings intersect for square. Then hang a line level on each length of string and check for level. Using the strings as a guide, drive a stake into the ground at the precise location of each post.

Determine the lowest point of your grade by measuring down from the level string to the ground. Keep in mind that the seating benches are attached directly to the posts. If your grade falls off radically, the benches will be uncomfortably low at one end or uncomfortably high at the other, or both. If you have a steep grade and want to duplicate this arbor precisely, then you'll have to level the area first.

Once you've established the low point, consult your local building department to determine the depth of the frost line in your area. Where we live it's about 36 in. deep. So, beginning at the lowest point, we excavated a 10-in.-dia. hole to a depth of 42 in.

Then we filled the bottom 4 in. with gravel, placed a 2-in.-thick flat stone on top of the gravel, and placed the post on top of the stone. By using a 12-ft.-long post, this yielded 9 ft. of post above grade, which was our goal. If your frost line is deeper, use longer posts.

Excavate the remaining holes using the same system. Then set each post in its hole and backfill around it with soil. Measure frequently back to the string to make sure the posts are in their precise locations.

If you did your initial layout carefully, there should be enough adjustment room in the holes to move the posts into

Fig. 5 *Locate the hinge positions for the storage doors on the rear support board. Then trace the leaf outline and mortise the board with a sharp chisel.*

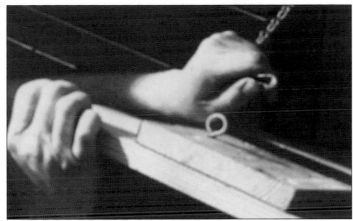

Fig. 6 *To support the door in the open position, attach a screw eye to the door cleat, then attach a chain with a spring snap hook to the inside of the post.*

Fig. 7 *Cut the privacy screen rails to size from 2x8 stock. Then lay out the position of all the screen slats using a protractor or framing square.*

perfect alignment. Temporarily brace the posts with 2x4s tack nailed 16 in. below the tops. Then measure 9 ft. above grade on the first post and attach one end of a mason's string to the mark. Wrap the string around the perimeter of the remaining posts. Level it with a line level, and mark the point where the string intersects each post. Remove the string and cut off each post at that point.

Louver Beams

Remove the temporary braces used for cutting the tops and reuse them as diagonal braces for the posts. It is crucial that the posts be absolutely square and plumb before attaching the louver beams. Cut all beams to the size and shape given in the drawing. Then bore louver rod holes through the beams that fall on the inside of the end posts, as shown in the exploded diagram Detail 1.

Fig. 8 *Cut the screen uprights to size and shape, then set the rail on edge and attach the uprights—at the layout marks—using galvanized nails.*

Next, rip 1¾ in. off the top of these two beams. This cut line should intersect the middle of the louver rod holes. Save the rippings because these form the hold-down strips for the louver rods that will be needed later. (Note: This step is necessary because once the louvers are installed, they are held captive in beam holes at both ends. By ripping off the strip, the louvers can be fitted into the holes in the middle beams and can simply rest on the ripped beams. When all the louvers are in place, they are secured by attaching the hold-down strips.)

Lift all the beams into place and tack nail them to the posts. Check for precise alignment, then attach with bolts, nuts, and washers as shown. Add blocking between the beam members to stabilize each pair and to ensure uniform alignment. Then nail the supports (see exploded diagram Detail 3) to the posts under each beam.

Finally, cut to size and shape the 2x6 bracing boards that fall in the notch on the bottom edge of beams. Nail these in place but do not install the louvers yet.

Fig. 9 *Construct the hole-boring jig as shown on the drawing, then clamp it over the ends of the louver boards and bore holes for copper tubing.*

Fig. 10 *Insert copper tubing into the end holes. Then build the second jig, clamp it in place and bore vertical holes through louver and tubing.*

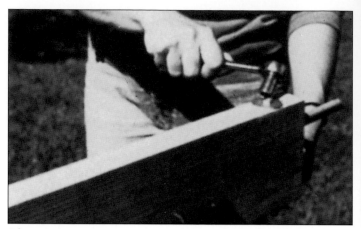

Fig. 11 *Secure the tubing in the ends of the louver boards by installing a bolt, washers, and nut. Tighten the bolt head with a socket wrench.*

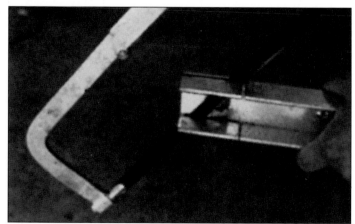

Fig. 12 *Cut the aluminum louver channel to length. Then cut 2-in.-long notches in both ends to allow clearance for washers and cotter pins.*

Fig. 13 *To make sure that the louvers align, attach a string to the end louver beams at the point where the louvers start. Mark the middle beams under the string.*

Fig. 14 *Use the jig for boring pivot holes in the middle beams. Bore the first hole, insert the dowel pin for alignment, and bore other holes through the jig.*

It's better to wait until after the benches and screens are built. These add stability to the structure, which makes installing the louvers easier.

Seating Benches

Cut the back braces and seat supports for the niches to the dimensions given on the drawing. Nail the braces in place (**Fig. 1**). Note that the two outside supports are longer than the middle ones because they cover the ends of the 2x6 stock used for the front seat support.

Similarly, the outside back braces are wider than the ones that fall on the middle posts, because they were designed to cover the ends of the 2x6 seat-back boards. Because of this, you have to cut two small filler strips (marked with a "C" on the drawing) and nail these against the end posts to maintain the proper slant.

Once the back braces are nailed to the posts, bolt the seat

supports into place using lagscrews and washers (**Fig. 2**). Next, nail the front seat support in place (**Fig. 3**) and cover the entire bench framing with 2x6 and 2x10 stock, as shown in the drawing.

Next, measure the opening between the posts, then cut the 1x3 and 1x6 stock to size for the fold-down doors. Join the door slats to the cleats with galvanized nails or brass screws and then carefully lay out the hinge position on the top of the back rail (**Fig. 4**).

Mortise one leaf of each hinge into the rail and the other into the support cleats on the inside surface of the seat doors (**Fig. 5**). Before attaching the doors, cut 1x6 stock to length to create the floorboards for both of the compartments. Bore several ½-in.-dia. holes in each floor for drainage. Toenail these into the posts.

Mount the hinges and check the doors for fit. When you are satisfied that they are snug and true, mount two chains with snap hooks to the inside of each compartment (**Fig. 6**). Add a matching screw eye to the inside of each door, then snap the hook over the eye to support the door when it's open.

Lastly, fabricate the louver-operating tools according to the diagram, and hang the tools in one of the compartments using large screw hooks.

Privacy Screen

Begin by cutting the upper and lower support rails to size and shape (**Fig. 7**). Any minor discrepancy between the dimensions we give and the actual dimension between your posts should be resolved in favor of the actual dimension.

Lay out the surface of the support rails to match the Screen Layout drawing. Note that all the screen parts are made of stock lumber except for the middle panels.

Each edge of the 2x10s must be beveled 45° to accept the 2x6 boards that abut them. Once the layout is complete and the screen boards have been cut to size and shape, nail the boards to the rails using galvanized nails (**Fig. 8**). Then toenail each assembly between the posts and add the trim boards around the bottom.

Louvers

Start by cutting all the louvers to size. Make sure your cuts are square and accurate because any minor error can cause the adjustment system to work poorly. Next, build the hole-boring jigs as shown (**Fig. 9**). These will ensure straight and square holes for the tubing rods.

Bore the holes in the ends of all louvers first, then cut the copper tubing lengths and drive them into the holes (**Fig. 10**). Be sure to shield the tubing ends with a scrap block of wood so that the hammer blows will not distort the copper.

Once all the tubing rods are in place, use the second jig to bore the bolt holes through the top edge of the louvers. Install the machine bolts, washers, and nuts, and tighten them in place (**Fig. 11**).

Fig. 15 *Install one set of louvers to stabilize the structure, then install the second set. Louvers must be pushed into middle beam holes first.*

Then bore cotter pinholes in the ends of the tubing rods as shown in the drawing.

Next, cut the adjustment channel from 1 x 2-in. aluminum stock, and drill the rod holes shown on the Channel Layout drawing. Establish the centerline of both channels and drill a ½-in.-dia. hole in the lower flange at this point.

Drill the same size hole ½ in. away on both sides. These holes will accept the slide-bolt latch that is used for adjusting the louvers. Complete the aluminum channels by cutting a notch in each end (**Fig. 12**).

Next, build the Beam Hole-Boring Jig. Before clamping it in place, run a string between the outside beams where the first rod hole is bored. Mark the spot where the middle beams fall under the string (**Fig. 13**). Use this as your reference point. Clamp the jig to the beam then bore the holes. Once you've reached the end of the jig, move it down the beam. Slide a wood dowel into the first jig hole and the last beam hole to ensure precise alignment (**Fig. 14**).

When you are finished boring the holes, temporarily attach the aluminum channels to the beams by wrapping wire around both.

Then slide the louvers into the holes in the beams and the channels, resting the other end on the beams that were ripped to width before (**Fig. 15**). Cover these rods with the hold-down strips then remove the wire supports from the channels. Install all of the washers and cotter pins, and the louver assembly is complete.

To hold the louvers in the three different positions, we used a slide-bolt latch for each channel. To this widely available stock item we added a light-duty spring to keep the slide bolt from dropping when installed in the vertical position.

Then, to hold the spring, we welded a washer to the bolt just under the padlock loop. We also welded another washer to the outside of the loop to make gripping it without a hook tool easier.

Backyard Barn

If you need lots of extra storage space or even an outbuilding workshop, this is the structure for you!

Homeowners complain about having too much storage space about as often as they do about having an overabundance of cash. Nearly every home, regardless of its size, has a shortage of accessible storage and workspace. Need proof? Take a peek into the average garage and you'll likely find it crammed full of bicycles, lumber, garden tools, trash cans, and power equipment. An occasional spring cleaning can help you reorganize, but it's only a matter of time before the clutter returns. What you need is more space, and a great way to find it is to build your own backyard barn.

*Key*POINTS

TIME
Prep Time	5 hours
Shop Time	10 hours
Assembly Time	35 hours

EFFORT
Skill Level	intermediate
Maintenance	light
Assistance	one-two

COST / BENEFITS
Expense: expensive
• Can serve **multiple functions**, as playroom, storage, or workshop.
• Best suited to **large properties** of one acre or more.

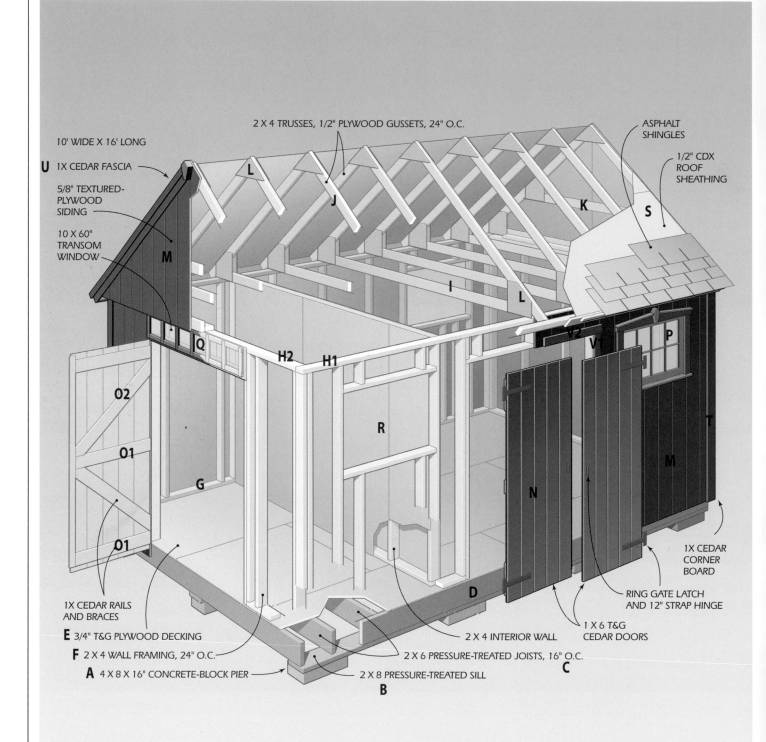

2 X 4 TRUSSES, 1/2" PLYWOOD GUSSETS, 24" O.C.

ASPHALT
SHINGLES

1/2" CDX
ROOF
SHEATHING

10' WIDE X 16' LONG

U 1X CEDAR FASCIA

5/8" TEXTURED-
PLYWOOD
SIDING

10 X 60"
TRANSOM
WINDOW

L

J

M

I

L

K

S

Q

H2

H1

V2

V1

P

O2

O1

R

T

G

M

N

O1

1X CEDAR
CORNER
BOARD

RING GATE LATCH
AND 12" STRAP HINGE

1X CEDAR RAILS
AND BRACES

1 X 6 T&G
CEDAR DOORS

E 3/4" T&G PLYWOOD DECKING

2 X 4 INTERIOR WALL

F 2 X 4 WALL FRAMING, 24" O.C.

D

2 X 6 PRESSURE-TREATED JOISTS, 16" O.C.

C

A 4 X 8 X 16" CONCRETE-BLOCK PIER

2 X 8 PRESSURE-TREATED SILL

B

At 10 x 16 ft., this handsome Colonial-style garden shed is large enough for all your backyard needs. This is a sizable outbuilding that can serve many different functions. The entire building could be used for storage, but we decided to divide the interior space into two separate areas: a 4 x 10-ft. tool-storage area, and a 10 x 12-ft. children's playroom.

Double doors on the side and gable end make it easy to access these spaces. It has easy-to-install plywood siding, three large windows, and two pairs of doors. Before starting construction, check local building codes to see if you need to get a building permit. You can get plans online or through several mail-order plan suppliers.

Starting at the Bottom

The shed we built rests on a foundation made up of 12 solid-concrete blocks. The 4 x 8 x 16-in. blocks are arranged in three rows spaced 59 in. apart. These blocks are typically set directly on the ground, but we put down a 4-in. bed of gravel first because our site occasionally receives groundwater. The gravel will keep the soil beneath the shed from eroding or becoming soggy.

After laying out the 12 blocks, use a straight 2x4 and a 4-ft. carpenter's level to ensure that all the blocks are level (**Fig. 1**). Shim up any low blocks with strips of asphalt roofing, cedar shingles, or 2-in.-thick concrete patio blocks.

Next, form each front and rear band joist by nailing a 2x6 to a 2x8 mudsill. Set the mudsills on top of the blocks running across the front and rear of the shed. Cut a third 2x8 mudsill to fit along the tops of the center row of

foundation blocks. Cut all the 2x6 floor joists to length and set them between the two band joists and on top of the mudsills (**Fig. 2**). Space the joists 16 in. on center and secure them with 16d galvanized nails (**Fig. 3**).

Before nailing down the plywood floor, secure the floor frame with four steel-cabled ground anchors, which are code-required in some areas and are a good idea no matter where

Fig. 1 *Use a 4-ft. level and a long, straight 2x4 to ensure that the concrete foundation blocks are level. Add shims to build up any low blocks.*

Materials List

Key	No.	Size and description (use)
A	12	4 x 8 x 16" concrete block (footing pier)
B	3	2 x 8 x 192" pressure-treated pine (mudsill)
C	12	2 x 6 x 116" pressure-treated pine (floor joists)
D	2	2 x 6 x 192" pressure-treated pine (band joists)
E*	6	³/₄ x 4 x 8" tongue-and-groove plywood (floor)
F	37	2 x 4 x 88" pine (studs)
G*	6	2 x 4 x 96" pine (sole plate)
H1	2	2 x 4 x 192" pine (top plate)
H2	2	2 x 4 x 112" pine (top plate)
I	12	2 x 4 x 120" pine (joist)
J	18	2 x 4 x 84" pine (rafter)
K	2	2 x 4 x 60" pine (end truss chord)
L**	2	¹/₂ x 96 x 48" plywood (gussets)
M*	14	⁵/₈ x 96 x 48" textured plywood (siding)
N	15	1 x 6 x 80" cedar tongue-and-groove (door panel)
O1	12	1 x 4 x 30" cedar (door rails)
O2*	8	1 x 4 x 36" cedar (door braces)
P	3	2 x 3" barn sash window
Q	1	10 x 60" transom window
R	3	³/₈ x 96 x 48" drywall sheets (interior wall)
S	8	¹/₂ x 96 x 48" CDX plywood (roof sheathing)
T	8	1 x 2 x 96" cedar (corner board)
U	4	1 x 2 x 84" cedar (fascia board)
V1	4	1 x 4 x 80" cedar (door side trim)
V2	2	1 x 4 x 60" cedar (door top trim)

Misc.: Gravel; 4 steel-cabled ground anchors and spikes; 6d galvanized nails; 8d galvanized nails; 16d galvanized nails; carpenter's glue; 1" roofing nails; barrel bolt for windows; glazing points; 6-12" strap hinges; asphalt shingles; ring gate latch; door hasp latch.

*Cut to fit.

**Individual gussets cut out of sheet.

TECH Tips

Know the Code

When you're building a shed like this one, there are more considerations than just the construction of the building. A number of factors will affect where you site the shed, how you use it, and may even affect whether you can build it in the first place. The place to start is your local building department. Before building a detached structure, you need to consult local zoning ordinances. Always have plans in hand when you go—whether you've had someone draw them up, or buy them through a mail-order vendor. Although many building codes will allow the construction of a building this small without permits, some zoning boards are peculiar about particular issues. In any given town or municipality, the local zoning ordinances may restrict outbuildings, so it's wise to check. The height of frustration would be having to take down this structure after you spend the time, money, and effort to build it. Even if they don't restrict the size of this outbuilding, your local codes may affect where it is placed on your property. Most local zoning boards create "setback" limits, defining how close any structure can be to the property line. Setbacks are generally measured from the property line to the foundation of the building. You also need to be aware of any utility easements governing your property. These supersede setback limitations, and provide access for things such as emergency services. Lastly, if you are running electrical (see the "Power Up" box) or plumbing to the building, those will also be regulated by local codes.

you're building. Bolt one anchor to each corner of the frame and drive the hold-down spikes deep into the ground.

For the shed floor, we used ¾-in. tongue-and-groove ACX plywood. Tongue-and-groove joints create a rigid floor that doesn't bounce or sag. Secure the plywood with 8d galvanized nails (**Fig. 4**).

Framing the Roof Trusses

The roof is constructed of a row of triangular trusses. The roof pitch is 40°, which is fairly steep and ensures that snow and rain runoff is good. Each truss is made up of two 2x4 rafters and one 2x4 ceiling joist. The three boards are joined together with ½-in. plywood gussets. To speed up the assembly process, build all the trusses on the shed floor before erecting the walls.

Start by cutting all the rafters to length with a 40° angle at one end of each. Cut 2x4s to 10 ft. long for the bottom chords of the trusses. Also, cut out all of the plywood gussets from full sheets.

Make a template on the shed floor for assembling the trusses. Begin by laying out the parts for one truss. Align the bottom chord with the edge of the plywood floor. Then cut four 24-in.-long 2x4s. Lay two alongside each rafter and screw them to the plywood floor. Now use these short boards as

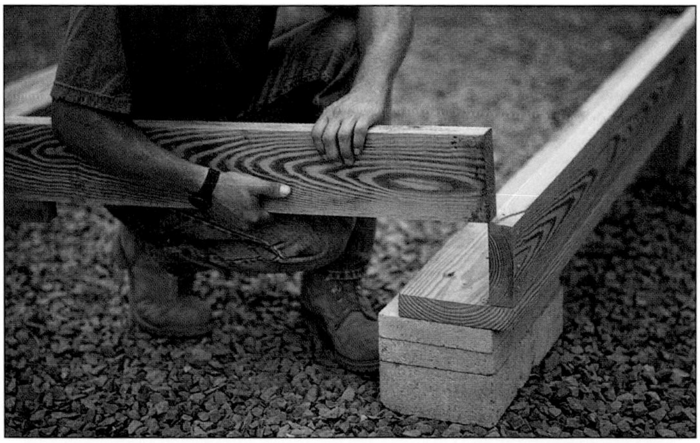

Fig. 2 ***Set the 2x6 floor joists on top of the 2x8 mudsills. These floor-frame members are cut from pressure-treated lumber.***

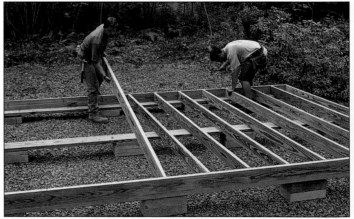

Fig. 3 ***Install a 2x6 floor joist every 16 in. Fasten the joists by nailing through the band joists with 16d galvanized nails.***

Fig. 4 Use ¾-in. exterior-grade, tongue-and-groove plywood for the floor. Secure the plywood to the frame with 8d nails.

Fig. 5 Assemble all of the roof trusses on the shed floor. Nail plywood gussets across the joints on both sides of the trusses.

Fig. 6 Build the exterior walls on the floor. Assemble the 2x4s with 16d nails and then add the plywood sheathing.

Fig. 7 Carefully raise the end wall into position. Note how the plywood siding hangs down to cover the floor framing.

stop blocks for laying out and assembling each truss. Fasten plywood gussets to each side of every truss with carpenter's glue and 1-in. roofing nails (Fig. 5) and set the trusses aside.

Building the Walls

Cut all the 2x4 parts for one side wall and lay them out on the shed floor. Space the studs along the sole plate and top plates, making sure they are precisely aligned 24 in. on center, and secure them with 16d nails (Fig. 6). Frame in the window at this time as well. Then cut the plywood siding to size and nail it to the wall framing with 6d galvanized nails.

Tilt the wall up into place (Fig. 7) and secure it with 3-in. deck screws (Fig. 8). Frame and erect the rear wall, followed by the front wall. For the front wall, you'll need to frame out an opening for the double doors, measuring 60 x 80 in. The top plate for the doorjamb will be positioned slightly more than 10 in. from the wall top plate, which will not only frame

the door, but also allow for a transom window over the door (although you can exclude this if you prefer).

Finally, frame the other side wall, including openings for the windows and double doors. Raise it in position and secure it to the other walls to complete the exterior framing.

Then frame out the interior partition wall. First nail the sole and top plates to the floor and outside members, and then install the studs, toenailing them top and bottom, 16 in. on center. If you're including a playroom, as we did, cover the partition side that faces that room with ⅜ in. drywall (or use plywood if you have extra sheets), and screw it in place.

Setting the Roof Trusses

Start framing the roof by installing a sheathed truss (with the exterior plywood sheathing cut and nailed into place) at each end of the shed (Fig. 9). Note that the end trusses include a center chord for structural stability. This is rough cut to

Fig. 8 *With the wall in position, secure it by screwing down through the bottom 2x4 sole plate and into the floor framing.*

Fig. 9 *Start the roof by installing the end trusses. The plywood siding is nailed on before the truss is raised. A central 2x4 chord stiffens the sheathing.*

Fig. 10 *Carefully slide the roof trusses onto the walls. Space them precisely 24 in. on center and secure them with 3-in. screws.*

Fig. 11 *Cover the plywood roof sheathing with asphalt shingles, using roofing nails. Eight bundles are needed to complete this roof.*

Fig. 12 *Install perforated hardboard to the partition wall in the tool-storage area, for hanging tools. Fasten it with 1¼-in. screws.*

60 in., with the ends cut to accommodate the 40° angle.

Secure the trusses with 3-in. deck screws driven into the top wall plate. Then install the remaining roof trusses (**Fig. 10**). Set one truss over every wall stud and fasten it by driving 3-in. deck screws up through the top wall plate. One or two helpers will not only make the installation of the trusses go quicker, they will also make the operation safer and easier. In this case, the more the merrier.

To finish the construction of the roof structure, cover the trusses with ½-in. CDX plywood, then nail on the asphalt roof shingles (**Fig. 11**).

Finishing Touches

Secure perforated hardboard to the partition wall in the tool-storage area (**Fig. 12**), and install a transom window over the gable-end doors (**Fig. 13**). Make the transom window by assembling a simple wood frame to hold a piece

Power Up

Outbuildings can be made even more useful with the addition of electrical outlets and lights to accommodate working at nights or on overcast days. Bring power to your backyard barn fairly easily with a buried power line from the main junction box in your house. Your local building department will explain requirements for the job, including underground options, and they will point out any buried utilities. Contact your local utilities to check out your property before you begin building. The depth of your trench depends on how you run your power line. If you opt for cable designed for direct burial, most codes will require a 30-in.-deep trench. For a shallower trench and the flexibility to modify the service at a later date, running wires through conduit is a better idea.

Conduit

Rigid steel conduit can be buried as shallow as 6 in., but it's hard to work with and must be coated with asphalt to make it watertight. Plastic conduit is preferable for outbuildings. Though it must be buried at least 18-in. deep, its glued joints are watertight and components are easy to assemble. Sweep fittings are available for 90° turns and the material can be bent with a heat gun. For a simple 120v circuit you need ¾-in. conduit. It comes in 10-ft. lengths, and each piece has a female hub on one end for joining with another section. To join full lengths, apply PVC cement to the hub of one piece and the plain end of the next. Push the pieces together and twist a quarter turn to spread the glue over the mating surface and speed the bond. Join cut lengths of conduit with couplings. After digging the trench, assemble the conduit and use 90° sweep fittings at the house and outbuilding foundations to bring the conduit up to the wall. Use PVC cement to join the sweeps to the horizontal run, then measure and cut vertical lengths to extend at least 1 ft. above grade. Most codes require a slip coupling at this point. Before gluing the vertical length, chamfer one end with a file. Glue the opposite end to the sweep. The slip coupling is a sleeve with a hub at the top and a lubricated O-ring near the bottom. It allows the buried conduit to move as the soil settles. Slide the coupling's lower end over the chamfered riser. Push it down to within an inch of bottoming out.

When bringing conduit into a building, use a weatherproof LB (line box) or a weatherproof junction box. We prefer to use an LB in the outbuilding and a weatherproof junction box in the home connection. Bore a hole directly above the conduit, about 40 in. above the floor. Cut and join a piece of conduit to the LB and slip coupling so that the height of the LB matches the hole. Then insert a short stub of conduit into the LB's right-angle fitting, without gluing it, and guide the stub through the hole in the wall. Secure the riser and LB to the siding with a galvanized metal strap. To determine the final length of the stub, slip a male box adapter over it, again, without gluing the fitting. Then remove a knockout from a metal junction box and set the box over the male adapter. The distance that the front of the junction box extends beyond the face of the nearest stud is the length you'll subtract from the stub. After shortening the stub, glue it to the LB and the male adapter. Press the box over the male adapter and screw the box to the stud through its side holes. Finally, thread a locknut onto the male adapter and tighten it. At the house, bore through the rim joist above the conduit. Install a 4-in. threaded-plastic nipple into the back of the weatherproof junction box and a plastic male adapter into the bottom of the box. Press the threaded nipple through the wall and screw the box in place. Run conduit to the box using another slip coupling, and carefully caulk the joint between the siding and box.

Pulling Wires

Once the conduit is in place, three color-coded wires must be run through it from the house to the outbuilding. To pull the insulated wires through the conduit, first feed a fish tape from one box to the other. Attach three 12-ga. wires (black, white, and green) to the end of the tape and wrap them together with vinyl electrician's tape. Then slowly pull the wires back through the conduit. Leave plenty of wire showing at each box. At the LB, carefully feed the wires through the wall and fasten the cover in place over its weather gasket.

of double-strength glass, and secure the glass in place with glazing points.

Next, build the doors from 1x6 tongue-and-groove cedar boards and 1x6 battens. Attach the battens with 1½-in. screws, and hang the doors with heavy-duty strap hinges (**Fig. 14**). Before hanging the doors, trim the door frames with 1x4 cedar trim.

The style of the building is such that a butt joint is fine for the trim—no need to spend time mitering the pieces.

Finish the outer walls with 1x2 cedar pieces used to create corner boards. Use the same boards for the roof fascia front and back.

Cut a crown piece for where the fascia boards meet at the peak of the roof. This can be a simple triangle of layered plywood glued up and nailed in place, or something fancier, depending on your tastes.

For the windows, we used wooden barn sashes, which tilt in for ventilation (**Fig. 15**). The 2 x 3-ft. windows are available at most lumberyards and many home centers.

Install a barrel bolt at the top of each sash so they can be locked shut.

The textured plywood siding we installed came with a factory-applied coat of primer. We finished it with two coats of barn-red acrylic latex paint. If you would prefer to stain your shed, be sure to buy unprimed plywood siding and finish as soon after construction as possible.

TOOL *Care*

Handle It
Unfortunately, a missed swing with a sledge hammer often means a broken handle. But handles, like most other things around the workshop, can be recycled for a new and useful life. Next time you break a handle from a sledge, ax, hammer, or baseball bat, save it. These are made from the best kind of wood—usually hickory or ash—for turning new file and chisel handles. The handle for a socket chisel is a simple tapered turning. To make the handle for a tang chisel, make the hole to receive the tang before you turn the stock, then plug the hole temporarily while you turn the handle. For a professional-looking handle, size the collar. For a drive-fit ferrule, cut from thin-wall conduit or brass tubing. After installing the chisel in the handle, apply a 50/50 solution of shellac and linseed oil to the wood.

Fig. 13 *Make the 5-ft.-long transom window from a wooden frame and a single piece of glass. Install it over the end doors.*

Fig. 14 *Use tongue-and-groove cedar to build the doors. Then hang the doors with heavy-duty strap hinges and install the door handles.*

Fig. 15 *Slip the barn-sash window into the window frame and set it down on the sill. A simple barrel bolt holds it closed.*

Wiring Your Outbuilding

Begin by fitting the junction box with two box connectors—one for the 12/2 w/g cable that powers the light, and the other for the cable that leads to the receptacles. Pull 8 in. of each cable into the box and strip the sheathing from both. Tighten the box connectors and strip ¹/₂ in. of insulation from each wire. Join like-colored wires in twist connectors, and join the green wire from the conduit to the bare cable grounds. With a metal box, add a length of green wire to connect all three ground wires with a grounding screw at the back of the box. Finish the box by installing a blank cover plate. Run the cable through the middle of the stud cavities and joist spaces where it can be protected and attach metal plates on the joist faces so no nails can be driven in through the cable. Staple the cable to structural members every 4 ft. and within 8 in. of each box. If you plan to run cable through holes in studs and joists, bore holes in the center. Use straight cable runs that won't be skewered by nails. Nail metal protection plates on edges at the points that cables run through the members. Although most localities don't require conduit in unfinished walls, it pays to ask. To power a single light fixture, first bring the cable from the junction box to a switch box centered 40 in. off the floor. Then add a second cable to carry power to the fixture. Run the cable to the light fixture. Continue along a joist and into the ceiling box, leaving 8 in. of unsheathed wire showing.

At the switch, join both neutral wires in a twist connector and ground wires in a second connector. Then attach the two black wires to the switch and install the switch in the box. At the light fixture, attach the black wire to the brass-colored terminal and the white wire to the silver terminal. With a non-metallic box, press the ground wire deep inside or secure it to the fixture grounding screw if provided.

Pigtails

If your wiring boxes—such as a plug outlet and light fixture— are in a series, you need to make the connections through pigtails. A pigtail is a short length of color-coded wire with one end connected to a receptacle terminal and the other joined with a like-colored wire from the circuit. In this way, a failed receptacle can't interrupt power to those after it. You don't use pigtails in the final receptacle in the circuit. Some codes require pigtails on the hot side only, while others require both hot and neutral pigtails. Ground wires are always pigtailed unless it's the last receptacle. Install the receptacles in the boxes and secure the receptacle covers. At the outdoor receptacle located on your house, run cable between the panel and box, using pigtails as described. The only difference is that you'll need to ground the metal junction box as well. Do this with an additional pigtail secured to a grounding screw in the box. Finally, install a weatherproof receptacle cover and rubber gasket to keep out moisture.

At the Panel

Outlets used in wet conditions must have built-in ground-fault protection. The device that provides this is a ground-fault-circuit-interrupter (GFCI). It's designed to sense a short circuit by monitoring the current in both hot and neutral wires. If a short circuit occurs, power is switched off. Either a GFCI breaker or a GFCI receptacle can be used depending on the situation. For all outbuildings, use a GFCI breaker to cover all the receptacles on the circuit. Unlike standard breakers that have one terminal for the circuit's hot wire, GFCI breakers have two terminals for both the hot and neutral wires. The breaker comes with its own neutral lead that's connected to the breaker panel's neutral bus bar. Begin wiring the panel by shutting off the main power disconnect switch. Then remove the panel cover and break a ¹/₂-in knockout from the top or side of the panel. Install a box connector and feed cable into the panel. Next, cut the ground wire to length and bind it under one of the lugs of the neutral bus, or the grounded bus if a separate one is provided. Next, bind the end of the GFCI breaker's neutral lead under a separate neutral bus lug. Follow by connecting the cable's hot (black) wire to its breaker terminal and the neutral (white) wire to its terminal. Then press the breaker into its slot on the hot bus bar and replace the panel cover. Make it a point to check the breaker and box every month or so for safety, to ensure that there are no shorts or water damage.

Waste Not

This workhorse quickly and efficiently turns yard waste into black gold.

In this day and age of bloated landfills and restricted curbside trash service, we're all being confronted with the high cost of dealing with waste. And while there are some things we'll always need taken away, leaves, grass clippings, table scraps, and most other organic materials can easily stay at home. All we have to do to recycle this waste is be willing to start a compost pile. Of course, backyard-composting facilities are often as ugly as they are functional, but not so with the version that's shown here. It's attractive enough to be prominently located anywhere on your property.

*Key*POINTS

TIME
Prep Time	2 hours
Shop Time	5 hours
Assembly Time	8 hours

EFFORT
Skill Level	basic
Maintenance	none
Assistance	none

COST / BENEFITS
Expense: low
- Functional structure designed to **blend in** with garden design.
- Built to facilitate the **process of composting**.

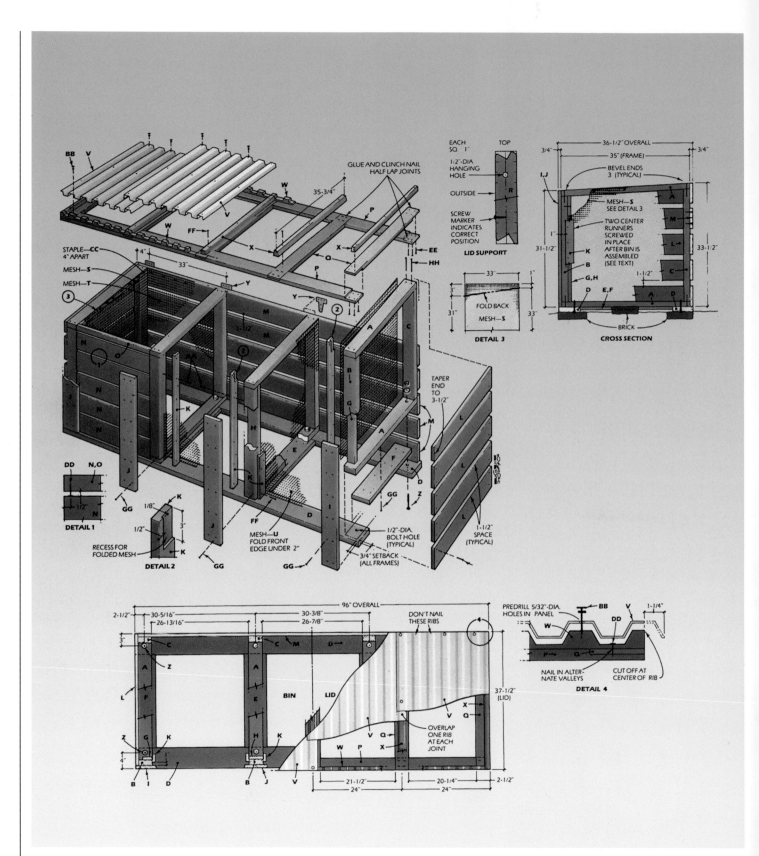

BB V

GLUE AND CLINCH NAIL
HALF LAP JOINTS

35-3/4"

W

V

W

FF

X

P

X

Q

EE

HH

STAPLE—CC
4" APART

MESH—S

MESH—T

3

4"

33"

Y

Y

2

2

M

M

1-1/2"

A

C

B

G

N

N

J

I

K

K

H

E

A

M

L

L

L

DD   N,O

N

1/2"

N

DETAIL 1

GG

1/8"

1/2"

K

3"

K

RECESS FOR
FOLDED MESH

DETAIL 2

J

K

FF

MESH—U
FOLD FRONT
EDGE UNDER 2"

GG

GG

D

I

1/2"-DIA.
BOLT HOLE
(TYPICAL)

3/4" SETBACK
(ALL FRAMES)

GG

F

D

GG

Z

TAPER
END
TO
3-1/2"

M

A

L

L

1-1/2"
SPACE
(TYPICAL)

EACH
SQ. 1"

TOP

1/2"-DIA.
HANGING
HOLE

OUTSIDE

SCREW
MARKER
INDICATES
CORRECT
POSITION

R

LID SUPPORT

33"

1"

3"

MESH—S

31"

FOLD BACK

33"

DETAIL 3

36-1/2" OVERALL

3/4"

35" [FRAME]

3/4"

BEVEL ENDS
3 (TYPICAL)

I,J

A

MESH—S
SEE DETAIL 3

M

TWO CENTER
RUNNERS
SCREWED
IN PLACE
AFTER BIN IS
ASSEMBLED
(SEE TEXT)

1"

K

L

31-1/2"

33-1/2"

B

G,H

1-1/2"

C

D

E,F

A

D

BRICK

CROSS SECTION

96" OVERALL

2-1/2"

30-5/16"

30-3/8"

DON'T NAIL
THESE RIBS

4

26-13/16"

26-7/8"

3"

C

C   M

D

A

Z

A

L

F

E

BIN

LID

Z

G   K

H   K

V   Q

OVERLAP
ONE RIB
AT EACH
JOINT

X   Q

B   I   D

B   J

V

W   P

X

V   Q

X

37-1/2"
(LID)

21-1/2"

20-1/4"

2-1/2"

24"

24"

PREDRILL 5/32"-DIA.
HOLES IN PANEL

BB

V

1-1/4"

W

DD

NAIL IN ALTER-
NATE VALLEYS

CUT OFF AT
CENTER OF RIB

DETAIL 4

The compost bin we've designed is meant to last many years, and its relatively simple construction requires only basic woodworking skills. It's dimensioned to process about ¾ of a cubic yard of organic material in each bin, yielding an ample supply of compost for the average garden on a continuing schedule. Be careful about modifying any of the dimensions or materials we've specified here—changes could affect the efficiency of the composting process.

Materials

This compost bin is built of redwood—the ideal lumber because of its pleasing appearance and remarkable resistance to decay and insect infestation, particularly termites. Not all redwood will serve the purpose, however. Only the reddish-brown heartwood from the tree's core contains the substances that render it decay-resistant. The creamy-colored sapwood that makes up the outer layer of the tree is not insect- or decay-resistant.

Therefore, try and get Construction Heart Grade redwood. If this is unavailable or too expensive, the next best grade is Merchantable Heart Grade. Both these grades are suitable for soil-contact applications. The former has knots of varying sizes and minor imperfections. The latter has larger knots, some splits, and some manufacturing flaws. Also, request either grade as surfaced, not unsurfaced (rough sawn).

The bin features removable front slats for easy access to the compartments, which are lined on the sides, back, and bottom with wire mesh (also known as hardware cloth). This keeps out animals while allowing air to circulate and water to

drain. The mesh floor prevents ground-burrowing pests from getting in, but allows beneficial earthworms to migrate up into the pile. The plastic Filon panel lid is extremely durable,

Fig. 1 *For neat crosscuts, make a T-guide from scrap wood. Run the saw's shoe against the guide for straight and bevel cuts.*

Materials List

Key	No.	Size and description (use)
A	8	1½ x 3½ x 35" redwood (frame)
B	4	1½ x 3½ x 28½" redwood (frame)
C	2	1½ x 3½ x 30½" redwood (frame)
D	2	1½ x 5½ x 96" redwood (base frame)
E	2	¾ x 5½ x 25½" redwood (mesh nailer)
F	2	¾ x 4½ x 25½" redwood (mesh nailer)
G	2	¾ x 2 x 28½" redwood (mesh nailer)
H	2	¾ x 3½ x 28½" redwood (mesh nailer)
I	2	¾ x 5¼ x 31½" redwood (front runner)
J	2	¾ x 5½ x 31½" redwood (front runner)
K	6	¾ x 2 x 31½" redwood (rear runner)
L	10	¾ x 5½ x 35¾" redwood (side slat)
M	5	¾ x 5½ x 94½" redwood (back slat)
N	15	¾ x 5½ x 26⅝" redwood (front slat)
O	3	¾ x 1½ x 26⅝" redwood (front slat)
P	25	¾ x 2½ x 96" redwood (lid frame)
Q	5	¾ x 2½ x 37½" redwood (lid frame)
R	2	¾ x 2 x 35½" redwood (lid support)
S	6	33 x 34" wire mesh (divider)
T	3	26½ x 32½" wire mesh (back)
U	3	26½ x 31" wire mesh (bottom)
V	2	26¾ x 96" corrugated panel cut to four 37½" lengths (cover)
W	3	6-ft. pieces corrugated redwood molding
X	3	6-ft. lengths vertical redwood molding cut to 35¾"
Y	4	3" Tee Hinge
Z	8	½"-dia. x 3½" carriage bolt, washer, and nut, zinc plated
AA	as reqd.	1⅝" galvanized drywall screws
BB	as reqd.	1¾" aluminum plastic panel nails
CC	as reqd.	¾" galvanized staples
DD	as reqd.	¾" nails
EE	as reqd.	3d galvanized common nails
FF	as reqd.	4d galvanized common nails
GG	as reqd.	6d galvanized common nails
HH	as reqd.	16d galvanized common nails

Misc.: Plastic resin glue; eight bricks.

Fig. 2 *Each frame section is made up of four pieces nailed together with 16d galvanized nails, and marked with chalk to indicate placement.*

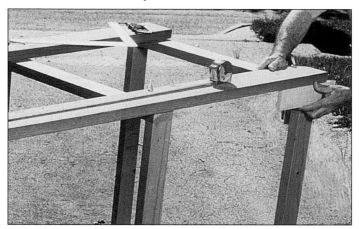

Fig. 3 *With the frame inverted, position the baseboards using a scrap block at the edge of the frame to gauge a ³/₄-in. overhang.*

Fig. 5 *With the frame inverted, attach the mesh nailers to the bottom of each frame using 6d galvanized common nails.*

keeps the compost from getting soaked when it rains, and tends to let through some solar energy—especially in cooler months—to keep the piles warm.

Frame Construction

The construction of this project is relatively simple and can be accomplished with tools that any home do-it-yourselfer is likely to have—a circular saw, an electric drill, and several hand tools.

Begin by cutting the 2x4s to length for each frame. The top of the frame is pitched down 2 in. across the bin's width. To achieve this pitch, crosscut the tops of the front and rear frame members at a 3° bevel. Use a crosscutting guide to ensure accurate, smooth cuts (**Fig. 1**).

Assemble the end and divider frames using two 16d common galvanized nails at each joint (**Fig. 2**). Label each frame, and position them bottom side up as they will be

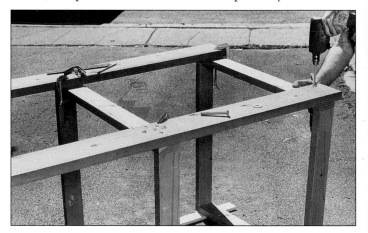

Fig. 4 *Clamp the baseboards to the frames and bore the ¹/₂-in. holes for the carriage bolts that attach the baseboards.*

Fig. 6 *Remove the baseboards from the frame and attach the front mesh nailers to each frame. Again, use galvanized nails.*

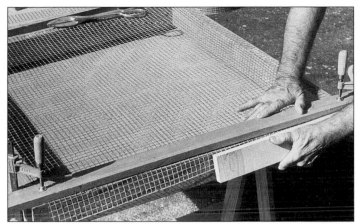

Fig. 7 *Position mesh over the frames with the overhang at the front. Clamp a board over the mesh and fold it with a scrap block.*

Fig. 8 *Place the mesh on a flat surface and hammer over the fold. It's faster to tap on the block than hammer the mesh itself.*

when assembled. Place the 2x6 base members on top of the frames using a scrap block to position them with a ¾-in. overhang at the ends, front, and back (**Fig. 3**).

Hold the frame and base pieces in position with a clamp at each point where the frame and base pieces overlap. Bore the ½-in.-dia. holes for the carriage bolts as indicated in the drawing (**Fig. 4**).

Temporarily insert the bolts, then rip and crosscut the bottom mesh nailers to size and attach them to the bottom frame members with 6d galvanized common nails (**Fig. 5**).

Attach Wire Mesh

Remove the frames from the base pieces to permit the nailing and stapling operations that follow. Start by securely fastening the nailer strip to the back of each 2x4 front vertical member (**Fig. 6**).

Next, cut six pieces of wire mesh 33 in. long from a 36-in.-wide roll. Lay the mesh across each frame, clamp a strip of wood across it, and fold over the mesh so that it conforms to the slope of the frame.

Use a block of wood to distribute the pressure evenly across the mesh (**Fig. 7**). Finish folding over the edge by placing the mesh on a flat surface and working over the fold with a block of wood and a hammer (**Fig. 8**). This produces a neat exposed edge, free of sharp points that could easily injure even the most careful user.

Use ¾-in. galvanized staples (also called poultry net nails) to attach the mesh, spacing them 4 in. apart. Attach the mesh to both sides of the dividers. Leave about 1 ft. unstapled at the bottom on one side of each divider frame, so later you can tighten the nut on each bolt that fastens the base pieces to the frames.

Rip and crosscut the rear and front runners to size. Chisel a slight recess at the top of the rear runners to allow them to fit tightly against the frame where the mesh is doubled over.

Fig. 9 *Nail the front and rear runners to the frame. The rear runner is notched to accommodate the mesh's fold at the corner.*

Fig. 10 *Bolt the end frames to the baseboards after the mesh is installed. On end frames, the bolts are positioned to clear the nailers.*

Nail the rear runners on the end frames and on one side of each divider frame, where the mesh has been fully attached (**Fig. 9**). Attach the remaining two rear runners with drywall screws after the divider frames have been securely bolted to the baseboards.

End Frames

Bolt the end frames to the baseboards (**Fig. 10**). Prop up the unattached mesh while you tighten the bolts that attach the divider frames to the baseboards (**Fig. 11**). Tighten the nut so that the square section of the carriage bolt bites firmly into the baseboards. After the frames are bolted in place, fold down the mesh on the remaining two divider frames and screw down the last two rear runners. This completes the bin subassembly (**Fig. 12**).

Use the same galvanized drywall screws to attach the side and rear slats. Screws are used in lieu of nails because the freestanding frames tend to bounce if nailed. Use a pair of 1½-in.-wide blocks to gauge the spacing between the side and back slats as you screw them in place (**Fig. 13**).

Attach the back mesh pieces after the rear slats are attached. The bottom mesh pieces go on last. Crosscut the drop-in front slats to size.

The drop-in slats are separated by nails that are driven partially into the edge of each slat. Leave ½ in. of each nail exposed to provide the needed ventilation gap. To drive these nails to a uniform height, butt a piece of ½-in.-thick hardwood against the nail after it has been started. Drive the nail until the head touches the guide block.

The Lid

Assemble the lid frame with half-lap joints. Mark the width of each frame member on the ends of the pieces where appropriate. Set the saw blade to cut a ⅜-in.-deep kerf (half

Fig. 11 *Don't nail the mesh at the bottom of the two center frames to retain access to nut. Tighten the nut until the bolt digs in.*

Fig. 12 *Complete the structural assembly of the compost bin before attaching the side and back slats and the rest of the wire mesh.*

Fig. 13 *Screw the slats to the end frames. For correct spacing, support each slat while fastening it with 1½-in.-wide spacer blocks.*

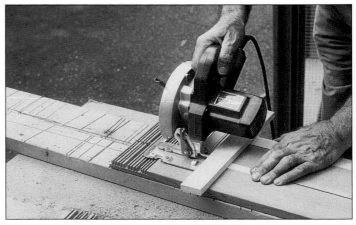

Fig. 14 *Use a T-guide to make the repeated kerf cuts in the lid frame. The kerfs should be no more than ¼ in. apart.*

Fig. 15 *After cutting the kerfs, clean out between the kerfs with a sharp chisel. The overlap's depth equals half the stock's thickness.*

Fig. 16 *Glue together the frame members with water-resistant plastic resin glue. Then clinch nail the pieces together.*

Fig. 17 *Support the panels on the corrugated molding. Mark a cutline with tape and run the saw's shoe against a fence.*

Fig. 18 *Nail the corrugated redwood molding through alternate valleys. The molding is sold with the corrugated panels.*

the thickness of the stock) and, running the saw against a T-guide, cut a series of kerfs no more than ¼ in. apart. Chisel out the waste (**Fig. 14 and 15**). Cut two or more frame pieces at a time during this operation. The combined width makes a more stable base for the saw, as opposed to cutting one piece at a time.

The five crossmembers are attached to the two lengthwise members with plastic resin glue and clinched nails (**Fig. 16**).

The lid is surfaced with four pieces of fiberglass-reinforced plastic Filon panel cut from two 8-ft.-long panels. These panels are sold at lumberyards and home centers. The panels are attached to matching corrugated redwood molding that is sold with the panels.

Lid Assembly

Support the panels while cutting them by resting them atop the corrugated redwood molding (**Fig. 17**). Cut two panels at

a time. Mark the appropriate length on one panel and fasten a piece of tape across its width. Mark the cutting line on the center of the tape and clamp a fence across the panel to run the saw against. Make the cut with a fine-toothed plywood or crosscut blade. To fit the four panels across the 8-ft. length of the lid with a 1-rib overlap, trim off 1¼ in. from the first and last rib using tin snips.

Nail the corrugated molding strips to the front and rear of the frame after cutting off the starting end to conform to the trimmed panel. Nail Filon vertical molding strips centered on the crossframe pieces (**Fig. 18 and 19**).

Use aluminum nails with neoprene washers to attach the Filon panels to the moldings (**Fig. 20**). Prebore the nail holes in the panels and the molding with a ⁵⁄₃₂-in. bit. Nail the panels as shown in the drawing, and, when this is completed, attach the lid to the bin with four hinges.

We leveled the bin across eight bricks, one under each

Fig. 19 *Vertical redwood molding is installed on the frame so that it aligns precisely with ridges on the corrugated molding.*

Fig. 20 *Prebore the clearance holes in the panel ridges and molding. Attach the panels with aluminum nails that have rubber washers.*

TECH *Tips*

Using the Three-Bin Composter
Food and yard waste account for about a quarter of our nation's garbage, so it's not surprising that states and municipalities are setting up programs that encourage composting. Composting not only helps our solid waste woes, it is also an inexpensive and effective way to improve soil. Compost loosens clay soil and improves water retention of sandy soil. It can supply nutrients, neutralize soil toxins and metals, and act as a pH buffer for your plants.

Materials
Collect a variety of organic materials. Leaves, grass clippings, tree and brush prunings, garden plants, manure, hay, straw, black-and-white newspaper (shredded, minus the colored advertising supplements), and even kitchen scraps (minus meat, bones, dairy, and fat) will turn into rich compost. The smaller the pieces, the faster the microorganisms break them down. Avoid colored and glossy papers because some inks contain heavy metals. Pet litter and sewage should be avoided because they contain toxins that a backyard pile cannot eliminate. When adding to your pile, consider the needs of the bacteria, the organisms that do most of the work of decomposition. They digest organic materials and release bound-up nutrients, and to do this efficiently

they need a certain ratio of carbon to nitrogen. Although difficult to measure exactly, the ratio that works best is approximately 30 parts carbon to 1 part nitrogen. Sawdust, leaves, and other dry, tough, fibrous materials are high in carbon. Manures, grass clippings, and green plant vegetation are high in nitrogen. Think of carbon as the food and nitrogen as the digestive enzymes, and add roughly 30 times as much carbon as nitrogen. Mix your materials on the ground and add them to the first bin. Or alternate layers of carbon and nitrogen materials. If there's too much nitrogen, you'll notice the unpleasant odor of ammonia gas as excess nitrogen is released. To remedy this, add more well-chopped carbon materials and mix them in. With too much carbon, decomposition slows down. In this case, try mixing in a nitrogen source, such as fresh grass clippings, fresh manure, or blood meal.

Activators
You may want to add an activator to make sure your pile has the necessary microorganisms. Finished compost, soil, and manure are good activators. Or use commercially available activators that contain dormant bacteria and fungi. These come in a powdered form, and a little will activate a large amount of compost. These are sprinkled on top of

Fig. 21 *Situate the bin on level ground and place a brick at the center of each bin to support the mesh. Nail in the bottom mesh.*

carriage bolt location. The bricks were slightly recessed into the soil and checked with a long board and level to obtain a true plane.

To prevent the weight of the compost from depressing the bottom mesh and loosening it, a brick was positioned under the center of each bin. Of course, you can substitute any large, flat stones for the bricks. Just be sure that the whole compost bin unit is relatively level so that the bin's lid will be able to work properly.

Complete the bin by nailing down the back and bottom mesh. The front edge of the bottom mesh is folded like the sides (**Fig. 21**). You can finish the bin with a stain if you like, but it's unnecessary. If you've used heart redwood, you don't even need to use a water sealer and—in keeping with the organic nature of the structure—it's best to leave the compost bin wood structure in its natural state. You can start putting organic material in immediately.

each layer of materials you add to your pile. Many garden centers carry activators, or you can order directly from manufacturers.

Moisture
Microorganisms need adequate moisture to decompose organic matter. Keep your pile as moist as a well-wrung sponge. As you build your pile, sprinkle water on top of each layer, but don't saturate. Reach into your pile every once in a while and squeeze a handful of materials. If they are too wet, turn the pile to help it dry out. If you need to add more water, insert your garden hose or watering can into the middle of the pile in a few places.

Oxygen
To stimulate the most efficient bacteria, keep your pile well aerated. The aerobic or oxygen-loving bacteria are 90 percent more efficient at breaking down organic matter than the anaerobic bacteria that take over in a pile devoid of oxygen. Furthermore, anaerobes produce substances that smell like ammonia and rotten eggs. Encourage airflow through the bottom of the pile by using bulky materials, such as corn stalks, for the bottom layer. Commercially available aerating tools are available from gardening catalogs.

Turning
Turn a pile to take advantage of the intensified microbial activity in the middle of the pile. Once the microorganisms break down materials in the center, their activity slows, and the pile begins to cool. Turning provides additional food for the microorganisms—as their activity increases, so does the temperature. Thus, turning can help raise the temperature high enough to kill weed seeds and disease organisms (about 150° F). To keep your pile at maximum heating capacity, it's worth investing in a compost thermometer, which is basically a round thermometer face with a long metal probe that reaches into the compost pile. Turn your pile whenever your thermometer tells you the temperature in the center of the pile has dropped below about 100°F. When turning no longer raises the temperature, your pile is probably well decomposed and ready to use. Keep in mind that turning is only beneficial up to a point. Turning too frequently can cause a disruption in the process that outweighs any benefit. In a fast-cooking pile, every three days is often enough. In a slower pile, every three weeks may be sufficient. Also remember that you can make compost year-round in moderate climates. But in colder regions, you and the microorganisms can take the winter off.

Basic Beauty

This small, well-tailored backyard deck can be the centerpiece of all your outdoor activities.

If the fronts of houses are more public and formal, the backs are decidedly private and informal, which explains why backyard decks are so popular in an age of instant access, crowded commutes, and information overload. A wooden deck can be a party center or a quiet retreat—a place to repair, to relax, or to socialize with a select group of family and friends. If your home and lifestyle are still waiting for that backdoor retreat, we have good news. Although the materials costs for a deck like this can be high, when properly finished, this deck can add much more than that cost to the value of your home.

*Key*POINTS

TIME
Prep Time	8-10 hours
Shop Time	4 hours
Assembly Time	15-20 hours

EFFORT
Skill Level	intermediate
Maintenance	light
Assistance	one-two

COST / BENEFITS
Expense: expensive
- Great **first deck project** for the home woodworker.
- **Specifications are flexible** depending on size and configuration of your deck.

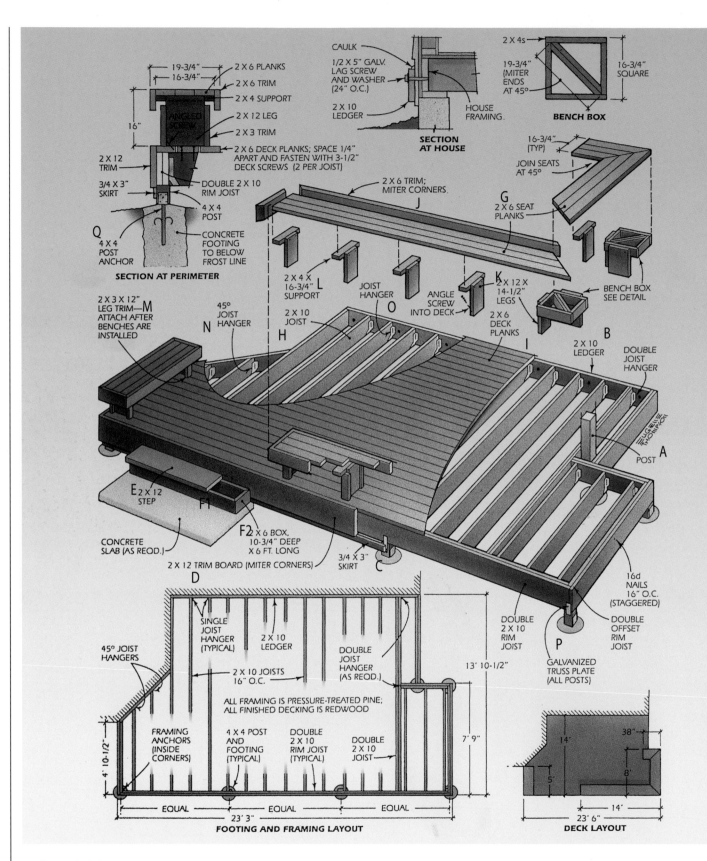

19-3/4"
16-3/4"
2 X 6 PLANKS
2 X 6 TRIM
2 X 4 SUPPORT
2 X 12 LEG
2 X 3 TRIM
16"
ANGLED SCREW
2 X 12 TRIM
2 X 6 DECK PLANKS; SPACE 1/4" APART AND FASTEN WITH 3-1/2" DECK SCREWS (2 PER JOIST)
3/4 X 3" SKIRT
DOUBLE 2 X 10 RIM JOIST
4 X 4 POST
Q
4 X 4 POST ANCHOR
CONCRETE FOOTING TO BELOW FROST LINE
SECTION AT PERIMETER

CAULK
1/2 X 5" GALV. LAG SCREW AND WASHER (24" O.C.)
2 X 10 LEDGER
HOUSE FRAMING.
SECTION AT HOUSE

2 X 4s
19-3/4" (MITER ENDS AT 45°)
16-3/4" SQUARE
BENCH BOX

16-3/4" (TYP)
JOIN SEATS AT 45°
G
2 X 6 SEAT PLANKS
2 X 6 TRIM; MITER CORNERS.
J
BENCH BOX SEE DETAIL

2 X 3 X 12" LEG TRIM—M ATTACH AFTER BENCHES ARE INSTALLED
45° JOIST HANGER
N
2 X 4 X 16-3/4" SUPPORT
L
JOIST HANGER
2 X 10 JOIST
O
ANGLE SCREW INTO DECK
K
2 X 12 X 14-1/2" LEGS
2 X 6 DECK PLANKS
I
B
2 X 10 LEDGER
DOUBLE JOIST HANGER
H
POST
A

E 2 X 12 STEP
F1
CONCRETE SLAB (AS REQD.)
F 2 X 6 BOX, 10-3/4" DEEP X 6 FT. LONG
2 X 12 TRIM BOARD (MITER CORNERS)
3/4 X 3" SKIRT
C
DOUBLE 2 X 10 RIM JOIST
P
GALVANIZED TRUSS PLATE (ALL POSTS)
DOUBLE OFFSET RIM JOIST
16d NAILS 16" O.C. (STAGGERED)

D
45° JOIST HANGERS
SINGLE JOIST HANGER (TYPICAL)
2 X 10 LEDGER
DOUBLE JOIST HANGER (AS REQD.)
13' 10-1/2"
4' 10-1/2"
FRAMING ANCHORS (INSIDE CORNERS)
4 X 4 POST AND FOOTING (TYPICAL)
DOUBLE 2 X 10 RIM JOIST (TYPICAL)
DOUBLE 2 X 10 JOIST
7' 9"
2 X 10 JOISTS 16" O.C.
ALL FRAMING IS PRESSURE-TREATED PINE; ALL FINISHED DECKING IS REDWOOD
EQUAL
EQUAL
EQUAL
23' 3"
FOOTING AND FRAMING LAYOUT

14'
38"
5'
8'
23' 6"
14'
DECK LAYOUT

We decided to build our deck superstructure out of pressure-treated pine because of its strength and high resistance to moisture and insects. But we also wanted the rich look and feel of redwood—to say nothing of its weather resistance—in the finished deck, so we came up with this box-like construction. The concealed pressure-treated lumber does most of the work, while the Construction Heart Grade redwood does most of the showing-off. When stepped in and out to echo the lines of the house and capped with a simple redwood bench, the deck manages an attractive complement of scale, with a look that is both satisfying and modest.

The deck as sized and configured in the drawing is for perspective. Your own deck's design and configuration will depend on where you site it, the shape and style of your home, and how much space you want to dedicate to the deck as opposed to the rest of your yard.

Getting Started

The first order of business is to lay out the perimeter. Measure out from the house, at each end of your future deck—in this case, 13 ft.,10½ in. Then drive wooden stakes and stretch a string line between them. This line will give you the exact outer edge of the double rim joist and the posts that will support it. A redwood 2x12 trim board will eventually bring the dimension to 14 ft.

Using this line as a guide, dig post-hole footings to frost level, usually 24 to 48 in. deep, depending on the climate of your location. Place one footing at each of the outside corners of the deck layout and equally space two more posts between these. Then, to accommodate the step and offset, dig two additional footing holes—one at the outside corner and one at the inside corner of the offset.

Fill these holes to about 1 in. above grade with concrete, and while the mix is still wet, insert metal 4x4 post brackets into the concrete, so that the outer edge of the bracket is aligned with the string line (**Fig. 1**). Then level each bracket in both directions with a torpedo level (**Fig. 2**). Finally, allow the footings to cure a day or two before building on them.

Because this deck is built at ground level, there will be no getting under it once it's finished. For this reason, it pays to strip the sod and cover the area with landscape fabric. The fabric will keep weeds from growing under the deck. Just roll out the fabric and pin it in place with galvanized nails (**Fig. 3**).

Fig. 1 *After pouring concrete into each footing hole, set a metal 4x4 bracket into the wet concrete. Align the brackets with the string line.*

Materials List

Key	No.*	Size and description (use)
A	6	4 x 4 x 48" pressure-treated pine (post)
B	1	2 x 10 x 210" pressure-treated pine (ledger)
C	4	¾ x 3 x 120" redwood (skirt)
D	4	2 x 12 x 120" redwood (trim board)
E	1	2 x 12 x 72" redwood (step)
F1	2	2 x 6 x 72" redwood (step base, front, and back)
F2	2	2 x 6 x 10¾" redwood (step base sides)
G	6	2 x 6 x 144" redwood (seat planks)
H	22	2 x 10 x 162" pressure-treated pine (joist)
I	54	2 x 6 x 144" redwood (deck planks)
J	5	2 x 6 x 144" redwood (bench trim)
K	11	2 x 14½ x 12" redwood (bench leg)
L	19	2 x 4 x 16¾" pressure-treated pine (bench leg support)
M	20	2 x 3 x 12" redwood (bench leg trim)
N	2	45° joist hanger
O	35	joist hanger
P	9	2 x 5" galvanized truss plate
Q	6	metal 4 x 4 post brackets

Misc.: Concrete for footings and step slab; landscape fabric; joist hanger nails; 3½" deck screws; 16d nails; ½ x 5" galvanized lagscrew and washer.

*Number of pieces depends on the exact size and shape of your deck.

Fig. 2 *Level the 4x4 brackets in both directions using a torpedo level, and let the concrete cure for at least a day before building on it.*

Fig. 3 *Remove the sod on the site, then cover the soil beneath the deck with landscape fabric. This keeps weeds from growing.*

Fig. 4 *Lay out the joist positions, then use a scrap of 2x10 joist to align each joist hanger. Use proper joist-hanging nails to install the brackets.*

Shovel a little sand over the fabric to hold it in place, or place small rocks on top as anchors.

The next step is to mount the ledger plate on the house. In our case, the first row of hardboard siding was not shimmed out at the bottom. If yours is, you'll need to either remove the shim or shim the top of the ledger plate. The point is that the ledger plate should be vertical, not canted inward.

To mount the 2x10 ledger, block under it or have a helper hold it up, then nail it to the siding-clad rim joist of the house with a few 16d galvanized nails. If your ledger will wrap around a trimmed corner, as ours did, use a circular saw to mortise out the depth of the vertical trim on the backside of the ledger. This need not be a perfect cut, as its only purpose is to allow the ledger to fit flush against the siding. In our case, we also continued the ledger partway around the cantilevered wall, stopping 1½ in. short of the adjoining 45° trim pieces. With the ledger tacked in place, bore a series of pilot holes every 24 to 32 in. along its length and lag the ledger into the rim of the house. Galvanized lagbolts, ½ x 5 in. long, will reach through all three layers of material. Back up each with a washer.

Installing Hangers and Posts

Start by laying out and marking all the joists along the ledger. A 14-ft. span requires joists set on 16-in. centers. With the layout complete, install a joist hanger at each marked location. To keep from getting a few of them too high or too low, use a short piece of 2x10 as a guide, aligning its top with the top of the ledger (**Fig. 4**). When positioned correctly, nail the hangers in place, using proper joist-hanger nails.

With the house side of the deck laid out and fitted with hangers, it's time to determine the height of the 4x4 posts that will support the double rim joists. Begin by cutting short lengths of 4x4 and setting them in the footing brackets. Then set a precut joist (13 ft., 6 in.) into one of the ledger hangers

Fig. 5 *Use a straight joist to level between the ledger and the support posts. Mark and cut the posts, then check the level again.*

Fig. 6 Anchor the footing bracket to the post with nails and the post to the double rim joist with a 2x5 galvanized truss plate.

Fig. 7 Use 45° joist hangers to attach the joists to the angled ledger. Nail the top half of the joist directly into the ledger for stability.

Fig. 8 Double joists require double-wide hangers. Install these hangers on the rim joist, then slide the two joists into place.

Fig. 9 Use a ¼-in. plywood spacer to maintain consistent gaps between the decking planks. Drive two screws through each board into each joist.

opposite a footing and place a 4-ft. level atop the joist. When the joist is level, mark the post and cut it to length, then set the joist on the post and check for level again (**Fig. 5**). When two such posts are marked and trimmed, use their elevations to snap a string line across the remaining posts. With all posts cut to length, nail two sets of 2x10s together with 16d galvanized nails to create the double rim joist. Alternate the nails, high and low, at 16-in. intervals. Make the outer 2x10 of the double rim 3 in. short of the overall length of the deck to accommodate the redwood trim joist. Then cut the inner joist 1½ in. short of the outer joist at each end. These stepped ends will allow you to nail the intersecting side joists from both directions.

With the posts cut and the double rim joist nailed together, set the rim on the posts and lay out the hanger locations to match those on the ledger. Then nail the posts through the footing brackets and join the posts to the rim joist with galvanized truss plates (**Fig. 6**). Nail the remaining floor joist hangers. Then check each joist to determine which side has the crown and set them into the brackets with the crown up. Nail all the joists to the joist hangers.

Building the Corners

Our deck has two corner details that required special attention. The first was the 45° extension around the cantilevered dining room wall. To build this section, just frame in a double rim joist to span between the ledger and outer double rim. Nail the intersecting corners, in both directions, and add a corner bracket to the inside of the double offset. Then use 45° joist hangers to support the joists set against the angled ledger (**Fig. 7**).

As for the step offset, frame-in a double joist on one side—in our case this was alongside our porch post—using a double-width joist hanger (**Fig. 8**). Then frame the outer edge of the offset conventionally, wrapping it back to the double

Fig. 10 *Trim the perimeter of the deck with 2x12 redwood boards. Screw these boards into the rim joists and also into the deck planks.*

Fig. 11 *Build the square corner bench boxes, then install two mitered crosspieces in each to support the mitered seat planks.*

Fig. 12 *Set the corner boxes in position and measure for the seat planks. Prebore the ends and screw the planks to the boxes.*

Fig. 13 *To make the bench legs, cut 14 ½-in.-long pieces from 2x12 stock and center them on the crossmembers. Then screw them in place.*

Fig. 14 *Bring the mitered bench sections together at the corners and screw them in place on top of the box supports.*

Fig. 15 *Bore the clearance holes diagonally through the bench legs and into the decking. Then drive screws into the holes.*

joist. A second double-width hanger makes this an easy connection. Then bridge between the return of the double rim joist and the ledger plate on the house with a second double rim. Finally, cut shorter joists to fill in the open spaces and hang them 16 in. on center.

Decking the Framework

Before decking over the pressure-treated undercarriage, thoroughly caulk the joint between the ledger plate and the house siding. This will keep rainwater from entering the joint and rotting the siding. Also, keep in mind that you'll find some warped lumber in every stack you buy.

These boards are still usable, but should be reserved for cutting into shorter lengths to fit tight spots. Use your straightest boards for the longest sections of exposed deck. To keep the decking running straight, measure out from the house at several points, and snap chalklines to establish a straight run across the joists. Every few boards, re-key your decking off of these lines.

Starting against the house, lay your first length of 2x6 redwood tight against the siding. Then nail or screw it down with two fasteners in each joist. Though nails work well enough, we used 3½-in. deck screws. They are harder to install, but galvanized screws hold longer and are better at coaxing warped lumber back in line.

For quick gapping of all subsequent decking planks, it pays to make two ¼-in. spacers. (We made ours from ¼-in. plywood.) Slide a spacer between the preceding plank and the latest plank and nail or screw the plank in place. Then slide the spacer down a joist and fasten the plank again (**Fig. 9**). When screwing the end of a plank, always prebore clearance holes to avoid splitting it. When fastening a plank away from the ends, place two screws at every intersecting joist, each ¾ in. in from the edge of the plank.

With all the decking in place, it's time to install the 2x12

Fig. 16 *Finish the legs with 2x3 vertical trim pieces. These pieces hide the leg screws and give the benches a more substantial feel.*

rim-joist trim boards (**Fig. 10**). Miter the corners and screw them to the pressure-treated rims, so that the top of each 2x12 is flush with the top of each decking plank. To keep the top edge of this trim board from warping outward, as it surely will, screw it to the decking planks as well, about every 18 in.

Building the Benches

The benches we built here are about as simple as they come. To construct the continuous J-shaped bench, start by building two redwood boxes, 16¾ in. square, using standard 2x4 lumber. Next, miter-cut two sets of 19⅜-in. crosspieces for each box. Join them back-to-back with galvanized nails. Finally, screw them into the boxes (**Fig. 11**).

Set each box in its corner, just inside the 2x12 trim board, and measure for the seat planks. Miter each plank at 45°, using the positions of the boxes to establish the length of the planks. Finally, screw these planks to the tops of the boxes, preboring clearance holes in the ends (**Fig. 12**). To build the long runs of the bench, boxes won't be necessary. Just lay out 2x4 braces (also 16¾ in. long) about 32 in. apart, and screw three deck planks over them. With all three planks assembled, cut one end at a 45° angle.

To build the bench legs, cut 14½-in.-long pieces of 2x12 planks and screw one to each 2x4 seat support (**Fig. 13**). Do the same with the boxes, placing one leg under the inside edge of each box, and one spaced between the boxes. Turn the assemblies upright and set them in position. Then join the two mitered corners and screw the seat planks in place (**Fig. 14**). Assemble the short end of the J in like fashion, and build the remaining bench without corner boxes. To anchor the bench to the deck, drill the face of each leg and drive 3½-in. screws at an angle into the deck planks (**Fig. 15**).

To trim out the bench, screw mitered 2x6 redwood planks to the sides of the seat, anchoring them at each crossmember location and at each mitered corner. Finish the bench by nailing 3-in. uprights to the faces of each 2x12 leg (**Fig. 16**). These vertical trim pieces not only bring the legs into a more satisfactory scale, but also hide the anchoring screws.

Finishing Up

All that remains is to conceal the truss plates nailed to the posts with a redwood skirt and to build two box steps. To install the skirt, simply rip a redwood 1x8 into two 3-in. strips and nail them to the fronts of the posts.

Because our deck is built so near the ground, we opted for a simple box step, set on concrete. If you prefer, you can rest your steps on concrete cap blocks, set in a bed of gravel. To make the steps, build two rectangular boxes as shown on the plans. Set these boxes on their supports and drill the back of each several times with a ¼-in. bit. Then screw through these holes into the face of the deck. The oversize screw holes will allow the step to float a bit with the seasons. Finally, screw a 2x12 tread to the top of each box.

Garage Overflow

No more room in the garage? Never fear—find handy storage space with this simple structure.

Consider the items we now store in garden sheds. In addition to the lawn mower, the selection may include a snowblower, leaf blower, wheelbarrow and, of course, the usual lawn-and-garden hand tools. The total value can easily run to several thousand dollars. With this in mind, the quality of the shed itself becomes a priority. You could, of course, choose from metal shed kits long offered at the retail level, or site-built woodsheds available at lumberyards. We opted for a third alternative—constructing a quality shed from scratch, using conventional house-building materials and methods.

*Key*POINTS

TIME
Prep Time . . . . **6 hours**
Shop Time . . . . **7 hours**
Assembly Time . . . . **24 hours**

EFFORT
Skill Level . . . . **intermediate**
Maintenance . . . . **light**
Assistance . . . . **one**

COST / BENEFITS
Expense: **expensive**
• **Plans can be customized** to suit your yard space and your own storage needs.
• The **more help** you have, the quicker the project will go.

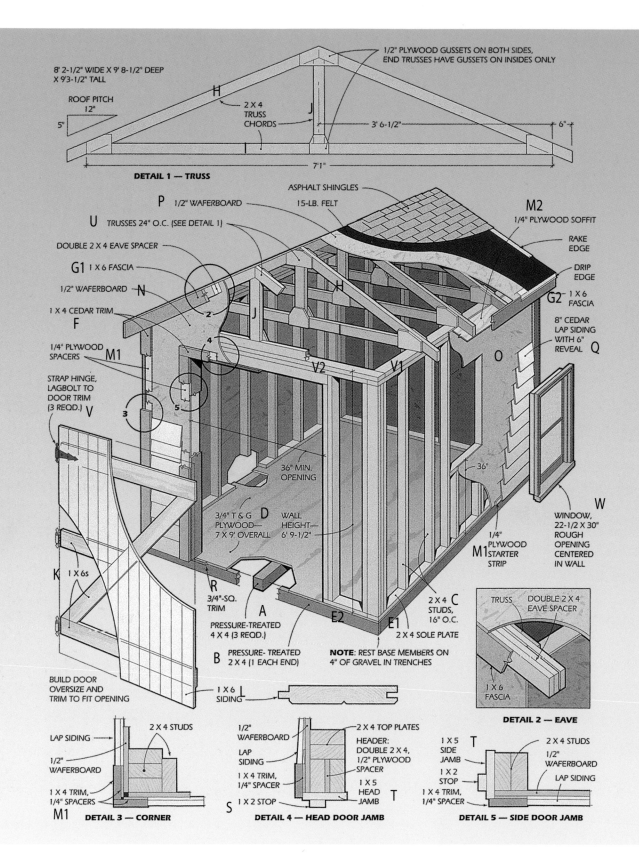

8' 2-1/2" WIDE X 9' 8-1/2" DEEP
X 9'3-1/2" TALL

ROOF PITCH
12"
5"

H
2 X 4
TRUSS
CHORDS

J

3' 6-1/2"

6"

7'1"

1/2" PLYWOOD GUSSETS ON BOTH SIDES,
END TRUSSES HAVE GUSSETS ON INSIDES ONLY

DETAIL 1 — TRUSS

ASPHALT SHINGLES
15-LB. FELT

P 1/2" WAFERBOARD

U TRUSSES 24" O.C. (SEE DETAIL 1)

DOUBLE 2 X 4 EAVE SPACER

G1 1 X 6 FASCIA

1/2" WAFERBOARD N

1 X 4 CEDAR TRIM
F

1/4" PLYWOOD
SPACERS
M1

STRAP HINGE,
LAGBOLT TO
DOOR TRIM
(3 REQD.) V

K 1 X 6s

BUILD DOOR
OVERSIZE AND
TRIM TO FIT OPENING

M2
1/4" PLYWOOD SOFFIT
RAKE
EDGE
DRIP
EDGE
G2 1 X 6
FASCIA

8" CEDAR
LAP SIDING
WITH 6"
REVEAL Q

H

J

2

4

V2

V1

3

5

36" MIN.
OPENING

3/4" T & G
PLYWOOD—
7 X 9' OVERALL D

WALL
HEIGHT—
6' 9-1/2"

O

36"

1/4"
PLYWOOD
STARTER
STRIP
M1

W

WINDOW,
22-1/2 X 30"
ROUGH
OPENING
CENTERED
IN WALL

R
3/4"-SQ.
TRIM

A
PRESSURE-TREATED
4 X 4 (3 REQD.)

B PRESSURE- TREATED
2 X 4 (1 EACH END)

E2

E1

2 X 4 C
STUDS,
16" O.C.
2 X 4 SOLE PLATE

NOTE: REST BASE MEMBERS ON
4" OF GRAVEL IN TRENCHES

TRUSS
DOUBLE 2 X 4
EAVE SPACER

1 X 6
FASCIA

DETAIL 2 — EAVE

1 X 6 L
SIDING

LAP SIDING

1/2"
WAFERBOARD

1 X 4 TRIM,
1/4" SPACERS

M1

DETAIL 3 — CORNER

2 X 4 STUDS

1/2"
WAFERBOARD

LAP
SIDING

1 X 4 TRIM,
1/4" SPACER

1 X 2 STOP
S

2 X 4 TOP PLATES

HEADER:
DOUBLE 2 X 4,
1/2" PLYWOOD
SPACER

1 X 5
HEAD JAMB
T

DETAIL 4 — HEAD DOOR JAMB

1 X 5
SIDE
JAMB

1 X 2
STOP

1 X 4 TRIM,
1/4" SPACER

T

2 X 4 STUDS

1/2"
WAFERBOARD

LAP SIDING

DETAIL 5 — SIDE DOOR JAMB

With this plan, it's possible to accommodate the shed's size to your collection of tools and machinery, and even tailor the trim and siding to match your home. Our shed is based on a 7 x 9-ft. floor frame with lapped siding. Frankly, this do-it-yourself option will cost more than purchasing a shed—for the materials alone. But in the end, you'll have an attractive, secure building that will outlast just about everything you put in it.

Materials List

Key	No.	Size and description (use)
A	3	4 x 4 x 105" pressure-treated pine (floor joist)
B	2	2 x 4 x 84" pressure-treated pine (floor end)
C	38	2 x 4 x 81½" pine (stud)
D	1	¾ x 7 x 9" tongue-in-groove plywood (floor)
E1	2	2 x 4 x 117½" pine (soleplate, side)
E2	2	2 x 4 x 20½" pine (soleplate, front)
E3	1	2 x 4 x 98½" pine (soleplate, rear)
F*	14	1 x 4 x 81½" cedar (trim)
G1	4	1 x 6 x 54½" cedar (fascia)
G2	2	1 x 6 x 116½" cedar (fascia)
H	18	2 x 4 x 54½" pine (rafter)
I	6	2 x 4 x 85" pine (roof joist)
J	6	2 x 4 x 24" pine (truss chord)
K**	4	1 x 6 x 73" pine (door struts)
L	13	1 x 6 x 73" tongue-in-groove pine (door siding)
M1***	1	¼ x 8 x 4" plywood sheet (starter strip, spacers)
M2	1	¼ x 6 x 116½" plywood (soffit)
N	2	½ x 116½ x 81½" waferboard (side)
O	2	½ x 98½ x 111½" waferboard (end)
P	2	½ x 116½ x 54½" waferboard (roofing)
Q***	50	8 x 120" cedar (lap siding)
R	1	¾ x ¾ x 36" cedar (bottom door trim)
S	1	1 x 2" pine (door stop)
T	3	1 x 5 x 81½" pine (side/head doorjamb)
U**	2	½" plywood sheet (spacers and trusses)
V	3	Strap hinge
W	1	22½ x 30" double-hung window
X1	4	2 x 4 x 117½" pine (top and cap plate, side)
X2	4	2 x 4 x 98½" pine (top and cap plate, front and rear)

Misc.: Gravel; lagbolts for hinge; roofing felt; asphalt shingles; sheet-metal strips (for rake edge and drip edge); construction adhesive; door handle; bolt and hasp; 16d galvanized nails; 8d screw-shank galvanized nails; 10d galvanized casing nails; 1⅜" coated screws; 7d galvanized nails; ¾" galvanized roofing nails.

*Cut to size around for door trim.
**Cut to fit pattern.
***Cut to suit as needed.

Because garden sheds are considered temporary structures, they're usually not constrained by building codes. Lacking code directives, we chose a pressure-treated pine framework for our base, set over shallow trenches filled with gravel. The gravel provides drainage away from the wood and accommodates the pitch and heave of the seasons. We also built our own roof trusses. Trusses are easy to build, even if you've never used a framing square or haven't mastered roof geometry. And the ones seen here are easy to install, even if you're working alone.

Setting the Base

Build the shed base frame using three pressure-treated 4x4s and two pressure-treated 2x4s. For a 7 x 9-ft. shed like ours, cut the 4x4s to 9 ft. less 3 in. for the 2x4s at each end. Cut the 2x4s to 7 ft. long. Nail the boards to the ends of two 4x4s using 16d galvanized common nails to make a rectangular frame. To provide extra floor support, nail the third 4x4 to the 2x4s along the frame centerline.

With the base frame assembled, level the ground at the shed site and dig a continuous 4-in.-deep trench to match the base frame perimeter and an additional trench that's aligned with the center 4x4 support. Fill the trenches with gravel, set the frame in place and level it in both directions (**Fig. 1**).

To make the floor, nail pieces of ¾-in. tongue-and-groove plywood onto the frame. Begin by trimming the groove from the starting sheet and nail that piece in place with 8d screw-shank galvanized nails. Using the two factory edges of the

Fig. 1 *Place the pressure-treated pine floor frame on gravel-filled, 4-in.-deep trenches. Then level the frame in both directions.*

plywood, check that the framework beneath it is square, and adjust if necessary. Then set the second piece in place, engage the tongue in the groove, and nail it down (**Fig. 2**).

Wall Construction

Cut the four 2x4 long-wall plates to the length of the floor. Then mark the stud positions on the plates. Position the first stud 15¼ in. from the leading end of each plate, and each subsequent stud at 16-in. centers.

To frame a utility-sash window, measure the width of the window, position a full-length stud on each side of the opening, and cut a sill plate—to span between them—for the window to rest on. Leave the area above the window open. Cut the wall studs to 78½ in. and build the corners by nailing three studs side by side. Lay each stud in position and nail to the plates with 16d nails (**Fig. 3**). Build the back wall in a similar fashion, but omit the triple studs. Place the second stud 12½ in. from the leading end of the top and bottom plates. Then place the remaining studs on 16-in. centers.

The door opening on the front wall should be at least 36 in. wide—wider if you have a riding mower. For a 36-in.-wide opening, laminate the door header by sandwiching 39-in. 2x4s around a piece of ½-in. plywood. To support the header, cut two jack studs 3½ in. less than the normal stud length, and nail these to full-length studs. Then frame the front wall with a centered opening, as shown. Finally, slide the header between the jack studs and the top plate, and nail it from the top and sides.

Nail ½-in. plywood or waferboard sheathing over the studs, using 8d galvanized nails. On the end walls, extend the

Fig. 2 *Nail ¾-in. tongue-and-groove plywood to the floor frame. After this is completed, coat the floor with an enamel porch paint.*

Fig. 3 *Nail each stud through the plates with two 16d nails per stud. Place triple studs at the ends of both long walls.*

Fig. 4 *After sheathing the wall, cut the window opening and use10d galvanized casing nails to secure the window to the wall.*

TECH *Tips*

On Stage

Complicated outdoor projects with many pieces can quickly go astray leading to frustration when you can't find the screws you saw just a minute ago, or when the second roof joist has just gone missing. Make your outdoor woodworking jobs go much smoother by establishing a well-defined staging area. This can be a large tarp, such as a painter's cloth, or a piece of plywood. Whatever it is, it should be white or brightly colored, so that pieces of lumber and smaller fasteners and tools stand out against the surface. Get in the habit of returning tools and unused materials to the staging area, and you'll soon cut out time wasted hunting for your hammer!

Fig. 5 *Set the first wall up and nail it through the soleplate. Then level and brace the wall with a 2x4 nailed to the floor.*

Fig. 6 *After the end walls are set up, add a cap plate on top of the top plate. Overlap the wall plates at the corners and nail in place.*

sheathing 3½ in. beyond the framing on both sides. This overhang will eventually cover the ends of the long walls.

At the window wall, cut out the sheathing over the opening and set the window in place. Nail through the trim with 10d galvanized casing nails (**Fig. 4**). Now tip up a long wall and align it with the floor. Secure it with 16d nails. Then plumb the wall and nail a diagonal brace to the floor (**Fig. 5**). With the side walls up, raise the end walls between them. Nail them to the floor and to the side walls. Finally, nail cap plates to the top plates, overlapping the side walls at the corners (**Fig. 6**).

Building the Roof

First, build a jig for assembling the trusses. Cut a sheet of plywood and a 2x4 to match the width of the shed, and nail the 2x4 to the plywood flush with an edge. Measure 24 in. from each end and mark the 2x4. To establish a 5-in. pitch, lay a framing square on the plywood and against the edge of the 2x4 at the 24-in. mark. Then mark the plywood 10 in. above the 2x4. Next, lay a straight 2x4 against the corner of the jig 2x4 and angle it to intersect the 10-in. mark. Butt a second 2x4 edge to edge against the angled 2x4, and nail the second piece to the plywood. Repeat from the opposite end of the jig and mark the vertical centerline on the plywood and 2x4s.

Cut all the pieces for the first truss to fit the space on the jig. Use the first set as a pattern for the rest. Lay the members in place, and nail the joints together with gussets that are made of ½-in. plywood (**Fig. 7**). Use 7d nails and construction adhesive on the gussets. Place gussets on both sides of each truss, except the two end trusses. Mark the wall top plates every 24 in. Lay the trusses upside down on the walls, and then tip up the end trusses and align them with the top plates. Toenail these trusses in place (**Fig. 8**).

Run a string between the rafter ends of the two end trusses, and align the remaining trusses with this string. When all are toenailed to the walls, plumb the first truss and position the

Fig. 7 *Build a roof truss jig on a plywood platform. Then nail and glue ½-in.-plywood gussets to the truss components.*

Fig. 8 *Lay the trusses between the walls and then tip up the end trusses. Center and toenail them to the wall top plates.*

Fig. 9 *Create a 3-in. roof overhang at the gable ends by adding double 2x4 rafters to the truss rafters already in place.*

Fig. 10 *Use 1x5 pine for the doorjamb. Align with ¹/₂-in. plywood face-trim shims. Place the shims under the corner trim as well.*

Fig. 11 *To keep the siding lapped uniformly, measure up from the starter row and mark the spacing on the trim in 6-in. increments.*

Fig. 12 *Caulk all siding-to-trim joints and soffit joints. Always apply caulk sparingly and avoid smoothing it with a finger.*

rest of the trusses to match. To create an overhang on the ends, nail doubled 2x4 rafters to each end truss rafter (**Fig. 9**). Then rip ¼-in. plywood to fit under the rafter ends to create a closed soffit. Finally, sheath the end walls as well as the roof and add the 1x6 fascia, as shown in the drawing.

Siding and Trimwork

Install ¼-in.-plywood trim spacers around the door opening and at the corners of the shed so that the ¾-in. trim will cover the ends of the lap siding. Then install the 1x5 doorjamb (**Fig. 10**). Add the door face trim over the plywood, and follow with the 1x4 corner trim. Use 8d casing or galvanized screw-shank nails.

Nail ¼- or ½-in. plywood spacer strips to the bottom of the sheathing and install the first siding row around the shed. Leave a ¹/₁₆-in. gap from where the siding abuts any trim and start the first row about ¼ in. below the sheathing.

Measure up from the starter row and mark the trim every 6 in. (**Fig. 11**). Install the siding against these marks with 8d galvanized siding nails. On the long walls, bring the siding up against the eave soffit. You'll need to finish the gable ends by trimming the final rows with angle cuts to match the roof pitch. Use a framing square or the roof truss jig to lay out the angle for the gable cuts.

When you've completed the siding, caulk all joints between trim and siding and between soffit and siding (**Fig. 12**). When the caulk skins over, prime and paint the shed.

Shingling the Roof

Cover the sheathing with roofing felt. Then nail galvanized rake edge along the gable ends and drip edge along the eave edges of the roof. This will prevent rainwater from seeping between the shingles and the roof sheathing.

Install a starter row by trimming the tabs from a few

shingles and nail what remains over the drip edge, with the grit facing up and the factory edge down.

Allow the shingle edge to extend over the drip edge by about ¼ in. (**Fig. 13**). Offset the starter row from the first full row of shingles by trimming 3 in. from the first starter shingle you install.

After you've put the starter row down, lay the first row of full shingles over it and nail those shingles in place. On each and every subsequent row, be sure to cut exactly 6 in. from the first shingle.

Align the shingles so that the bottom of the latest row lies across the top of the tab slots of the previous row. Nail each shingle with four ¾-in. galvanized roofing nails.

To cap the ridge of the roof, cut shingles into three pieces along the tabs. Then nail the tabs along the peak at 5-in. intervals (**Fig. 14**).

Building a Door

Assemble tongue-in-groove pine boards to create a rectangular panel that's slightly larger in height and width than the trimmed door opening. Then secure two horizontal 1x6 battens across the boards with 1⅜-in. coated screws. Use four screws at each junction.

Next, mark and cut the door squarely to size. Finish by adding a diagonal brace between the cross battens to further stiffen the door and help prevent sagging. Add an additional short crossmember at the center of the hinge side to support a third hinge (**Fig. 15**).

Attach gate hinges to the door over the battens. Position the door in the opening and lagbolt the hinges to the door trim (**Fig. 16**). Then install a handle, bolt, and hasp. Finally, when the door swings easily and closes squarely, nail a 1x2 stop to the hasp side of the doorjamb.

Fig. 13 *After nailing the drip edges in place, trim the tabs from the shingles and then install a starter row along the eaves.*

Fig. 14 *Cut the shingles into three tab-size pieces and use the tabs to cap the peak. Be sure to space each piece 5 in. apart.*

Fig. 15 *Build the door by using tongue-and-groove pine. Attach the crossmembers and a diagonal brace with screws.*

Fig. 16 *Hang the door with three steel gate hinges. Secure it to the trim with lagbolts, then add the handle, bolt, and hasp.*

Small Addition

This simple deck is ideal for barbecues, sunbathing, or as a stage for a lovely container garden.

One area where builders often economize lies just beyond the back door. Open that door and it's usually one or two steps down to a modest concrete slab. These patios are often thrown down for cheap, and spend the ensuing years creeping steadily away from the foundation. Even when they don't crack or separate, they remain unsightly and uninviting. If this sounds familiar, you might consider forsaking that patio entirely and building a deck on top of it. Though decks can be obscenely expensive, they don't need to be—the modest size of this one translates to a reasonable cost.

*Key*POINTS

TIME
Prep Time	4 hours
Shop Time	6 hours
Assembly Time	12 hours

EFFORT
Skill Level	intermediate
Maintenance	light
Assistance	one

COST / BENEFITS
Expense: moderate
- Simple home addition that adds far more in **usability and enjoyment** value than you'll expend in money and effort.

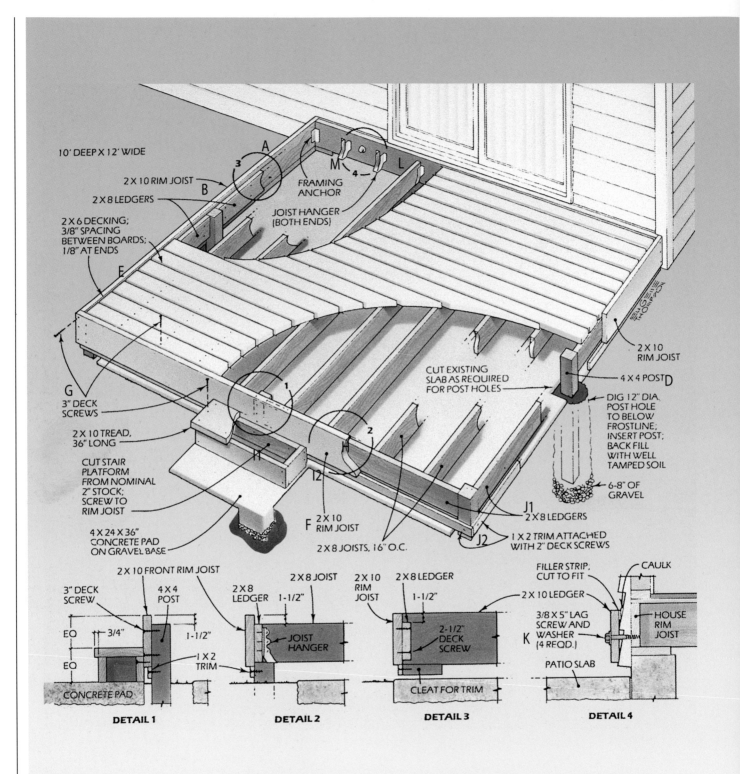

10' DEEP X 12' WIDE

2 X 10 RIM JOIST

2 X 8 LEDGERS

2 X 6 DECKING;
3/8" SPACING
BETWEEN BOARDS;
1/8" AT ENDS

FRAMING
ANCHOR

JOIST HANGER
(BOTH ENDS)

3" DECK
SCREWS

2 X 10 TREAD,
36" LONG

CUT STAIR
PLATFORM
FROM NOMINAL
2" STOCK;
SCREW TO
RIM JOIST

4 X 24 X 36"
CONCRETE PAD
ON GRAVEL BASE

CUT EXISTING
SLAB AS REQUIRED
FOR POST HOLES

2 X 10
RIM JOIST

4 X 4 POST

DIG 12" DIA.
POST HOLE
TO BELOW
FROSTLINE;
INSERT POST;
BACK FILL
WITH WELL
TAMPED SOIL

6-8" OF
GRAVEL

2 X 8 LEDGERS

1 X 2 TRIM ATTACHED
WITH 2" DECK SCREWS

2 X 10
RIM JOIST

2 X 8 JOISTS, 16" O.C.

3" DECK
SCREW

2 X 10 FRONT RIM JOIST

4 X 4
POST

EO

3/4"

1-1/2"

1 X 2
TRIM

EO

CONCRETE PAD

DETAIL 1

2 X 8
LEDGER

2 X 8 JOIST

1-1/2"

JOIST
HANGER

DETAIL 2

2 X 10
RIM
JOIST

2 X 8 LEDGER

1-1/2"

2-1/2"
DECK
SCREW

CLEAT FOR TRIM

DETAIL 3

FILLER STRIP;
CUT TO FIT

CAULK

2 X 10 LEDGER

3/8 X 5" LAG
SCREW AND
WASHER
(4 REQD.)

HOUSE
RIM
JOIST

PATIO SLAB

DETAIL 4

O ne of the major advantages of this deck is that it is at floor level—it will never rot and it has frost footings, so it will stay put. Even though it's small, it can still accommodate a gas grill, a few chairs, and a small table for that morning newspaper and first cup of coffee. You'll be surprised at just how much relaxation and enjoyment you can crowd on a small space.

Location

With a relatively small concrete slab, you can simply dig the post footings outside the slab perimeter. In our case, a footing placed outside the slab would have extended the deck past the house by several inches. With this in mind, we opted to cut the slab at each footing location, so that we could maintain the original 10 x 12-ft. footprint.

Material Selection

Although galvanized casing nails are acceptable, we chose to use rustproof, coated screws in all instances where fasteners would be visible. These were coarse-thread deck screws, driven in with a screw gun. Where joist hangers were needed, we used code-required hanger nails, which are shorter and heavier than common nails.

The lumber you choose will need to be rot-resistant. The

Materials List

Key	No.	Size and description (use)
A*	3	2 x 10 x 116" pressure-treated pine (rim joist)
B	2	2 x 8 x 116" pressure-treated pine (ledger sides)
C	2	2 x 8 x 140" pressure-treated pine (ledger)
D	5	4 x 4 x 48" pressure-treated pine (post)
E	20	2 x 6 x 127³/₄" pressure-treated pine (decking)
F	8	2 x 8 x 116" pressure-treated pine (joist)
G	1	2 x 10 x 36" pressure-treated pine (tread)
H	1	2 x 10 x 140" pressure-treated pine (rim joist)
I1	2	2 x 5¹/₂ x 32" pressure-treated pine (step box)
I2	2	2 x 5¹/₂ x 4" pressure-treated pine (step box sides)
J1	2	1 x 2 x 143" pressure-treated pine (trim, side)
J2	1	1 x 3 x 120" pressure-treated pine (trim, front)
K	4	³/₈ x 5" lag screw and washer
L	16	Metal joist hanger
M	4	Framing anchor

Misc.: Concrete; gravel; 3" deck screws; 2¹/₂" deck screws; hanger nails; caulk; oil-based stain.

*Cut to size.

Fig. 1 *Begin by laying out the deck location. If concrete must be cut, use a masonry blade in an old circular saw to score the surface.*

Fig. 2 *Use a post-hole digger to dig pier footing holes below the frost line. Square off the bottoms of the holes in preparation for the posts.*

Fig. 3 *If the house siding leaves a large gap between the siding and the ledger, tack a strip of treated lumber to the ledger.*

TECH *Tips*

Boring Deep
When you need to drill a deep hole, use the tools that electricians and plumbers use. Typical twist drills have effective depths of 2 to 3 inches, but you can go much deeper with a bell-hanger bit. These twist drills are available in diameters from ¼ inch to ⅝ inch and in lengths up to 18 inches. Another alternative is the powered drill bit extension. These are sold in lengths of 12 and 18 inches. Just fasten the bit in the extension and you have dramatically increased depth capacity. For large diameter holes, use a powered ship auger bit. These heavy hitters bore holes from ⅝ inch in diameter up to 1¼ inch. These bits are typically 18 inches long.

most common choices are cedar, redwood, and pressure-treated pine (CCA). Each has its advantages and its shortcomings. Redwood and cedar make the most attractive decks when new, but are a little pricey. Because we wanted to keep costs as low as possible, we chose pressure-treated stock. We used 2x10s, 2x8s, and 4x4s for the structural components, and 2x6s for the decking.

Frost-Proof Footings

As mentioned earlier, we decided to cut the slab at each footing location. Although sawing concrete may seem daunting, it's really fairly easy. All it takes is a circular saw and one or two masonry blades. Though you can rent a demolition saw, we used an old circular saw that had been dropped from a ladder once too often. Its bent base-plate makes ugly work of lumber, but it handles concrete just fine. The goal is to score the concrete roughly one-third of the way through (**Fig. 1**). Then break the slab inside the score lines with a 3-pound hammer.

With the concrete removed from the footing locations, use a post-hole digger to dig holes past the frost level in your area (**Fig. 2**). Acceptable footing designs vary, but we chose to fill the bottom 8 in. of our 36-in.-deep holes with gravel. Then we set the 4x4 posts on this gravel base and packed soil firmly around each post. The rigidity of the deck will keep them from moving laterally.

As for the number of footings, we placed one at each outside corner and centered one along the front of the deck. We also installed one post on each side, halfway between the corner posts and the house. As such, our longest rim joist span was less than 6 ft.

Easy Framing Method

Framing methods vary, but we chose to build a deck that hides the end cuts of the decking lumber. To achieve this no-reveal look, we built the perimeter frame with 2x10 lumber. We then lined them with 2x8 ledgers, securing them to the inside of the rim joists with 2½-in. screws.

Step by Step

After digging the post footings and adding the gravel, we put off installing the 4x4 posts until the box was built and squared up. To build the box, start by trimming a 2x10 joist (because of its position against the siding, now called a ledger) 3 in.

Fig. 4 *Attach the ledger to the house siding with a couple of screws, then bore four lagbolt clearance holes in the ledger.*

Fig. 5 *Slide a lagbolt and washer into each ledger hole and tap the bolt with a hammer. Then drive it into the rim joist with a wrench.*

Fig. 6 *After screwing the side rim joists to the house ledger from the outside, nail a corner bracket to both on the inside.*

Fig. 7 *After setting the 4x4 posts, plumb them in place. Then screw the rim joists to them with three or four long screws.*

Fig. 8 *With the rim joists squared and fastened to the posts, mount the 2x8 ledger plates to the inside with screws.*

Fig. 9 *Lay out the outside rim joist for the deck joists and install a joist hanger at each mark. Slide the joists into place.*

short of the overall deck width. If your home has lap siding, and if the gap left between the top of the deck ledger and the siding is more than ¼ in., you'll want to cut a strip of lumber to fill this gap. The best approach is to tack this strip to the rim before mounting it on the siding (**Fig. 3**).

Keeping it level, screw or nail this ledger to the house (**Fig. 4**). Then bore holes through the ledger at four points along its length, and use 5-in. lagbolts to bind it to the rim joist of the house (**Fig. 5**).

With the 2x10 ledger mounted on the house, cut the side joists to length and prop them up temporarily. Then screw them to the ends of the ledger on the house. For extra strength, nail a corner bracket to the inside of this joint (**Fig. 6**). Finally, cut the front rim joist and screw it to the front of the side joists, using 3 in. screws.

With the basic box completed and propped up temporarily, measure from corner to corner to square it. If necessary, tack braces diagonally across the corners to keep it square while you install the posts. At this point, you'll also want to level the deck in all directions.

To install the posts, simply set them in the post holes and mark and cut them to the correct length. Be sure to hold the tops of the posts 1½ in. below the rim to accommodate the decking. Finally, plumb each post in its hole and secure the rim to the posts with 3-in. deck screws (**Fig. 7**). Screw the corner posts from both directions. With all posts secured, backfill around them.

Your next step will be to screw the 2x8 ledger plates to the three 2x10 rim joists (**Fig. 8**). Remember to hold these exactly 1½ in. down from the top of the rim joists. (The 2x10 ledger on the house will not need an additional 2x8 ledger, because the joist hangers can be tacked directly to it.)

With the ledgers in place, lay out the 2x8 joists on 16-in. centers along the front rim and on the house-side ledger. Then cut the joists to length and set them in the hangers (**Fig. 9**).

Fig. 10 *Use spacer sticks to maintain a ³/₈-in. gap between the deck boards and a ¹/₈-in. space alongside the rim joists.*

Fig. 11 *To keep the screw rows straight, draw a line across the boards above each joist. We used a drywall square to do this.*

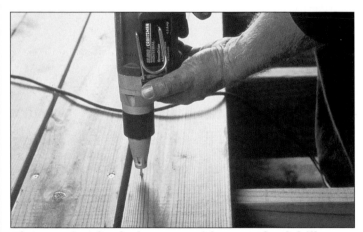

Fig. 12 *Drive the deck screws with a standard drill or a screw gun like we did. Set the screws just below the wood's surface.*

Fig. 13 *Preassemble a box step using the drawing as a building guide. Set the step on a poured concrete pad or a few concrete blocks.*

Fig. 14 *Make sure the top of the step box is truly parallel to the top of the deck. Then attach it to the deck with screws.*

Finally, nail the joists through all openings in the hangers, using the special hanger nails.

Decking

With the deck frame box essentially complete, and the joists in place, it's time to cut the 2x6 decking planks to length. Choose the straightest 2x6 you can find for the first deck plank. Then screw it to the joists and ledgers using 3 in. screws. Start the decking at the front of the deck and proceed toward the house.

Although the first plank can be placed against the rim, all subsequent planks should be spaced roughly ³/₈ in. apart. To maintain this spacing, make a spacer stick and use it at each screw location (**Fig. 10**). When dealing with warped lumber, screw the nearest point and pry the rest of the plank over one joist at a time, securing it as you go. Use two screws per plank, per joist.

For the best nailing, it's a good idea to draw a straight line across the boards above each joist (**Fig. 11**). And for ease of installation, you can use a screw gun instead of a standard drill to drive in all of the deck screws (**Fig. 12**).

Building a Step

Most do-it-yourselfers find stair building a frustrating experiment, because of the need for a precise tread-to-riser ratio. With that bit of discouragement behind us, here's the good news. When we're only talking about a step or two, a simple box will work just fine. All you need to do is build an open box (**Fig. 13**) and screw a plank on top of it. If you need two steps, build two boxes. You can set the box on buried concrete blocks, or you can pour a small concrete pad, as we did. Just make sure your step support is level.

As a general rule, a step's rise should not exceed 7½ in. and its tread should be at least 10 in. deep x 36 in. wide. Minor compromises are acceptable. Major ones are not. To split the difference between pad and deck, which was 14 in., we built our box 5½ in. high. After securely screwing the box to the deck (**Fig. 14**), we screwed a 2x10 plank over it, making an even 7-in. rise (**Fig. 15**).

Finishing Touches

Ask around and you're sure to hear that deck lumber needs to cure for six months before being stained or sealed. Our recommendation is that you not ask around. Months of sun and rain will only degrade the surface of the lumber, and it's the surface that the sealant is designed to protect. Besides, these are exactly the conditions that cause lumber to cup and warp.

Before applying deck stain or waterproofing, take the time to caulk the top of the ledger board (**Fig. 16**) and to sand away any imperfections on the surface of the deck. These include rough spots, grade stamps, and pencil marks. This preparation will help ensure that your final deck surface is comfortable to walk on, and prevents any moisture from getting into the wood. Then apply an even coat of oil-base stain and keep off the deck for several days (**Fig. 17**).

Fig. 15 *Complete the step by installing a tread. Use at least three screws on the sides, and several along the front and back.*

Fig. 16 *To protect the siding behind the ledger from water exposure, seal the top joint with a bead of silicone caulk.*

Fig. 17 *After sanding away any rough spots and removing the dust, cover the deck with wood sealer or an oil-base stain.*

Outdoor Furnishings

Under Cover

An umbrella table let's you put shade where you want it for fine dining in the brightest sun.

It's easy to understand the appeal of outdoor dining. Think of fresh air and bright sunshine with a soft breeze keeping pesky insects at bay. Then think of yourself surrounded by your family and friends. You're sitting there with a cold drink while some sumptuous food sizzles on the grill. Few of us would wish for much more than that. Of course, to complete the picture, you need a table and a place to sit. This cedar table and bench set provides a perfect foundation for that alfresco dining experience. It accommodates up to eight people, but maintains a sense of intimacy if used by two.

*Key*POINTS

TIME
Prep Time	5 hours
Shop Time	13 hours
Assembly Time	20 hours

EFFORT
Skill Level	advanced
Maintenance	light
Assistance	none

COST / BENEFITS
Expense: expensive
- One of the most **useful** outdoor projects you can make.
- Designed for **durability and longevity**.

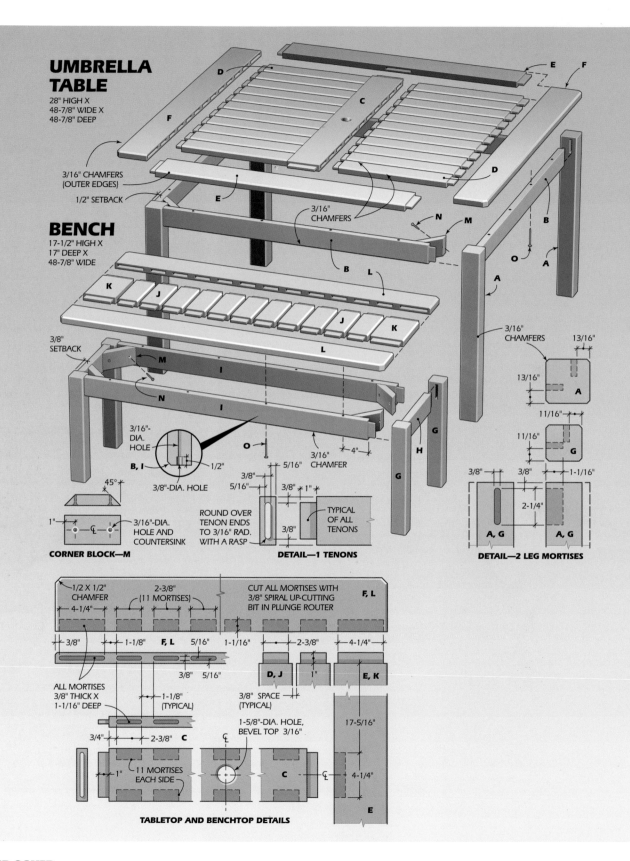

UMBRELLA TABLE

28" HIGH X
48-7/8" WIDE X
48-7/8" DEEP

3/16" CHAMFERS
(OUTER EDGES)

1/2" SETBACK

BENCH

17-1/2" HIGH X
17" DEEP X
48-7/8" WIDE

3/16" CHAMFERS

3/8" SETBACK

3/16"-DIA. HOLE

B, I

1/2"

3/8"-DIA. HOLE

45°

1"

3/16"-DIA. HOLE AND COUNTERSINK

CORNER BLOCK—M

3/16" CHAMFERS

13/16"

13/16"

A

11/16"

11/16"

G

3/8"   3/8"   1-1/16"

2-1/4"

A, G   A, G

DETAIL—2 LEG MORTISES

5/16"

3/8"   1"

3/8"

ROUND OVER TENON ENDS TO 3/16" RAD. WITH A RASP

TYPICAL OF ALL TENONS

DETAIL—1 TENONS

O

3/16" CHAMFER

4"

1/2 X 1/2" CHAMFER

2-3/8" (11 MORTISES)

4-1/4"

CUT ALL MORTISES WITH 3/8" SPIRAL UP-CUTTING BIT IN PLUNGE ROUTER

F, L

3/8"   1-1/8"   F, L   5/16"

3/8"   5/16"

1-1/16"   2-3/8"   4-1/4"

ALL MORTISES 3/8" THICK X 1-1/16" DEEP

1-1/8" (TYPICAL)

D, J   1"   E, K

3/8" SPACE (TYPICAL)

3/4"   2-3/8"   C

1-5/8"-DIA. HOLE, BEVEL TOP 3/16"

17-5/16"

1"   11 MORTISES EACH SIDE

C

4-1/4"

E

TABLETOP AND BENCHTOP DETAILS

This outdoor table is designed to accept an umbrella to shelter you from the hot summer sun, or from an untimely shower. Best of all, the project is not too time-consuming. Four weekends part-time should be enough to build the set. As far as the table umbrella is concerned, you can order it from a number of different mail-order suppliers, or at any large home center. Just be sure that the spread of the umbrella when open is 3 to 4 feet greater in total diameter than the table.

We chose red cedar for this project. This wood resists rot and insect infestation and it's readily available at lumberyards and large home centers. If you can't purchase kiln-dried cedar for your project, you should buy the material several weeks before starting and stack it someplace where it will have a chance to sufficiently air-dry. Place evenly spaced strips of wood between each layer of boards to allow air to effectively flow through the stack of lumber.

Other suitable wood species for this project are redwood, teak, and cypress. These woods are more expensive than cedar, however, and you may have a hard time finding them at lumberyards and home centers.

We should mention that we used single-part waterproof wood glue to assemble the furniture joints. This is waterproof for all but the most extreme situations, such as when joints are subject to continuous submersion in water. Unlike epoxy or resorcinol adhesives that are completely waterproof, this glue is easy to use and readily available.

Making the Parts

The table legs are cut from 4x4 stock (or they can be glued up from thinner material). When using 4x4 stock, cut each leg to rough length. Next, clamp a fence to the band saw table, and rip the blanks to a 2¾ x 2¾-in. square (**Fig. 1**). Then clamp the leg to a workbench and use a razor-sharp plane to remove the saw marks (**Fig. 2**). Unless you are very experienced with a

Fig. 1 *Rip the table leg stock out of a 4x4 piece of lumber. Clamp a temporary rip fence to the band saw table to do this.*

Fig. 2 *Clamp a table leg to the benchtop and remove all the saw marks with a hand plane. To make a smooth cut, push the plane at an angle.*

Materials List

Key	No.	Size and description (use)
A	4	2³/₄ x 2³/₄ x 27" cedar (leg)
B	4	1 x 3 x 43⁷/₈" cedar (apron)
C	1	1 x 5 x 40⁷/₈" cedar (rail)
D	22	1 x 3¹/₈ x 18¹⁵/₁₆" cedar (slats)
E	2	1 x 5 x 40⁷/₈" cedar (rail)
F	2	1 x 5 x 48⁷/₈" cedar (stile)
G	16	2¹/₄ x 2¹/₄ x 16¹/₂" cedar (leg)
H	8	1 x 3 x 12" cedar (apron)

Key	No.	Size and description (use)
I	8	1 x 3 x 44⁷/₈" cedar (apron)
J	44	1 x 3¹/₈ x 9" cedar (slats)
K	8	1 x 5 x 9" cedar (rail)
L	8	1 x 5 x 48⁷/₈" cedar (stile)
M	20	1 x 2³/₄ x 5¹/₄" cedar (block)
N	40	2" No. 8 fh galvanized screw
O	48	3" No. 8 fh galvanized screw

Misc.: Table umbrella and base; sandpaper; waterproof wood glue.

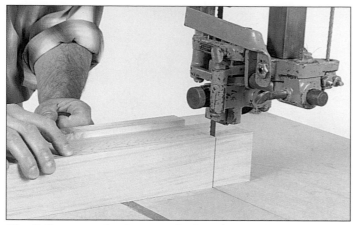

Fig. 3 *Crosscut the legs on the band saw. Here, a shopmade crosscutting table and a miter gauge are used to make the cut.*

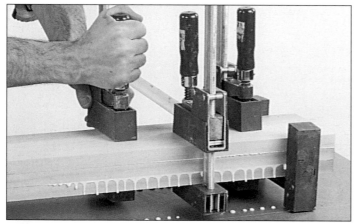

Fig. 4 *For the bench legs, spread glue on ¾-in.-thick stock. Lay disposable material under the pieces and clamp them together.*

Fig. 5 *Rip and crosscut the individual bench legs to size, and then clamp them together. Mark out mortise locations on the legs.*

hand plane, check the workpiece often as you go. The edges of the leg must remain square to one another. Remember that you are only smoothing the surface, so do not remove too much material.

Use a miter gauge on the band saw to crosscut the leg blanks to finished dimension (**Fig. 3**).

Because the bench legs are smaller than the table legs, it is a better use of materials to glue them up from three pieces of ¾-in.-thick stock. You can simplify the job if you plan to make the blanks large enough to cut four legs from each glued-up stack.

Rip and crosscut material for the leg blanks slightly oversize, then use a foam roller to spread glue on the mating surfaces of each piece.

Assemble the pieces into a stack, and securely clamp the pieces together (**Fig. 4**). After about 20 minutes, scrape off the glue that has squeezed out from the joints, then allow the glue to fully set.

Now use the table saw to rip the blanks to 2¼ in. wide, and crosscut the bench legs to finished length.

Lay out the mortise locations in all the legs for the apron joints. You can speed the process by clamping four legs together with their ends perfectly aligned. Then mark across the stack using a square (**Fig. 5**).

Next, use the router and edge guide to cut the leg mortises (**Fig. 6**). It's best to use a spiral up-cutting bit in the router because that type of bit pulls the dust and chips out of the cut, and reduces the strain on the motor. This also keeps the bit's cutting edge cooler.

SHOP*Helper*

Copy Cat
If your project plans involve creating multiple turned pieces, such as table and chair legs, it may make sense for you to invest in a pantograph. This useful draftsman's tool is a set of folding arms attached in a series of connected "X"s, with simple fasteners that serve as adjustable pivot points. To use a pantograph, attach one end to a fixed surface, such as the edge of a worktable, and then use the center tracing point to copy the design or physical part you want to replicate. Place a piece of paper under the graphite tip on the end opposite the fixed pivot point, and as you trace the shape with a fixed point, it will be dutifully copied to the paper. You can use a pantograph to enlarge, reduce, or copy to the exact same size.

Fig. 6 *Using a spiral up-cutting bit in a plunge router, cut the table leg mortises. Two legs clamped together provide a stable base.*

Fig. 7 *Use a dado blade setup in the table saw to cut the tenons on the apron pieces. Butt each apron to the fence, and make the cut.*

Rip and crosscut 1-in.-thick stock for the table and bench aprons as well as for the top frames and slats. Install a dado blade in the table saw, and then use the miter gauge to guide the workpiece over the saw blade when you are cutting the tenons (**Fig. 7**).

Note that you can use the rip fence as a stop to gauge the tenon length. Because the tenons are 1 in. long, you need to make two passes to complete each cheek.

Cut the tenons across the width of each workpiece, then adjust the blade height and move each workpiece over the blade on edge to cut the shoulder (**Fig. 8**). Clamp each workpiece upright in a vise and gently round over the tenon's edges using a wood rasp (**Fig. 9**).

Lay out the mortise locations for the tabletop and benchtop joints. Use a router with an edge guide and a spiral up-cutting bit to cut the mortises (**Fig. 10**). It is best to clamp three workpieces of the same width together when routing to

Fig. 8 *To cut the shoulders on a tenon, stand the apron on edge, and hold it firmly to the miter gauge. Butt it to the fence and make the cut.*

Fig. 9 *Round off a tenon with a rasp. The tenon's radius matches the radius left by the spiral up-cutting bit used to cut the mortise.*

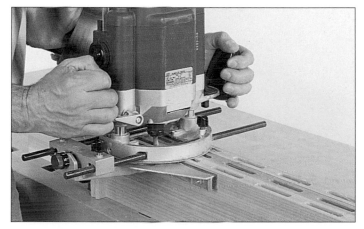

Fig. 10 *To cut the long row of mortises in each stile and rail, clamp three of the workpieces together to support the router.*

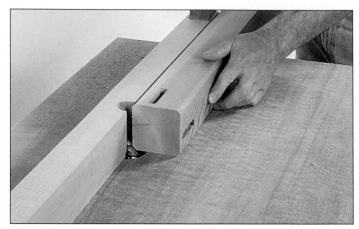

Fig. 11 *Use a chamfer bit in the router table to cut the chamfer on all four edges of the legs for the benches and table.*

Fig. 12 *Glue and clamp together a pair of the bench legs and one short apron. Make two of these subassemblies.*

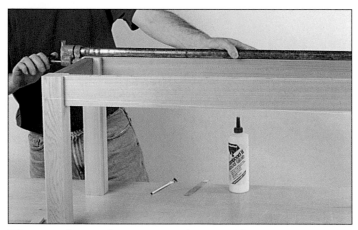

Fig. 13 *Join two leg-apron subassemblies spanned by a long pair of aprons. Glue and clamp this to complete a bench base.*

TECH *Tips*

Hide-and-Seek
To hide a nail hole in paint-grade woodwork, build up a mound of putty over the nail and sand the workpiece. The filler is leveled with the surrounding area. An alternative when a clear finish is used is to take a $\frac{1}{4}$-in. wide chisel and cut a shallow trench. Gently peel the shaving back then drill a hole under it, drive the nail then bend the shaving back and glue it down. It's an delicate procedure, and if you use too much glue, you'll blow it. You can buy an invisible nailing kit, which provides a specialized tool and fish glue, or, an easy alternative is to use oil-based model makers paint. Fill the nail holes with a neutral-color filler, then apply the finish. Before the last finish coat, blend paint to match that spot and apply it with an artist's brush. Then brush on the last coat of finish.

form a wide and stable base for the plunge router to move along. Mark the location of the umbrella hole in the center rail of the tabletop, and then use a Forstner bit in the drill press to bore the hole.

After laying out the locations of the holes in the aprons for mounting the top, use a Forstner bit in the drill press to counterbore a recess for each screw head. Next, use a $\frac{3}{16}$-in.-dia. bit to drill the pilot holes for the screw shanks. Each of these holes is centered in a recess.

To complete the part-making process, install a chamfer bit in the router table, then use it to cut the $\frac{3}{16}$-in.-deep chamfer on the table and bench legs, aprons, and top parts as shown in the plans (**Fig. 11**). Note that not all edges are chamfered.

Assembly

Begin assembly with the benches, because they are smaller and are much easier to work with. After you refine your technique on them, you can assemble the table.

It's worth noting that all the parts for the table and benches should be dry assembled before glue is applied. With the assemblies joined in this manner, make reference marks and numbers on the backs of the parts or in some other discreet location. Before proceeding to gluing and clamping, gather the parts together in batches so they are not confused during the assembly process.

In some cases, you'll want to make a second dry fit midway through the assembly process, such as when gluing and clamping a stile or rail to multiple slats that have been glued

Fig. 14 *The first stage in assembling a benchtop is to glue and clamp slats to one stile. Use one clamp in the center of each slat.*

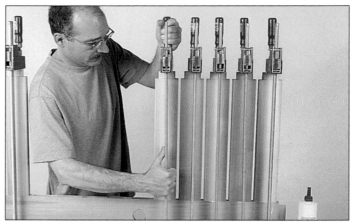

Fig. 15 *Multiple subassemblies are made in the process of assembling the tabletop. First, slats are joined to the center rail.*

to a stile or rail on the opposite side. This is a necessary evil to ensure that the parts go together smoothly—the parts may have fit the first time you tried them but shifted slightly when they were glued up as a subassembly.

Apply glue to the mortises of two bench legs and on the tenons of one short apron. Use a small wood shim to spread glue on the mortise walls, and use a small brush to coat the tenons. Press together the apron and legs, and then clamp the subassembly to pull the joints tight (**Fig. 12**).

When the glue is dry on these parts, glue and clamp the long bench aprons to the end subassemblies (**Fig. 13**). It's best to do this on a flat work surface to ensure that the base assembly is not twisted.

Assemble the table base in the same manner as the bench bases. Make two subassemblies consisting of a pair of legs and one apron. When the glue has set on these, join the subassemblies spanned by a pair of aprons.

Fig. 16 *A second set of slats is glued and clamped to the center rail. Again, use one clamp in the center of each slat.*

MATERIAL*Matters*

Sandpaper Quick Cuts
Cutting sheets of sandpaper to size is one of the more troublesome little tasks around the workshop. To quickly cut stiff sheets of abrasive to custom sizes—for your pad sanders or sanding blocks—use your saw table. Most saw tables have a right-angle edge that is perfect for neatly tearing sandpaper to often-used sizes. Simply scribe lines on the table's surface to mark the width and length of the sheets that your pad sander or block require. Use a framing square to ensure that the scribe marks are completely accurate. Make the marks with a sharpened awl, ice pick, or nail. If you're a little touchy about your tabletop, there's another option. If you just want to cut a single sheet of sandpaper easily and quickly, don't use a knife, shears, or scissors—the sandpaper will dull them. Instead, use a scriber, such as an awl, and a metal straightedge. Score the back of the sheet, then fold the paper to make a sharp crease along the line. Finally, carefully tear the sandpaper as scribed.

TOOL*Care*

Belt Sanding Basics

As unpleasant a chore as sanding may be, it is made a whole lot easier and acceptable with the use of a good sander. One of the most efficient at sanding large surfaces, such as those associated with outdoor projects, is the belt sander. These handy tools are the most popular for removing stock and smoothing surfaces because they work so quickly. They are designed around different size sanding belts, and a little insight into how they do what they do can go a long way to cutting down on your outdoor woodworking workload.

Available Sizes: The three most popular sizes are 2½ x 16 in., 3 x 21 in., and 3 x 24 in. (The smaller number represents the belt width; the larger equals the belt circumference.)

Available Grits: Abrasive belts commonly range from 50 grit to 180 grit. Use a medium-grit belt to smooth rough surfaces and remove minor surface scratches and irregularities. For final sanding, use a fine-grit belt (higher than 120). Most home centers and hardware stores carry a selection of sander belts, but for the best price—and to ensure you have the belt you need on hand when you need it—buy in bulk through mail-order woodworking supply companies. Find them on the Internet.

Ratings: Belt sanders are rated by amperage and belt speed. The amperage rating is an indicator of pure power. Generally, the higher the amps, the more power. Amperage ranges from 3-10 amp, depending on the sander. Belt speed is measured in surface feet per minute (sfpm), and varies from 600 to 1600 sfpm. For most jobs, you'll set the sander to the maximum speed.

Special Features: The most convenient features to get on a belt sander include an extra-long power cord, a belt-release lever, and a dust collection bag. The last is perhaps the most important, because belt sanders produce an incredible amount of dust.

Working Tips: The most common mistake made with these sanders is to press too hard, which can result in quick clogging of the abrasive surface, and puts additional load on the motor. Use a light touch and let the sander do the work. Avoid another common mistake by sanding cleanly off the ends of boards. If you let the sander tilt, it will quickly round the edges of your board. Keep the sander moving at all times, because if it sits too long in one spot, it will make a noticeable depression. Lastly, although it usually isn't recommended to sand across grain, you can do so when you are removing stock with a belt sander.

Fig. 17 *Carefully glue and clamp a side rail to the center rail. One clamp, precisely centered, should provide enough force.*

Fig. 18 *Clamp one stile at each end of the top subassembly. Space the bar clamps evenly and at the center of each tenon.*

Fig. 19 *A corner block is installed at each leg on the table and the benches. A pair of screws holds each block to the aprons.*

Fig. 20 *Attach the tabletop to the base with several screws. Drive each screw into its matching counterbored hole in the apron.*

Now move on to assembling the benchtops. Because there are several slats in each top, assemble each top in stages. First, glue and clamp the slats to one long rail (**Fig. 14**). After the glue sets on those joints, apply the opposite rail.

Approach the tabletop assembly in the same manner. Begin by gluing and clamping a slat at each end of the center rail. Fill in between these two slats with more slats (**Fig. 15**).

When the glue is dry on this subassembly, glue and clamp slats to the opposite side (**Fig. 16**). Next, glue and clamp the side rails to this subassembly (**Fig. 17**). When the glue is set on that subassembly, position clamps across it and then glue and clamp one stile to it (**Fig. 18**). Complete the top by gluing and clamping the second stile.

Using this technique, you will not have to worry about getting all the parts together before the glue begins to set. Your results will be better, and the stress of a frantic assembly is eliminated.

Mark the benchtops and tabletop for the 45° corner cuts, and make these cuts with a sabre saw. Sand the cut corners smooth, then use the chamfer bit in the router to shape the table edges and benchtops. Use the router and chamfer bit to shape the top edge of the umbrella hole as well.

Rip, crosscut, and miter the 1-in.-thick stock to make corner blocks. Bore and countersink pilot holes in each block, and then attach them with screws to the aprons for the table and benches (**Fig. 19**).

Invert the tabletop on a padded surface, then place the base over it. Adjust the base so that there is an even reveal on all sides of the top, and then attach the base to the top with screws (**Fig. 20**). Assemble the benches in the same manner.

Sand all surfaces with 120-grit and 140-grit sandpaper, and remove all dust with a tack cloth. Although cedar is resistant to rot and insect infestation, it will weather if left untreated. To preserve its natural color and protect it from the elements, apply a penetrating finish with a high-quality brush.

A pigmented stain could easily be used on this project. In fact, pigmented finishes provide greater protection against weather damage—even if they do obscure the wood's grain. Although most people prefer white, green, or redwood-colored finishes for outdoor wood furniture, there's nothing to prevent you from being a bit more creative. The finish could be color matched to other outdoor furnishings, or to the house itself.

For maximum protection against the elements, use a paintable water repellent preservative, followed by a compatible primer and topcoat. Visit your paint store or a large home center to buy these three products and check that they are fully compatible.

SHOP*Helper*

Big Vac
If you're tired of frequently emptying your shop vac because the waste containment chamber is so small, consider this modification. Run your vac through a steel garbage can to increase the amount of waste that can be collected at any one time. Simply cut two round holes in the lid of the can and then caulk in connectors, such as those used in whole-house vacuum systems. Run the input hose from your vacuum to one of the inlets on the lid, and then connect a suitable length of vacuum hose to the other connector. Finally, seal the lid in place securely with duct tape to create an airtight fit (and a quick-remove connection for easy emptying).

Bench Mark

A nice place to sit in the garden only increases the enjoyment of your blooms and birds.

One of the many accents to a complete garden—like a birdbath or decorative edging—is an attractive garden bench. The difference between a bench and the other accents, though, is that you can get a lot of use out of a bench. We've specifically designed this piece of outdoor furniture to be not only extremely comfortable, but to also add a handsome touch to any garden setting—from a formal herb garden to the typical backyard layout of grass bordered by perennials and annuals. And, even if you don't have a garden, build it anyway. It's just as good for lazy afternoons on your porch or deck.

*Key*POINTS

TIME
Prep Time . . . . 3 hours
Shop Time . . . . 12 hours
Assembly Time . . . . 10 hours

EFFORT
Skill Level . . . . advanced
Maintenance . . . . paint 2-3 years
Assistance . . . . none

COST / BENEFITS
Expense: moderate
• **Complementary style** will suit a range of garden types, from simple backyard annual beds and borders to a profuse cottage garden.

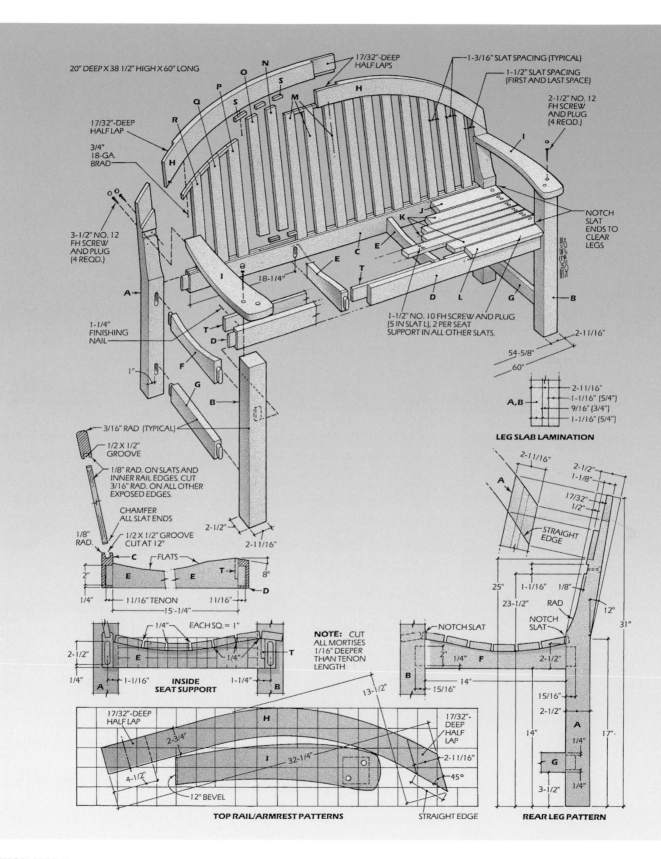

20" DEEP X 38 1/2" HIGH X 60" LONG

17/32"-DEEP HALF LAPS

1-3/16" SLAT SPACING (TYPICAL)

1-1/2" SLAT SPACING (FIRST AND LAST SPACE)

2-1/2" NO. 12 FH SCREW AND PLUG (4 REQD.)

17/32"-DEEP HALF LAP

3/4" 18-GA. BRAD

3-1/2" NO. 12 FH SCREW AND PLUG (4 REQD.)

NOTCH SLAT ENDS TO CLEAR LEGS

1-1/4" FINISHING NAIL

1-1/2" NO. 10 FH SCREW AND PLUG (5 IN SLAT L), 2 PER SEAT SUPPORT IN ALL OTHER SLATS.

18-1/4"

1"

54-5/8"

60"

2-11/16"

3/16" RAD (TYPICAL)

1/2 X 1/2" GROOVE

1/8" RAD. ON SLATS AND INNER RAIL EDGES. CUT 3/16" RAD. ON ALL OTHER EXPOSED EDGES.

CHAMFER ALL SLAT ENDS

1/8" RAD.

1/2 X 1/2" GROOVE CUT AT 12°

FLATS

2"

1/4"

11/16" TENON

11/16"

15-1/4"

8°

2-1/2"

2-11/16"

LEG SLAB LAMINATION

2-11/16"
1-1/16" (5/4")
9/16" (3/4")
1-1/16" (5/4")

A,B

2-11/16"

2-1/2"

1-1/8"

17/32"

1/2"

STRAIGHT EDGE

25"

23-1/2"

1-1/16"

1/8"

RAD

NOTCH SLAT

12°

31"

EACH SQ. = 1"

2-1/2"

1/4"

1/4"

1/4"

1-1/16"

INSIDE SEAT SUPPORT

1-1/4"

NOTE: CUT ALL MORTISES 1/16" DEEPER THAN TENON LENGTH

NOTCH SLAT

2"

1/4"

15/16"

14"

2-1/2"

15/16"

2-1/2"

14"

15/16"

2-1/2"

1/4"

17"

1/4"

3-1/2"

17/32"-DEEP HALF LAP

2-3/4"

32-1/4"

4-1/2"

12° BEVEL

13-1/2"

17/32"-DEEP HALF LAP

2-11/16"

45°

TOP RAIL/ARMREST PATTERNS

STRAIGHT EDGE

REAR LEG PATTERN

We chose poplar, a moderately priced hardwood, for this project because it's easy to work with and takes paint well. Other woods will work as well, such as clear redwood and cedar, though these woods are more expensive. Also, these woods require a special primer to keep any stains from bleeding through. Painting the bench is a good idea because it helps it stand up to the elements. A clear finish like spar varnish will also work well. But no matter what finish you choose, be sure to use waterproof plastic resin glue if you're going to keep the bench outside. If you build it for interior use, you can use regular yellow glue.

The Legs

Begin by making the legs. Glue together three pieces of lumber surfaced on two sides (S2S): One piece of ¾-in. stock (nominal) surrounded by two pieces of 5/4 stock (nominal). This works out to be, in actual dimensions, one piece 9/16-in. thick sandwiched between two pieces 1 3/16-in. thick.

The back legs are cut from a blank 8 in. wide x 34 in. long, and the front legs from a blank 5½ in. wide x 26 in. long. Rip and crosscut the leg blanks, then stack the pieces and bore pilot holes for 2-in. finish nails spaced ¼ in. in from the side and ends (for alignment during gluing). Spread plastic resin glue on the stock with a paint roller (**Fig. 1**). Be careful not to spread glue around the work surface.

Make a template of the back legs on cardboard. Cut out the template, and, when the glue has dried, trace two legs on the blank, leaving about ½-in. space between them (**Fig. 2**). Separate the two legs by band sawing between them.

Next, make a ripping platform from plywood ¼ in. thick x 8 in. wide x 35 in. long. Tack nail the blank to the platform so that the outside of the leg is parallel to the saw blade. Rip one face of the leg (**Fig. 3**), reposition the leg, and then rip the other face.

Make the inside cuts in two stopped passes. Raise the blade as high as possible, then set the rip fence for a 2½-in.-wide cut. Stick a piece of masking tape to the saw table and draw a line on the tape where the blade meets the table. Also, mark a line on the leg to indicate the back of the leg's knee. Rip the leg, stopping just short of where the two reference lines meet. Flip the work end for end, and make the second pass (**Fig. 4**). Complete the cut on the band saw.

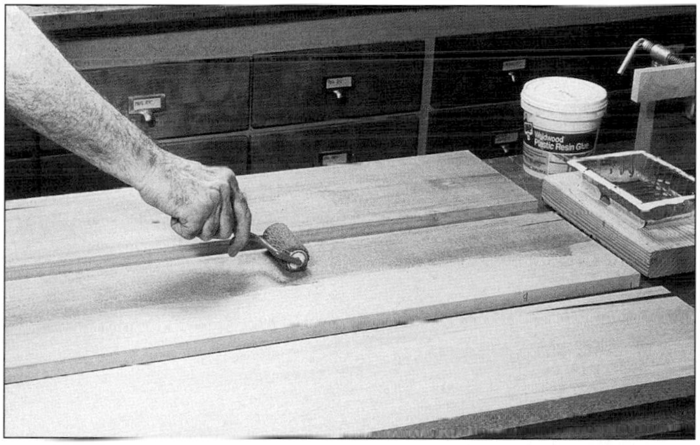

Fig. 1 ***Use a paint roller to quickly spread the plastic resin glue on boards that will be clamped together to form the leg blanks.***

Materials List

Key	No.	Size and description (use)
A	2	2½ x 2 11/16 x 31¼" poplar (back leg)
B	2	2½ x 2 11/16 x 23½" poplar (front leg)
C	1	1 1/16 x 3½ x 56½" poplar (lower back rail)
D	1	1 1/16 x 3 x 56½" poplar (front rail)
E	2	1 1/16 x 3 x 16⅝" poplar (seat support)
F	2	1 1/16 x 3 x 15⅞" poplar (seat support)
G	2	1 1/16 x 2 x 15⅞" poplar (stretcher)
H	2	1 1/16 x 2¼ x 64½" poplar (curved rail)
I	2	1 1/16 x 4 x 20" poplar (armrest)
J	1	¾ x 2¾ x 60" poplar (rear seat slat)
K	5	¾ x 2⅛ x 60" poplar (seat slat)
L	1	¾ x 2⅛ x 54⅝" poplar (front seat slat)
M	5	½ x 1¾ x 19⅜" poplar (back slat)
N	2	½ x 1¾ 19¼" poplar (back slat)
O	2	½ x 1¾ x 18⅞" poplar (back slat)
P	2	½ x 1¾ x 18" poplar (back slat)
Q	2	½ x 1¾ x 16⅝" poplar (back slat)
R	2	½ x 1¾ x 14⅞" poplar (back slat)
S	32	½ x ½" (length cut to fit) poplar (filler block)
T	3	⅜ x 2 x 17" poplar (slat support cleat)

Misc.: 49-1½" No. 10 fh wood screws; 4-2½" No. 12 fh wood screws; 4-3½" No. 12 fh wood screws; ½"-dia. wood plugs; ¾" 18-gauge brads; 1¼" finish nails; plastic resin glue; oil-based primer/sealer/stain killer; white latex high-gloss enamel.

Fig. 2 *Make the patterns for the rear legs, including mortise positions, from cardboard. Trace the patterns onto the stock.*

Fig. 4 *Mark the workpiece and saw table to prevent overcutting the rear leg face. Stop the cut before the marks line up.*

Fig. 5 *Hold the legs on a sliding platform and make repeated deep kerf cuts to form the angled half-lap for the arched back rail.*

Fig. 3 *Mount the blank on a ripping platform with its front edge aligned with the saw blade. Rip one edge, then the other.*

Next, cut the angled end half-laps on the leg tops. To do this safely and easily, make a jig from ½-in. plywood, measuring 12 in. wide x 20 in. long.

The plywood slides smoothly on two wood runners that ride in the saw table's miter gauge slots. Place the runners in the slots, then tack nail the plywood to them. Screw a 2-in. wide and high x 12-in.-long block to the plywood at a 43° angle to the saw blade. Reverse the block when cutting the other leg.

Make a series of cuts 1 in. deep and ⅛ in. apart (**Fig. 5**). The waste at the top of the leg is retained to keep the leg level. Clean out the waste between the saw kerfs with a chisel.

When the laps have been cut, cut off the waste at the legs' tops, leaving a bit extra to allow flush trimming later when the top rail is attached. Band saw the tapers on the legs.

Next, cut the front legs to size, and mark the mortise locations for the rails, seat supports, and stretchers on the front and rear legs. Cut the bulk of the mortises on the drill press by boring overlapping holes, then chisel the mortise sides flat (**Fig. 6**).

Rails and Supports

Rip and crosscut the lower back rail, front rail, seat supports, stretchers, and armrests from 5/4 stock. Cut the beveled ends on the rear of each armrest.

Do not cut the profiles on the top edges of the seat supports until their tenons have been cut. Also, carefully bore out and cut the mortises for the seat supports in the front and rear rails.

Cut the tenons on the table saw using a dado head and miter gauge. Clamp a small stop block on the miter gauge fence. Rotate the stretcher after each pass.

Using a ½-in.-wide dado blade, make one pass with the stretcher butted to the block and a second pass holding it away from the block. Chisel the corners of the tenons round to match the round ends of the mortises (**Fig. 7 and 8**). Now, tilt the dado head to 12° and cut the ½-in.-wide angled groove in the top edge of the lower rear rail.

Use the band saw to cut the six flats on the top edge of each seat support. If necessary, use a file or a narrow belt sander to true each flat (**Fig. 9**). Next, rip an 8° bevel on the top edge of the front rail.

The Arched Rail

Draw a half section of the arched rail on paper. Cut out the template and trace the outline on two boards, each measuring a minimum 8½ in. wide x 38 in. long.

On both pieces, draw two straight lines approximately tangent to the rail's outside curve. Band saw these lines, then joint them flat.

The jointed surface serves to rest against the miter gauge fence for cutting the half-laps at the center and at the ends where the arched rail joins the rear leg assembly. The angle at which these flats are cut is not critical. Adjust the miter gauge as required for the shoulder cut.

Before cutting the half-laps, band saw the inside curve on each half to make it easier to grip. Cut the ends flat where they butt against the shoulders on the leg half-laps.

Cut the laps on the dado head (**Fig. 10**). Make a test cut an inch away from the marked line on the shoulder and check that it's parallel to the shoulder. If not, adjust the miter gauge.

Now, band saw the rail's outside curves and remove any saw ripples with a spokeshave (**Fig. 11**). Use a drum and disc sander to smooth the edges, then glue and clamp the two sections (**Fig. 12**). Drive two ¾-in. brads into the joint to keep the pieces from sliding.

After the glue has dried, use the router and slotting cutter to cut the groove for the slats in the rail's bottom edge (**Fig. 13**). Adjust the router base so that a cut from each face of the rail forms the outside edges of a ½-in.-wide groove. Readjust the router and remove the waste between the grooves. Clamp a stop block at each end to control the cut.

Assembly

Dry assemble the bench and butt the armrests against the rear legs. Mark their position (**Fig. 14**). Disassemble the bench. Prop up the leg on the drill press with a wedge left from

TECH Tips

See-Through Stains
Use a latex or oil-based "stain-blocking" primer when painting redwood and cedar. Follow this with two applications of the same type topcoat.

Fig. 6 Remove the bulk of the mortise on the drill press by boring overlapping holes, then smooth the mortise with a sharp chisel.

Fig. 7 Use a miter gauge and stop block to cut the tenons on the table saw. Butt the rail to the block on the first pass, then cut the remainder of the tenon.

Fig. 8 Round off the edges of the tenons with a chisel to fit the mortises. Another option is to square the ends of the mortise instead.

Fig. 9 *The curved seat supports are really a series of six flats. Saw the supports, then use a strip sander or a file to true each flat.*

Fig. 10 *On each half of the arched rail, first cut the inside curve. Make a flat edge tangent to the curve, then cut the half-lap.*

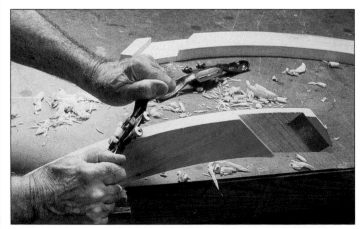

Fig. 11 *Cut the rail's outside curve on the band saw, then use a spokeshave to smooth away the saw marks and refine the curve.*

cutting the leg (**Fig. 15**). Bore ³⁄₁₆-in.-dia. holes in the leg and push dowel centers in the holes.

Securely clamp a 12° beveled block to the leg and slide the armrest against it to mark pilot hole centers (**Fig. 16**). Use a doweling jig to bore holes on the marks (**Fig. 17**). Chisel notches in the legs.

Use the router with a ³⁄₁₆-in.-rad. rounding-over bit to ease the corners on the legs, stretchers, seat supports, and front rail. Use a ⅛-in.-rad. bit on the groove edges of the arched rail and the rail below it. Finish sand all completed parts.

Glue and clamp the rear legs to the lower rear rail. Temporarily clamp the arched rail in place to ensure that the entire assembly is square. Glue and clamp the front legs to the front rail.

Fasten each spacer in the lower rail with glue and a ¾-in. 18-gauge brad. Use a slat cutoff to alternately space the blocks (**Fig. 18**). Tip the assembly on its back. Use a framing square to carry the spacer locations to the curved rail (**Fig. 19**).

Rip the ½-in.-thick back slats to width and crosscut them 1 in. oversize. Starting at the center slat and working to the ends, use two ¼-in.-thick gauging sticks to mark the length

Fig. 12 *Glue and clamp the halves of the arched rail together with blocks on each side. Wax paper keeps glue off the blocks.*

Fig. 13 *Cut the groove in the arched rail using a slotting cutter and router in a series of passes. Clamp the stop block to the rail.*

Fig. 14 *Dry assemble the bench with the arched rail clamped in place. Lay the armrest on the front leg and trace the position on the rear leg.*

and curved end of each slat. Spread the sticks apart in each slat position and trace the rail's curve (**Fig. 20**). Saw the curve on the gauging stick, and refit the stick to mark the slat's length. Transfer the length and curve from the gauging sticks to the slat, and cut it to shape.

Slide the slats and spacers in place, and trace the arched rail's curve on the spacers. Cut them to shape (**Fig. 21**), and fasten them with glue and brads. Chamfer the slat ends and use a ⅛-in.-rad. rounding-over bit on their exposed edges.

Insert the slats dry in the lower rail. Fit the arched rail on

Fig. 15 *Use the drill press to bore pilot holes for the screws that attach the armrest to the rear leg. A scrap wedge positions the leg.*

SHOP*Helper*

Quick Blade Adjustment

To make quick work of adjusting heights on a table saw or router, create a custom, quick-reference, all-purpose blade depth gauge. Using a foot-long section of 2x4 or 1x2, sit the board on edge and run it through the saw or router at decreasing heights, from 1" stepped down to ¼"—or any other heights you need. Looking at the board in profile, you will have created upside-down steps. Now just mark the heights you've cut on the end, and you'll be able to use the board as a quick depth gauge any time you need one. To make it even handier, drill a hole in the board and hang it right by your saw or router table. If you use many different sizes, you may want to make more than one depth gauge.

Fig. 16 *Lean the armrest against an angled block to mark the pilot holes in the end grain. Dowel centers are pushed into pilot holes in the leg.*

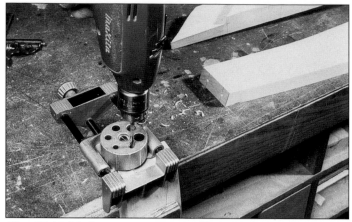

Fig. 17 *Hold the armrest vertically in a vise, and use a doweling jig to bore the pilot holes on the marks left by the dowel centers.*

Fig. 18 *Using a dummy slat for spacing, glue and nail spacer blocks in the bottom rail groove. The blocks negate the need for mortising.*

TECH *Tips*

Handy Clamp
Outdoor projects are often odd shapes that are difficult to clamp. If you need to clamp pieces but the clamps you have won't reach or won't work for some other reason, create your own with some nylon clothesline or rope and a scrap piece of wood. Simply tie the line to the pieces that need to be clamped, and then twirl the wood scrap until the structure is tight. Then brace the end of the wood scrap against a crossbrace or wall.

the slats and clamp two sticks across them to hold them parallel. Use masking tape on front and back to secure the slats' tops to the arched rail.

Raise the arched rail until the slats clear the mortises (**Fig. 22**). Brush glue into the mortises. Lower the top rail and seat the slats. When the glue has dried, lift off the rail. Apply glue to the slat mortises, the half-laps on the rail, and the rear legs. Clamp the rail in place (**Fig. 23**). When the glue is dry, pare the rail flush to each leg with a chisel. Sand the rail/leg corners and use the ³⁄₁₆-in.-rad rounding-over bit on the rail's top corners.

Glue and clamp the rear leg assembly to the front assembly, spanned by the stretchers and seat supports.

Next, mark the screw locations on all of the slats and use a ½-in.-dia. bit to clearly bore ³⁄₈-in.-deep plug holes, as indicated in the drawing.

Bore through pilot holes in the slats with a ⅛-in.-dia. bit.

Fig. 19 *Ensure perpendicular alignment of the slats in the bottom rail with a framing square. Mark the slat positions on the arched rail.*

Fig. 20 *Hold the gauging sticks in the bottom rail and mark the curve at the arched rail. Cut the curve on the sticks and use them to mark slat length.*

Position the slats on the bench, with ¼-in. spacer blocks between them.

Bore ⅛-in. pilot holes in the supports. Remove the slats and enlarge the ⅛-in. holes to fit the screw shank. Round over the top slat corners, then screw them down. Glue and screw in the armrests. Glue the plugs into the screw holes, and when the glue is dry, pare the plugs flush with a chisel.

We finished up by applying a coat of sealer, followed by two coats of white latex high-gloss enamel.

MATERIAL *Matters*

Sticky Situation
Glue serves so many functions in woodworking that it's easy to forget that it can also complicate situations. A bad glue job, or allowing glue to go where it's not supposed to, can seriously detract from the appearance of your finished piece. Here are a few dos and don'ts for working with glue, to ensure a problem-free finish:

Do allow standard yellow carpenter's glue to harden for about half an hour, and then remove it with a chisel, being sure not to scar the surface of the work.

Do use wax paper when gluing up several pieces of a project together. The paper will ensure that any runout does not end up on the surface of the pieces. You can also wax the pieces to ensure glue doesn't stick.

Do use a razor or X-acto blade to remove squeeze-out in tough-to-reach corners. This sort of detail makes the difference between a mediocre and great job.

Do keep your clamps clean. Clamping up glued work can contaminate the pads, spreading the glue to other surfaces and causing deep stains. Be sure that the clamp pads and bars are clean everywhere they will come into contact with wood.

Don't try to wipe off squeeze-out from joints while the glue is wet. More than likely, you'll spread the wet glue and seal the wood pores in that area—the area will take stain inconsistently and will mar the final appearance.

Don't work with glue on your hands. Be very careful to remove glue from your hands when you move to the next stage after gluing up pieces. Even a small bit of glue on your hand can cause an ugly mess on a subsequent work surface.

Fig. 21 *Cut spacer blocks for the top rail overwide, mark the rail's curve on the blocks, then cut them to fit. Number the blocks in sequence.*

Fig. 22 *Raise the arched rail with the slats taped and clamped to it. Brush glue into the slat mortises, and lower the slats into position.*

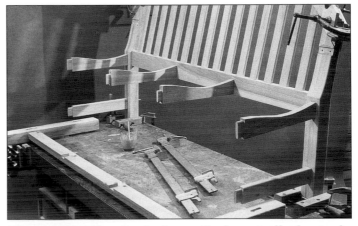

Fig. 23 *When the glue is dry on the lower rail, glue and clamp the arched rail to the rear legs and slats. Next, glue and clamp the remaining pieces.*

Laid Back

Finish this project and you'll have a perfect excuse to take the rest of the summer off—a laze-around chair!

The combination of straight lines, flat planes, and gentle curves that is the signature of the Adirondack chair is familiar even to those who have never had the good fortune to visit the Adirondack Mountains of New York State. Elegant and functional, these chairs complement any style of yard. Though many variations can be found, the essential spirit of the chair has not changed much from its earliest form as outdoor seating for modest cabins, rustic mountain hotels, and elegant "great camps" (as luxurious mountain retreats were known in the late 19th and early 20th centuries).

*Key*POINTS

TIME
Prep Time	2 hours
Shop Time	10 hours
Assembly Time	8 hours

EFFORT
Skill Level	intermediate
Maintenance	light
Assistance	none

COST / BENEFITS
Expense: moderate

• A **classic** outdoor chair that is both comfortable and stylish.
• Construction design and use of cedar ensure chair **can last decades**.

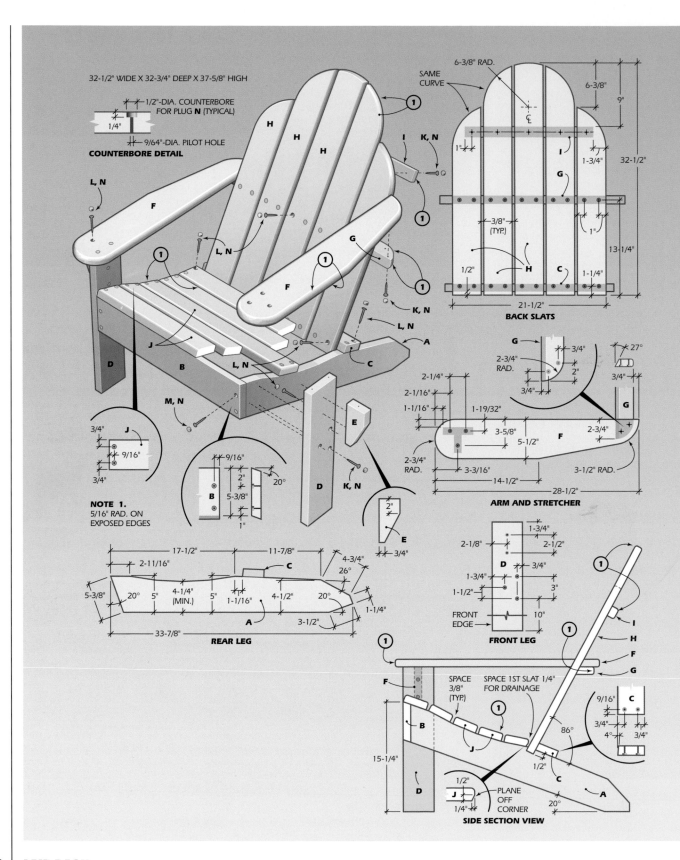

32-1/2" WIDE X 32-3/4" DEEP X 37-5/8" HIGH

1/2"-DIA. COUNTERBORE FOR PLUG **N** (TYPICAL)

1/4"

9/64"-DIA. PILOT HOLE

COUNTERBORE DETAIL

NOTE 1.
5/16" RAD. ON EXPOSED EDGES

6-3/8" RAD.

SAME CURVE

6-3/8"

9"

1"

1-3/4"

32-1/2"

3/8" (TYP.)

1"

1/2"

1-1/4"

13-1/4"

21-1/2"

BACK SLATS

G

3/4"

27°

2-3/4" RAD.

2"

3/4"

3/4"

G

2-1/4"

2-1/16"

1-1/16"

1-19/32"

3-5/8"

5-1/2"

F

2-3/4"

2-3/4" RAD.

3-3/16"

14-1/2"

3-1/2" RAD.

28-1/2"

ARM AND STRETCHER

3/4"

J

9/16"

3/4"

9/16"

2"

5-3/8"

B

1"

20°

2"

E

3/4"

17-1/2"

11-7/8"

2-11/16"

C

4-3/4"

26°

5-3/8"

20°

5"

4-1/4" (MIN.)

5"

1-1/16"

4-1/2"

20°

1-1/4"

A

3-1/2"

33-7/8"

REAR LEG

1-3/4"

2-1/8"

2-1/2"

D

3/4"

1-3/4"

3"

1-1/2"

FRONT EDGE

10"

FRONT LEG

1

F

SPACE 3/8" (TYP.)

SPACE 1ST SLAT 1/4" FOR DRAINAGE

1

I

H

F

G

B

J

86°

9/16"

C

3/4"

4°

3/4"

15-1/4"

1/2"

J

PLANE OFF CORNER

1/4"

C

1/2"

A

20°

D

SIDE SECTION VIEW

The flat back and the severely sloping seat might lead you to expect some discomfort in a chair like this. In reality, these seats are extremely comfortable, and they will provide you with hours of pleasant summer sitting on a porch, lawn, poolside, or at the edge of a mountain lake. And these chairs are as durable as they are comfortable.

We chose white cedar as the material for these chairs. Cedar is naturally resistant to rot and insect damage. Depending on your location, you might find white or red cedar at the lumberyard. Either species is fine for this project. In either case, be fussy when going through the lumber pile, and select boards that are as close to being free of knots as you can get.

The joinery for the chair is very simple. All the joints are screwed together with galvanized deck screws. The screws are set into counterbored holes and covered with cedar plugs that are glued in place. For additional strength, especially in endgrain joints, we used polyurethane glue in addition to the screws. This glue is an excellent choice for outdoor construction because it is waterproof, and you don't have to rush during assembly.

In addition to these favorable characteristics, it cures in the presence of moisture. Cedar, like most softwoods, is dried to about 14 percent moisture content, compared to about 7 percent for kiln-dried hardwood.

Materials List

Key	No.	Size and description (use)
A	2	1¹/₁₆ x 5 x 33⁷/₈" white cedar (rear leg)
B	1	1¹/₁₆ x 5³/₈ x 23⁵/₈" white cedar (rail)
C	1	1¹/₁₆ x 4¹/₄ x 20⁷/₁₆" white cedar (stretcher)
D	2	1¹/₁₆ x 4¹/₄ x 20⁷/₁₆" white cedar (front leg)
E	2	1¹/₁₆ x 2¹/₂ x 6" white cedar (bracket)
F	2	1¹/₁₆ x 5¹/₂ x 28¹/₂" white cedar (arm)
G	1	1¹/₁₆ x 2¹/₂ x 27" white cedar (stretcher)
H	5	1¹/₁₆ x 4 x 32¹/₂" white cedar (slat)
I	1	1¹/₁₆ x 1¹/₂ x 18" white cedar (support)
J	5	1¹/₁₆ x 3³/₈ x 23⁵/₈" white cedar (hinge block)
K	as reqd.	1¹/₂" No. 10 galvanized fh screw
L	as reqd.	2" No. 10 galvanized fh screw
M	as reqd.	2¹/₂" No. 10 galvanized fh screw
N	as reqd.	¹/₂"-dia. wood plug

Misc.: Polyurethane glue; primer; paint; sandpaper.

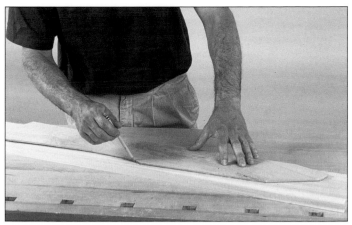

Fig. 1 *Begin by making a plywood or cardboard pattern of the chair sides and, once precisely finished, trace it onto the workpiece.*

Sides, Rails, Arms

Begin by making a pattern for the chair sides. The sides of this chair also function as the rear legs and are the real foundation of the chair. You can use heavy cardboard or ¼-in.-thick plywood for the pattern.

Though plywood is obviously more difficult to cut than cardboard, the advantage of using it is that it is easy to make fine adjustments to the shape using sandpaper and a block plane. With cardboard, once the pattern is cut, it's difficult to adjust. Trace the shape on the pattern material and cut it out. Trace the completed pattern on the side blanks (**Fig. 1**).

Make the angled cuts on the ends of the side blanks using a sliding miter saw, table saw, or circular saw. Next, cut the workpiece to shape using a sabre saw (**Fig. 2**). Cut to the waste side of the line and then work down to the line using a block plane and sandpaper. The finished piece should be well shaped with smooth edges that are free of saw marks.

Fig. 2 *Clamp the workpiece to the bench, and saw the chair sides to shape using a sabre saw held to the waste side of the line.*

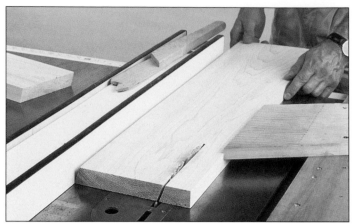

Fig. 3 *Cut the beveled edge on the front seat support rail. Use a featherboard to prevent the workpiece from kicking back.*

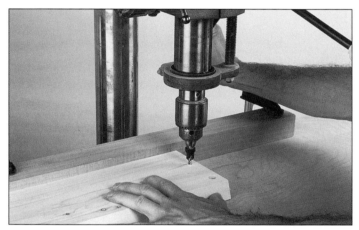

Fig. 4 *Bore and counterbore pilot holes for joining chair parts using a combination tapered drill and countersink.*

Fig. 5 *In two stages, apply polyurethane glue to the end of the leg. Allow some glue to be absorbed, and then apply more.*

Proceed now to making the front rail. Rip it to width, but make it slightly oversize. Then cut the beveled edges on it using the table saw (**Fig. 3**). Use a featherboard firmly clamped to the saw table to ensure that the workpiece moves firmly along the fence, and also to ensure that it doesn't kick back. And always use a pushstick at the end of the cut to keep your hands a safe distance from the saw blade.

Bore and counterbore pilot holes in the front rail for fastening it to the sides. The most efficient tool for this is a combination drill and countersink bit chucked in a drill press (**Fig. 4**), but the holes can be made accurately with a portable drill, or a drill and drill stand. Limit the counterbored portion of the hole to about ¼ in. deep.

Next, clamp one of the chair sides in a workbench vise with its front end pointing up. Place the front rail over the side, and bore pilot holes into the endgrain of the side.

Driving screws into endgrain is generally not considered to be the best method of fastening. In this case, however, there isn't much stress on the joint, and by combining the mechanical fastening of a screw with the glue bond, we can achieve a good joint for this application.

Apply polyurethane glue to the end of the chair side (**Fig. 5**). There is a strong tendency for the endgrain to absorb liquid, so the best technique is to spread some glue on the piece, then wait a minute or two and reapply a bit more.

Position the front rail over the side, and drive the screws to fasten the two pieces (**Fig. 6**). Repeat the procedure for the opposite side.

Cut the back stretcher to size. Then rip the angle on its front edge as shown in the plan. Bore and counterbore the pilot holes, and apply some glue to the joints. Then fasten the stretcher to the chair sides.

Rip and crosscut the front legs to size. Then bore the pilot holes in them. Apply glue to the joint surfaces, and use clamps to temporarily hold the legs to the chair side assembly while

Fig. 6 *Clamp the chair sides and rail in a vise, and drive the deck screws that fasten together the rail and the chair sides.*

Fig. 7 *Spread glue on the joint between the front leg and the chair sides. Hold the parts with a clamp, and drive the screws.*

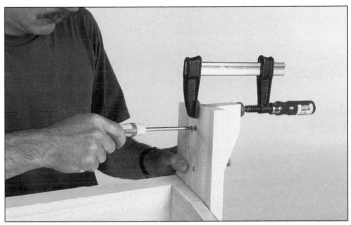

Fig. 8 *Cut the arm brackets to size, and hold them in place with clamps while you attach them to the front leg with screws.*

you drive the screws to fasten the legs (**Fig. 7**). Use a sabre saw to cut the arm brackets, and remove any saw marks with a pass from a block plane. Apply glue to the brackets, clamp them to the front legs, and drill pilot holes for the screws. Drive the screws through each leg and into a bracket (**Fig. 8**).

Transfer the arm profile to the arm blanks, and cut the arms to shape using a sabre saw. Again, stay to the waste side of the line, and then refine the shape after the arm is cut. To remove the sharp corner from each arm's edge, use a router and a ⁵⁄₁₆-in.-rad. rounding-over bit.

Cut the arm stretcher slightly oversize, and use the table saw to rip the angle on its front edge. Trace the radius profile on either end of the stretcher, and then use the sabre saw to cut the shape. Use the router and rounding-over bit to round the edges of the piece. Fasten the stretcher to the underside of the arms with screws and glue. Note that since the screws on the bottom of the stretcher will not be visible, or directly exposed to moisture, they don't need plugs. Just countersink the screw heads slightly below the wood surface. Check that the arms are square to the stretcher before fastening.

Temporarily position the arm assembly over the chair base. Cut a scrap stick to support the back of the assembly. Then bore pilot holes through the arms and into the endgrain of the leg and arm bracket. Remove the arms and apply glue to the joint. Position the parts and screw them together (**Fig. 9**).

Making the Back

Rip the stock for the back slats to width, but leave the workpieces long. They will be cut to finished length later. Clamp the three center slats together with a ³⁄₈-in.-thick spacer between each. Use a large compass to mark the curved profile across them (**Fig. 10**). Cut the curve with a sabre saw. Mark the curve on the two outer slats, and cut them to shape.

Use a ⁵⁄₁₆-in.-rad. rounding-over bit in the router to cut a curved edge on the front and back of each slat. Then crosscut

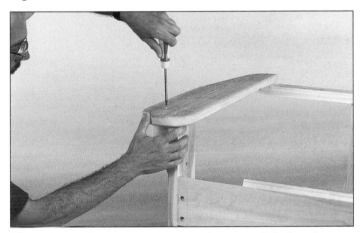

Fig. 9 *Once the arms are cut to shape and their edges are completely rounded off, they can be attached to the front legs.*

Fig. 10 *Clamp together the back slats, positioning spacers between them, and use a large compass to mark their curve.*

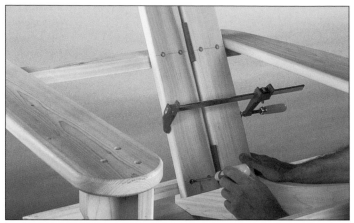

Fig. 11 *Fasten the first back slat with screws. Place spacers between it and the next slat. Clamp them, and screw securely in place.*

Fig. 12 *After all the back slats are installed, clamp the back support in place, and attach it to the back slats with screws.*

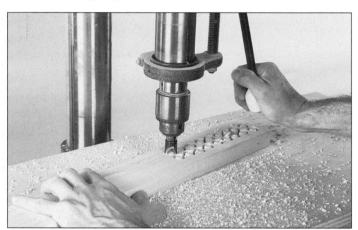

Fig. 13 *Use a ½-in.-dia. plug cutter chucked in a drill press to cut out the plugs that will be glued over the screwheads.*

Fig. 14 *Use a small disposable brush to apply a liberal glob of polyurethane glue on top of each screw head before covering with plugs.*

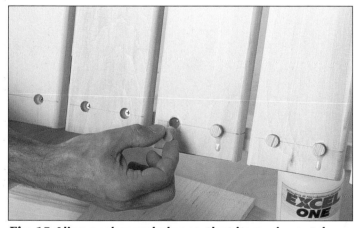

Fig. 15 *Align each wood plug so that its grain matches the direction of the workpiece. Then push it securely into place. Repeat over all the screw holes.*

Fig. 16 *Place a veneer shim under a fine-cutting pull-stroke saw, and cut the plug nearly flush with the workpiece surface.*

Fig. 17 *Plane a bevel on the back bottom edge of the first seat slat. This creates a space that effectively allows water to drain.*

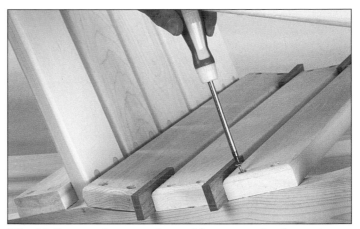

Fig. 18 *Fasten the seat slats with screws. Again, note the use of ⅜-in.-thick blocks to ensure uniform spacing between slats.*

them to finished length. Lay out and bore the pilot holes in the slats for fastening them to the chair base.

Hold the first slat in position on the chair, and fasten it to the stretchers with screws. Clamp the second slat to the first with ⅜-in. spacers between them, and screw that slat in place (**Fig. 11**). Proceed across the chair back driving four screws through the front of each slat into each stretcher.

Cut and install the upper back support stretcher to the back side of the slats. Use clamps to hold the part in place while you drive in the screws (**Fig. 12**).

Seat Slats, Plugs, and Finish

Before installing the seat slats, you must install the plugs in the back slats because they will be inaccessible after the seat slats are installed. Cut all the plugs you need at this point using a plug cutter in a drill press (**Fig. 13**).

Use a small brush to spread a bit of polyurethane glue in each screw hole, and install the plugs (**Fig. 14 and 15**). Align the grain of the plugs with the surrounding wood to make them less visible. Plug all the existing holes in this fashion. After the glue has dried, saw them nearly flush (**Fig. 16**). Finally, pare off the remaining material using a chisel.

Cut the seat slats to size, bore and counterbore pilot holes in them, and round over their top edges as you did with the other chair components. Plane a bevel on the back bottom edge of the first seat slat to create a drainage space where the slat meets the chair back (**Fig. 17**).

Install the seat slats by screwing them to the chair sides with ⅜-in. spacers between them (**Fig. 18**). Plug the screw holes, and proceed to finish the chair.

Sand the chair with 120-grit sandpaper to remove rough spots and machine marks from the face of the lumber. Dust off the chair thoroughly, and apply an oil-based primer and two coats of oil-based gloss exterior paint to all the chair's surfaces, including the leg bottoms.

TECH *Tips*

Block Plane Adjustments
One of the most useful tools in a workshop is the block plane. It's worth spending a little more to get a model that does what you need it to do. Better block planes include a depth-of-cut adjustment nut, lateral adjustment lever, and an adjustable mouth opening. Knowing how to adjust these features ensures you get the results you want and keep the plane working well. To adjust the depth of cut, sight along the bottom of the plane while turning the adjustment nut. Rotate the nut until the cutting edge appears just above the plane's sole. If necessary, move the lateral adjustment lever to the left or right until the edge projects evenly and is parallel with the sole. The mouth opening is adjustable for coarse or fine work. For heavy cuts, loosen the locking knob at the front and shift the lever to open the mouth. Set the mouth to a narrow slit for fine, extra-smooth cuts. Proper adjustment is only possible with a razor-sharp cutter. For consistent sharpening, use a honing guide to hold the cutter at the correct angle. Hone the bevel on a whetstone until a wire edge forms. Then remove the blade from the guide and stroke the back along the stone to remove the wire edge.

Dining Out

Nothing says summer like a meal eaten outside—
especially when it's served on a redwood dining set.

One of life's simple pleasures is to dine outdoors on a beautiful warm day. And whether your tastes run to hot dogs on the grill or chilled strawberry soup, it is always nice to have a pleasant place to sit. To that end, we offer this redwood table and bench set. Functional and handsome, the set is not too difficult to build. It's a good project for intermediate woodworkers; the construction is straightforward and requires mostly mortise-and-tenon joints. Because the project has so many joints and slats, however, it does require that you prepare your stock uniformly and accurately.

*Key*POINTS

TIME
Prep Time	2 hours
Shop Time	7 hours
Assembly Time	10 hours

EFFORT
Skill Level	intermediate
Maintenance	light
Assistance	one (optional)

COST / BENEFITS
Expense: moderate

• **Informal** style is well suited to almost any outdoor patio or deck.
• Table's **size accommodates** groups small and large.

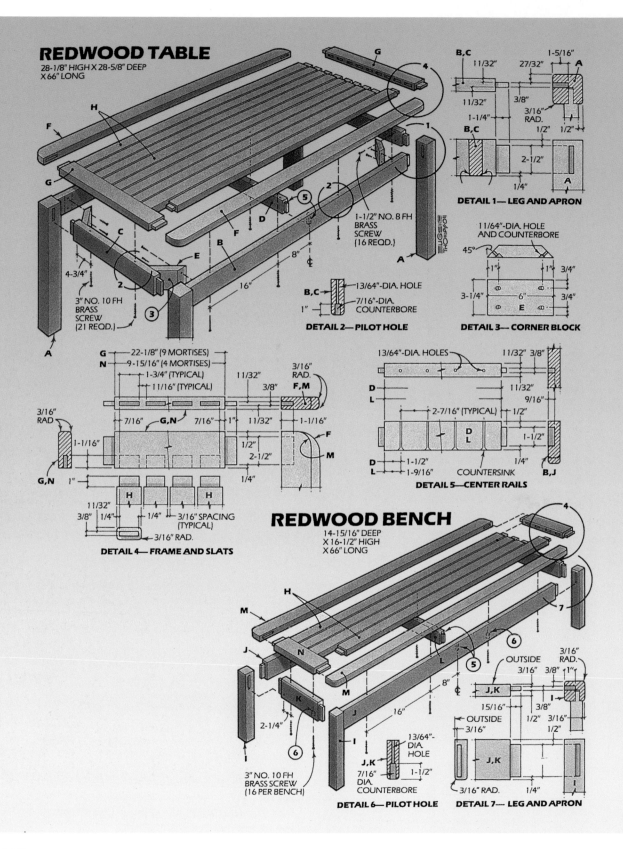

REDWOOD TABLE
28-1/8" HIGH X 28-5/8" DEEP
X 66" LONG

G

H

F

G

C

E

2

4-3/4"

3" NO. 10 FH
BRASS
SCREW
(21 REQD.)

3

A

1

2

5

D

F

B

8"

16"

1-1/2" NO. 8 FH
BRASS
SCREW
(16 REQD.)

A

EUGENE
THOMPSON

B,C

13/64"-DIA. HOLE

7/16"-DIA.
COUNTERBORE

1"

DETAIL 2— PILOT HOLE

DETAIL 1— LEG AND APRON

B,C   11/32"   27/32"   1-5/16"   A

11/32"   3/8"   3/16"
RAD.

1-1/4"

B,C   1/2" 1/2"

2-1/2"

1/4"

A

11/64"-DIA. HOLE
AND COUNTERBORE

45°

1"   1"   3/4"

3-1/4"   6"   3/4"

E

DETAIL 3— CORNER BLOCK

DETAIL 4— FRAME AND SLATS

G 22-1/8" (9 MORTISES)
N 9-15/16" (4 MORTISES)
1-3/4" (TYPICAL)
11/16" (TYPICAL)
11/32"

3/16"
RAD.

F,M

3/16"
RAD.

1-1/16"

G,N

7/16"   G,N   7/16"   1"   11/32"   1-1/16"

1/2"
2-1/2"

F

M

G,N   1"

H   H

11/32"
3/8" 1/4"   1/4"   3/16" SPACING
(TYPICAL)

3/16" RAD.

1/4"

DETAIL 5— CENTER RAILS

13/64"-DIA. HOLES   11/32" 3/8"

D
L

11/32"

9/16"

2-7/16" (TYPICAL)   1/2"

D
L

D
L

1-1/2"

D   1-1/2"
L   1-9/16"   COUNTERSINK

1/4"

B,J

REDWOOD BENCH
14-15/16" DEEP
X 16-1/2" HIGH
X 66" LONG

4

H

M

N

J

K

M

L

5

6

7

2-1/4"

6

I

8"

16"

J

I

3" NO. 10 FH
BRASS SCREW
(16 PER BENCH)

13/64"-
DIA.
HOLE

J,K

7/16"
DIA.
COUNTERBORE

1-1/2"

DETAIL 6— PILOT HOLE

DETAIL 7— LEG AND APRON

3/16"
RAD.

J,K   3/16" 3/8" 1"
OUTSIDE

15/16"   3/8"

1/2" 3/16"

OUTSIDE
3/16"

1/2"

J,K

3/16" RAD.   1/4"

I

The table is large enough to seat six to eight adults, and the benches can be used with the table, or as casual seating on their own.

Materials

We chose heart redwood as the material for this furniture because of its resistance to rot and insect damage (other grades of redwood are not rot- and insect-resistant). Redwood is generally available from lumberyards or large home centers, but you can also order it through mail-order outlets.

We used 5/4 stock for the table and bench tops, aprons, and center rails, and 8/4 stock for the table and bench legs. If you can get rough 8/4 stock, cut the bench legs from a single piece. However, if you can only buy surfaced lumber (normally 1½ in. thick), you will have to glue up the leg stock from two pieces. Throughout the construction of these pieces, use glue that has a waterproof rating.

We used epoxy for gluing up the leg stock, and a waterproof glue for the remainder of the joint assembly. This adhesive offers good weather resistance in combination with low toxicity and a relatively fast setup. The epoxy seemed a better choice for the legs because the table and bench legs may often be standing in water long after the rest of the pieces have dried off.

Legs and Aprons

Begin by gluing up stock for the table legs and bench legs. You can save time by gluing up blanks that are wide enough to provide two legs each. Mix the resin and hardener for the leg

Materials List

Key	No.	Size and description (use)
A	4	2¾ x 2¾ x 27¹/₁₆" redwood (leg)
B	2	1¹/₁₆ x 3¼ x 60" redwood (apron)
C	2	1¹/₁₆ x 3¼ x 22⁵/₈" redwood (apron)
D	1	1¹/₁₆ x 2¼ x 23½" redwood (support)
E	4	1¹/₁₆ x 3¼ x 6" redwood (corner block)
F	2	1¹/₁₆ x 3¼ x 66" redwood (stile)
G	2	1¹/₁₆ x 3¼ x 24⅛" redwood (rail)
H	13	1¹/₁₆ x 2¼ x 61½" redwood (slat)
I	4	1¾ x 1¾ x 15⁷/₁₆" redwood (leg)
J	2	1¹/₁₆ x 3¾ x 62⁵/₈" redwood (apron)
K	2	1¹/₁₆ x 3¾ x 11⁵/₁₆" redwood (apron)
L	1	1¹/₁₆ x 2¼ x 11⁷/₁₆" redwood (support)
M	2	1¹/₁₆ x 2½ x 66" redwood (stile)
N	2	1¹/₁₆ x 3¼ x 11¹⁵/₁₆" redwood (rail)

Misc.: 53-3" No. 10 fh brass screws (enough screws for two benches); 16-1½" No. 8 fh brass screws; epoxy; decking stain.

Fig. 1 *Unless you can purchase very thick redwood stock, use waterproof epoxy and clamp up the leg blanks from two pieces.*

Fig. 2 *Clamp a stop block to the saw table. Butt each workpiece that will have a tenon to the block, and then cut the tenon.*

Fig. 3 *Tip the workpiece on edge, butt it to the stop block, and move the piece over the dado head to finish the tenon.*

Fig. 4 *Clamp a rail to the bench top with a scrap block next to it, and then cut the mortises in the rail with a router.*

Fig. 5 *Finish each mortise by chopping its ends square with a sharp chisel. Be sure to clear out the waste chips before assembly.*

blanks in the proportions suggested by the manufacturer, then spread liberally on both mating surfaces. Clamp the pieces together, then let them set overnight (**Fig. 1**). Be sure to wear gloves when working with the epoxy, as the hardener can be irritating to your skin. Also, ensure good ventilation when using epoxy, and place some old newspapers under where you are gluing up the legs.

Because the table and benches have many similar parts, cut out all the parts at one time. First, rip and crosscut the leg stock for both table and benches. Next, rip and crosscut all the slats for the table and bench tops. Then rip and crosscut the pieces for the top frames. Finally, rip and crosscut the aprons and crossrails. To keep from confusing the groups of workpieces, identify them with masking-tape labels, or write on them with a piece of white chalk.

Install dado blades in the table saw to cut the tenons on the aprons, slats, top end rails, and cross support rails. Study the

plans carefully, noting how the tenons differ on the various parts. Even though all tenons in this project are ⅜ in. wide, the length, shoulders, and offsets change from piece to piece. Cut all like parts with a single setup on the table saw, using a stop block clamped to the saw table for repeat cuts (**Fig. 2 and 3**).

Readjust the saw and block as necessary for each different part. As usual, because the dado blades leave small ridges on the surface of the cuts, it is good practice to cut the tenons just a bit oversize and pare them to fit with a sharp chisel.

Next, lay out the mortises, bench legs, and top frame pieces. Because quite a few mortises are required, the most expedient method of cutting these joints is to use a plunge router with a straight bit and edge guide.

Use a scrap block to test the router setup for each different joint, then clamp the workpiece between bench dogs to cut the mortises. When working on the narrow top frame members, clamp a scrap block to the side of the workpiece to

Fig. 6 *Mark out the apron mortises with pencil lines, and remove the bulk of the mortise by boring holes on the drill press.*

Fig. 7 *Finish the apron mortises with a sharp chisel. Pare down to flatten the mortise sides and square the mortise ends.*

help support the router base (**Fig. 4**). Complete each mortise by squaring the ends with a sharp chisel (**Fig. 5**).

Lay out the mortises in the aprons to house the center support rails. Use the drill press to remove waste from these mortises and finish them with a chisel (**Fig. 6 and 7**).

The table and bench tops are fastened to the base by driving long screws up through the aprons into the tops. Use the drill press and a long 1⅗⁄₆₄-in.-dia. bit to bore the pilot holes through the aprons. Then counterbore the holes from the bottom with a ⁷⁄₁₆-in.-dia. bit (**Fig. 8 and 9**).

Note in the plans that all exposed edges are rounded to a ³⁄₁₆-in. radius. Use the router table and rounding-over bit to cut this radius on all legs, slats, and apron bottom edges (**Fig.10**). The inside edges of the long sides of the table and bench top frames can also be rounded over, although you must stop just short of the joint with the end rails.

Base Assembly

Start assembling the base for both the table and the bench by joining a long apron to a pair of legs. Apply glue to the tenons and mortises with a small brush, then use a long clamp to pull the joints tight (**Fig. 11 and 12**). Use scrap blocks between the clamp jaws and the work because redwood is a soft material and can be easily dented or scratched. Compare opposite diagonal measurements of the leg-apron assembly to be sure that it is square before leaving the glue to set (**Fig. 13**). If the diagonal measurements differ slightly, shift the clamps and re-measure. Complete the bases by joining the short aprons and center support rails to the long side assemblies (**Fig. 14**). Apply glue to the joints, slide the pieces together, and clamp firmly. Be sure to assemble the bases on a flat, even surface, checking that all legs sit firmly and that the base does not rock. Readjust the clamps if required to eliminate any twist in the base. Check the assembly for square as before, then let the glue set.

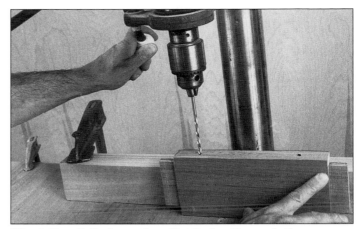

Fig. 8 *Carefully bore the pilot holes through the width of the aprons using a long bit chucked into the drill press.*

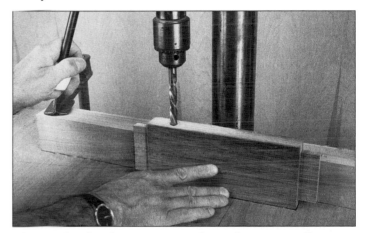

Fig. 9 *Take the time to counterbore the apron pilot holes. The counterbored holes will hide the screw heads from view.*

Fig. 10 *Cut a radius on the leg, slat, and lower apron corners using a rounding-over bit in the router table. Move slowly to avoid tearout.*

Fig. 11 *Use a small brush to apply glue to the apron tenons without getting it all over. Also apply a little glue to the mortise walls.*

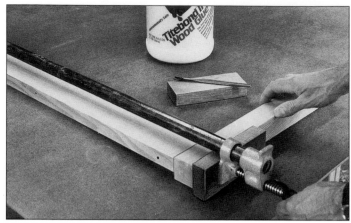

Fig. 12 *Redwood dents easily. Protect work surfaces during assembly by positioning a scrap block under the clamp jaws.*

Fig. 13 *Compare diagonal measurements of each leg-apron assembly to check it for square. Adjust the clamps if necessary.*

Fig. 14 *Glue and clamp together the leg-apron assemblies spanned by the short aprons and center support rails.*

Fig. 15 *Place a long scrap block of wood against the top frame rail while gluing and clamping the slats to the rails.*

Fig. 16 *Glue and clamp the stiles to the rails to complete the top assembly. Again, use a block under the clamp jaws.*

Fig. 17 *Carefully cut the radius on each top corner of the table using a sabre saw and staying just to the waste side of the line.*

Rip, crosscut, and miter the table's corner blocks. Bore and counterbore pilot holes and screw the blocks to the aprons.

Top Assembly

Begin assembling the tops by joining the slats to the end rails. In order to glue and clamp the many pieces together before the glue sets up, you must have all the parts ready. Position the glue, scrap blocks, and clamps within easy reach of each other. Begin by applying glue to the mortises in the end rails and the slat tenons. Slide the parts together. If the joints have been cut accurately, the proper spacing between slats will be automatic.

Place a scrap block across the ends of the rails to distribute the clamping pressure, then pull the joints tight with long clamps (**Fig. 15**). After the glue has set, apply glue to the end rail tenons and the mortises on the long side, and complete the top assembly (**Fig. 16**). Glue will squeeze out of the joints, but don't wipe it off. Wait until the glue gets rubbery, then cut it off with a chisel.

Trace the radius on the corners of the tops and use a sabre saw to make the cuts (**Fig. 17**). Remove saw marks with a file or a belt sander. Next, use the ³⁄₁₆-in.-rad. rounding-over bit in the router to shape the curved top and bottom edges of each top (**Fig. 18**).

Finishing

Because it is likely that these pieces will be exposed to wet grass or a wet patio or deck surface, it's a good idea to seal the bottom ends of the table and bench legs. If left unsealed, these endgrain surfaces will readily absorb water, with stains, mildew, and rot all as possible consequences. To seal the legs, we painted on two coats of epoxy, letting the first coat harden completely before applying the second (**Fig. 19**). The epoxy actually absorbs into the endgrain of the wood, effectively sealing the surface from moisture penetration.

Sand the tops and bases with 120- and 150-grit sandpaper, then dust off thoroughly.

Although heart redwood is naturally resistant to rot, if it is left untreated, the wood weathers and changes color. In addition, the glue in the joints—as well as the epoxy— degrades with exposure to the sun's ultraviolet rays. To protect the pieces, yet preserve their natural appearance, we applied a penetrating decking stain.

Complete assembly of the pieces by joining the tops to the bases. Invert a top on a padded surface and place the appropriate base over it. Adjust the base for equal overhang on all sides and attach the top by driving screws through the apron holes into the top frame.

Next, cut ³⁄₁₆-in.-thick spacers from scrap stock and place them between the slats, near the center of their span, to maintain proper spacing. Bore pilot holes and screw through the center support rail into each slat, again using 3-in. No. 10 fh screws (**Fig. 20**). Remove the spacer blocks and the pieces are now complete.

Fig. 18 *Use a rounding-over bit in the router to put a curved edge along the top and bottom edges of each top surface.*

Fig. 19 *To prevent water penetration and the resulting staining, apply two coats of epoxy on the bottom of each leg.*

Fig. 20 *Insert small thin blocks as spacers between the slats, and then drive screws through the rails and into the slats.*

Refined Recline

This classic redwood recliner will stand the test of time for many summer seasons.

B eing equipped for warm weather fun doesn't just mean that you know where your tennis racket is, or that the pool toys are inflated and afloat. For many of us, fun in the sun takes on a more civilized quality, where time is spent just laying around. Our outdoor chaise lounge (or, more properly, chaise longue— meaning "long chair" in French) has a three-position back that suits everything from reading to sky gazing. For creature comfort we added a long cushion, but with the chaise back fully lowered and the cushion removed, the unit converts to an attractive bench for your deck or poolside.

*Key*POINTS

TIME

Prep Time	5 hours
Shop Time	8 hours
Assembly Time	10 hours

EFFORT

Skill Level	intermediate
Maintenance	waterproof yearly
Assistance	none

COST / BENEFITS

Expense: moderate

• Best suited for **contemporary surroundings**—ideal pool furniture.

• Extremely portable, allows you to **follow the sun**.

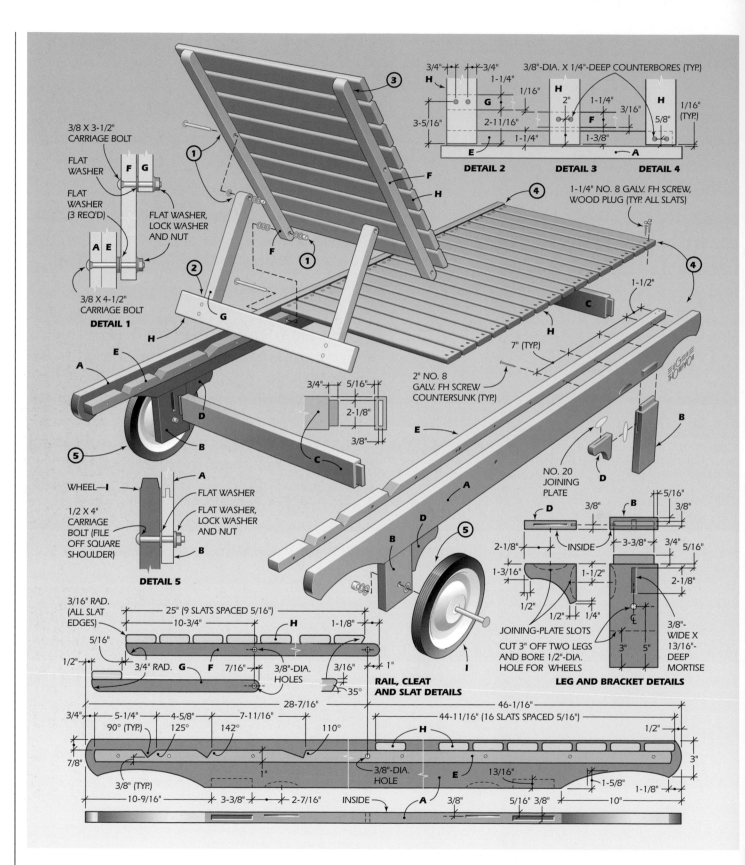

3/8 X 3-1/2"
CARRIAGE BOLT

FLAT
WASHER

FLAT
WASHER
(3 REQ'D)

F G

FLAT WASHER,
LOCK WASHER
AND NUT

A E

3/8 X 4-1/2"
CARRIAGE BOLT

DETAIL 1

3/8"-DIA. X 1/4"-DEEP COUNTERBORES (TYP.)

H   3/4"   3/4"
1-1/4"
1/16"
G
3-5/16"
2-11/16"
1-1/4"
E

DETAIL 2

H
2"   1-1/4"
3/16"
F
1-3/8"

DETAIL 3

H
1/16"
(TYP.)
5/8"

A

DETAIL 4

1-1/4" NO. 8 GALV. FH SCREW,
WOOD PLUG (TYP. ALL SLATS)

1-1/2"

7" (TYP.)

2" NO. 8
GALV. FH SCREW
COUNTERSUNK (TYP.)

3/4"   5/16"
2-1/8"
3/8"

NO. 20
JOINING
PLATE

D

B

WHEEL—I

A

1/2 X 4"
CARRIAGE
BOLT (FILE
OFF SQUARE
SHOULDER)

FLAT WASHER

FLAT WASHER,
LOCK WASHER
AND NUT

B

DETAIL 5

D   3/8"   B   5/16"
3/8"
INSIDE   3-3/8"   3/4"
2-1/8"   5/16"
1-3/16"   1-1/2"   2-1/8"
1/2"   1/4"
1/2"   3/8"-
WIDE X
13/16"-
DEEP
MORTISE
3"   5"

JOINING-PLATE SLOTS

CUT 3" OFF TWO LEGS
AND BORE 1/2"-DIA.
HOLE FOR WHEELS

LEG AND BRACKET DETAILS

3/16" RAD.
(ALL SLAT
EDGES)

25" (9 SLATS SPACED 5/16")

10-3/4"   H   1-1/8"

5/16"

1/2"   3/4" RAD. G   F   7/16"   3/8"-DIA.   3/16"   1"
HOLES   35°

**RAIL, CLEAT
AND SLAT DETAILS**

28-7/16"   46-1/16"

3/4"   5-1/4"   4-5/8"   7-11/16"   44-11/16" (16 SLATS SPACED 5/16")   1/2"
90° (TYP.)   125°   142°   110°
3"
7/8"   H
3/8"-DIA.   13/16"
HOLE   E   1-5/8"
3/8" (TYP.)   1"   1-1/8"
10-9/16"   3-3/8"   2-7/16"   INSIDE   A   3/8"   5/16" 3/8"   10"

We built the chaise frame, backrest, and back support out of solid redwood and assembled them with stainless steel fasteners.

Redwood is available at many lumberyards, home centers, and specialty lumber dealers. The highest grade is called "clear, all heart, vertical grain." Like pine, redwood comes in nominal sizes. However, the actual thickness of the stock will be less. For example, 1x redwood stock will be about ¹¹/₁₆ in. thick and 5/4 redwood will be about 1-in. thick.

Building the Frame

Rip 5/4 stock to width for the side rails and crosscut the rails a few inches longer than the finished dimension. Make a pattern of the rail-end shape from ¼-in. plywood and trace the shape onto each rail. Use a sabre saw to cut the rail-end profiles, and remove the saw marks with a spokeshave and sandpaper. Lay out the mortises for joining the legs to the rails. Then use a plunge router with an edge guide to make the cuts (**Fig. 1**). Rout each mortise in several passes to avoid overloading the motor and bit. Square the mortise ends with a sharp chisel. Cut the legs and crossrails to finished size. Then install a dado blade in your table saw and make the broad tenon cheek cuts on the two faces of each piece (**Fig. 2**). Next, cut the tenon shoulders in the same way.

Lay out the crossrail mortises on the leg inner faces. Rout the mortises and square the ends with a chisel. Test fit all the mortise-and-tenon joints to make sure they're snug, yet go together without excess force. Make a template for the leg bracket and trace the shape onto redwood stock. Orient the template so that the grain of the stock runs diagonally, and

Fig. 1 *Use a plunge router with an edge guide to cut the mortises for the legs. Clamp the rails side by side to provide good router support.*

Fig. 2 *Cut the leg tenons with a dado blade and table saw. A stop block clamped to the miter gauge ensures consistent tenon lengths.*

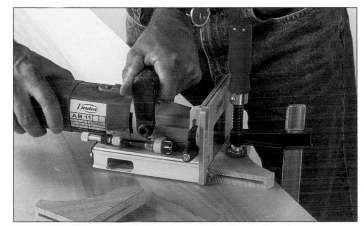

Fig. 3 *Cut the plate joint slots for attaching the brackets to the legs and rails. Register the joiner and work against the bench surface.*

Materials List

Key	No.	Size and description (use)
A	2	1 x 4 x 74¹/₂" redwood (side)
B*	4	1 x 4 x 9¹/₄" redwood (leg)
C	2	1 x 2³/₄ x 25" redwood (crossrail)
D	4	¹¹/₁₆ x 3¹/₄ x 4¹/₄" redwood (brace)
E	2	1 x 1¹/₄ x 73" redwood (side cleat)
F	2	1 x 1¹/₄ x 26¹/₈" redwood (back cleat)
G	2	1 x 1¹/₄ x 14" redwood (support leg)
H	26	¹¹/₁₆ x 2¹/₂ x 23³/₈" redwood (slat)
I	2	10"-dia. wheel

Misc.: ¹/₂ x 4" carriage bolts; ¹/₂" flat washers, lock washers, and nuts; ³/₈ x 3¹/₂" carriage bolts; ³/₈ x 4" carriage bolts; ³/₈" flat washers, lockwashers, and nuts; 1¹/₄" No. 8 fh galvanized screw; 2" No. 8 fh galvanized screw; ³/₈"-dia. redwood plugs; No. 20 joining plates.

*Cut two legs 3" shorter for wheels.

Fig. 4 *Apply glue to the joining-plate slots and the plates, and join each bracket to a leg. Clamp until the glue sets.*

Fig. 5 *When the leg/bracket assemblies are finished, join them to the rails. Apply glue to the plate and mortise-and-tenon joints, then clamp.*

Fig. 6 *After cutting the rail cleats to length and shaping the backrest notches, glue and screw each cleat in place on its rail.*

Fig. 7 *Use carriage bolts to join the backrest cleats to the support legs. Use a washer between parts to create a ¹/₁₆-in. space.*

Fig. 8 *Bolt the backrest and support leg assemblies to the rails. Align and clamp the parts while attaching the first slat.*

Fig. 9 *Use ⁵/₁₆-in. blocks between the slats to create uniform spaces, and screw the slats in place. Keep the ends of slats ¹/₁₆ in. from the rails.*

cut out the brackets. Mark the joining-plate positions on the legs, brackets, and side rails. Clamp each piece to your bench to cut the slots (**Fig. 3**). Hold the plate joiner against the benchtop to ensure accurate slot registration.

Spread glue in the plate slots of a leg and adjoining bracket, and spread glue on the plate. Assemble the parts, clamp, and repeat the process on the other legs (**Fig. 4**). Prepare to join a leg/bracket subassembly to a rail by spreading glue on the mortise-and-tenon joint mating surfaces in the two plate slots and on a joining plate. Join the leg and bracket to the rail, and clamp (**Fig. 5**). Repeat the procedure for each leg.

Rip 5/4 stock to width for the rail cleats and cut them to length so that their ends match the rail ends. Lay out the angled notches for the back-support assembly, make the cuts, and sand each notch to remove the saw marks.

Use an exterior glue and galvanized screws to fasten the cleats to the side rails. Countersink the screw holes so that the screw heads are just below the wood surface (**Fig. 6**). Mark the locations of the carriage bolts that fasten the chaise back to the side rails and bore the holes through the side/cleat subassembly. Apply glue to the crossrail joints, assemble the base frame, and clamp until the glue sets.

The Back and Slats

Cut the backrest cleats and support legs to size. Use a sabre saw to trim the ends of each piece to the profiles shown in the drawing. Then bore the bolt holes and join the support legs and back cleats with the bolts. Use one flat washer between each leg and cleat (**Fig. 7**). Rout the long edges of each slat with a $\frac{3}{16}$-in.-rad. rounding-over bit. Bore screw pilot holes in each slat and counterbore for $\frac{3}{8}$-in.-dia. plugs to cover the screws. Install the bolts to hold the back cleats to the frame sides. Use three washers between each back cleat and main side-rail cleat. Clamp the cleats to the chaise sides. Then screw the first slat to the back-support legs (**Fig. 8**).

Use $\frac{5}{16}$-in. blocks to space the slats, and screw each slat in place (**Fig. 9**). Bevel the last slat on the back to provide clearance for the back to move to the highest position. Leave a 1-in. space between the beveled slat and the first slat on the chaise seat (**Fig. 10**). Use a $\frac{3}{8}$-in.-dia. plug cutter in a drill press to cut plugs for all the slat screw heads. Glue the plugs in place so that the grain of each aligns with the slats. Saw each close to the surface, and pare flush with a sharp chisel.

Lay out and bore the holes in the legs for mounting the wheels as shown in the drawing. Then cut these legs 3 in. shorter (**Fig. 11**). Use a file or small grinding wheel to remove the square shoulder on two $\frac{1}{2}$ x 4-in. carriage bolts. Then install the wheel with the modified bolts, washers, lock washers, and nuts (**Fig. 12**). Sand all surfaces with 120- and 220-grit sandpaper. To protect the redwood, we applied a coat of clear decking stain. Let the finish thoroughly saturate all surfaces and allow it to dry at least 48 hours.

Fig. 10 *Where the backrest joins the fixed seat portion, leave a 1-in. space so that the backrest has room to pivot to its highest position.*

Fig. 11 *To provide clearance for the wheels, cut 3 in. from each rear leg with a sabre saw. Smooth the sawn edges with sandpaper.*

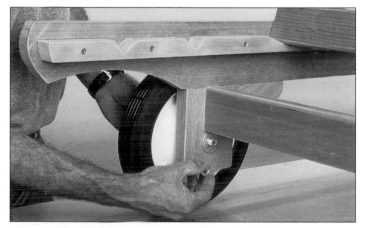

Fig. 12 *After filing away the square shoulder on $\frac{1}{2}$-in. carriage bolts, use the bolts as axles to support the wheels.*

Sitting Around

A summer meal just seems to taste better on this comfortable outdoor dining set.

Outdoor dining is one of the great pleasures summer has to offer, and it's a pastime with almost universal appeal. From crowded city sidewalk cafes to the quiet backyard barbecues of Middle America, people love to gather, celebrate, and dine outside. Although preparing the meal is a great part of the fun, the real pleasure comes in the leisurely dining, and that's where our project shines. This set is built for comfort, and built to last. With a minimal amount of maintenance, it should see you through a decade or more of outdoor meals.

*Key*POINTS

TIME
Prep Time . . . . 10 hours
Shop Time . . . . 18 hours
Assembly Time . . . . 12 hours

EFFORT
Skill Level . . . . advanced
Maintenance . . . . light
Assistance . . . . none

COST / BENEFITS
Expense: expensive
• The table and chairs dominate and set the style for a patio or deck.
• Add more chairs to the project to accommodate a bigger family or more guests.

131

TABLE
50-1/4" DIA. X 30" HIGH

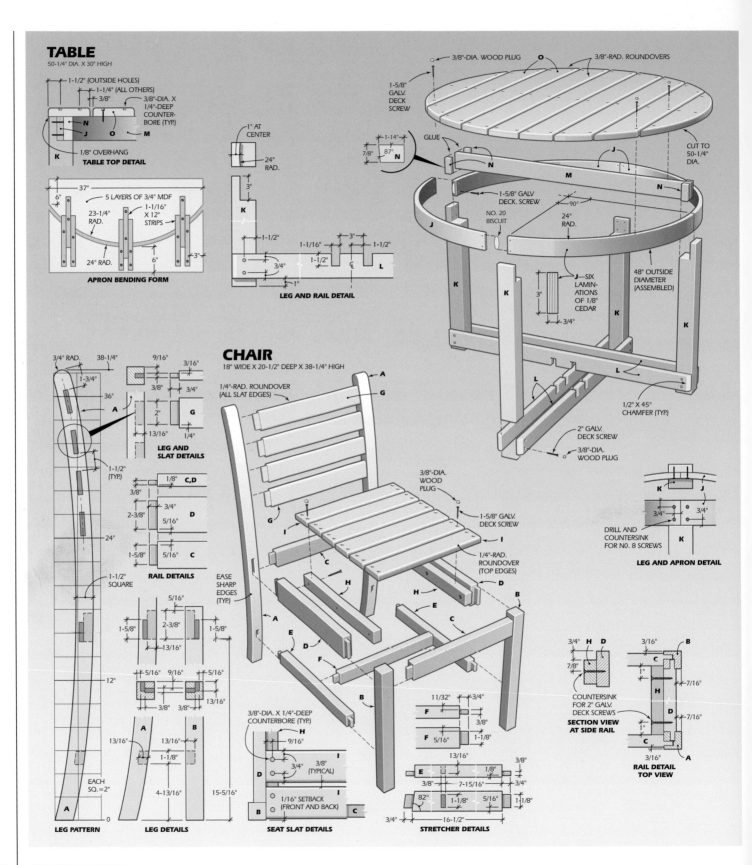

TABLE TOP DETAIL

1-1/2" (OUTSIDE HOLES)
1-1/4" (ALL OTHERS)
3/8"
3/8"-DIA. X 1/4"-DEEP COUNTER-BORE (TYP.)
1/8" OVERHANG
N J O M K

APRON BENDING FORM

37"
6"
5 LAYERS OF 3/4" MDF
23-1/4" RAD.
24" RAD.
1-1/16" X 12" STRIPS
6"
3"

LEG AND RAIL DETAIL

1" AT CENTER
24" RAD.
3"
K
1-1/2"
3/4"
1-1/2"
1-1/16"
3"
1-1/2"
1"
L

3/8"-DIA. WOOD PLUG O
3/8"-RAD. ROUNDOVERS
1-5/8" GALV. DECK SCREW
GLUE
7/8" 1-14" 87° N
CUT TO 50-1/4" DIA.
N M N
1-5/8" GALV. DECK SCREW
NO. 20 BISCUIT
90°
24" RAD.
48" OUTSIDE DIAMETER (ASSEMBLED)
J K K K K
J SIX LAMINATIONS OF 1/8" CEDAR
3" 3/4"
L
1/2" X 45° CHAMFER (TYP.)
2" GALV. DECK SCREW
3/8"-DIA. WOOD PLUG

LEG AND APRON DETAIL
K J
3/4" 3/4"
K
DRILL AND COUNTERSINK FOR NO. 8 SCREWS

CHAIR
18" WIDE X 20-1/2" DEEP X 38-1/4" HIGH

LEG PATTERN
3/4" RAD.
38-1/4"
1-3/4"
36"
A
24"
1-1/2" (TYP.)
1-1/2" SQUARE
12"
EACH SQ.=2"
A
0

LEG AND SLAT DETAILS
9/16"
3/16"
3/8" 3/4"
2"
13/16" G
1/4"

RAIL DETAILS
1/8" C,D
3/8"
3/4" D
2-3/8" 5/16"
1-5/8" 5/16" C

LEG DETAILS
5/16"
1-5/8" 2-3/8" 1-5/8"
13/16"
5/16" 9/16" 5/16"
3/8" 3/8" 13/16"
13/16" A 13/16" B
1-1/8"
4-13/16"
15-5/16"
A

1/4"-RAD. ROUNDOVER (ALL SLAT EDGES)
A
G
EASE SHARP EDGES (TYP.)
3/8"-DIA. WOOD PLUG
1-5/8" GALV. DECK SCREW
1/4"-RAD. ROUNDOVER (TOP EDGES)
G
I
C
H
D
H
E
B
A
E
C
D
B
F
B

SEAT SLAT DETAILS
3/8"-DIA. X 1/4"-DEEP COUNTERBORE (TYP.)
H
9/16"
3/4" 3/8" (TYPICAL)
D I
B I C
1/16" SETBACK (FRONT AND BACK)

STRETCHER DETAILS
11/32" 3/4"
F 3/8"
F 5/16" 1-1/8"
13/16" 3/8"
E 1/8"
3/8" 7-15/16" 3/4"
82° 1-1/8" 5/16" 1-1/8"
3/4" 16-1/2"

SECTION VIEW AT SIDE RAIL
3/4" H D
7/8"
COUNTERSINK FOR 2" GALV. DECK SCREWS

RAIL DETAIL TOP VIEW
3/16" B
C
1"
H 7/16"
D 7/16"
1"
C
3/16" A

O ur table and chairs provide a great spot for outdoor dining. Whether you indulge in elegant or simple fare, this set provides a wonderful place to enjoy it. The table combines an ample serving surface with an intimate seating arrangement, and the chairs are extremely sturdy, yet lightweight. For added comfort, the chairs are dimensioned to work with outdoor seat cushions.

The table and chairs are built from red cedar, a wood known for its resistance to rot and insect damage. The pieces need little maintenance—their slat construction allows water to drain off them. If left untreated, the chairs will weather to a pleasant shade of gray, but their surface will become rough. To maintain their appearance, apply an exterior sealer every year or two.

Building the Table

We used air-dried, clear red cedar for our project. Although normally we use kiln-dried stock for woodworking, we couldn't locate kiln-dried material in the sizes we needed. Besides, using kiln-dried lumber is not that important for outdoor furniture because these pieces are subjected to wide variations in humidity.

To stabilize the air-dried stock, we brought it into the shop and stacked it neatly in a dry space out of direct sunlight, with

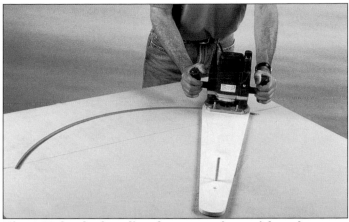

Fig. 1 *Make the bending form template with a plunge router connected to a trammel arm. Then cut an arc in a sheet of MDF.*

Fig. 2 *The remaining pieces of the form are trimmed to size using the template, router, and a flush-trimming router bit.*

evenly spaced strips of wood between each board. This is known as "stickering."

Start by making the laminating form. We chose MDF (medium-density fiberboard) for the form because it is inexpensive. First, make the trammel base for the router. Install a ¾-in.-dia. straight bit in the router, and bore a ⅜-in.-dia. hole through the trammel so that the hole's center is 24 in. from the outside of the router bit. Use a short length of ⅜-in. dowel to pin the trammel to a large piece of MDF. Now make three passes with the router to cut an arc through the stock (**Fig. 1**). Temporarily leave a section of the panel connected at each end of the arc. Make a set of alignment marks across the arc, and use the router to cut the panel into two sections. Use the two sections as templates. Cut slightly oversize blanks from the remaining panel stock.

Screw a template to each blank and use the router with a flush-trimming bit to cut them to finished radius (**Fig. 2**).

Materials List

Key	No.	Size and description (use)
A	2	1½ x 3½ x 38¼" cedar (leg)
B	2	1½ x 1½ x 18" cedar (leg)
C	2	1¹⁄₁₆ x 2¼ x 16½" cedar (rail)
D	2	1¹⁄₁₆ x 3 x 17" cedar (rail)
E	2	1¹⁄₁₆ x 1¾ x 18" cedar (stretcher)
F	1	1¹⁄₁₆ x 1¾ x 16½" cedar (stretcher)
G	4	¾ x 2½ x 16½" cedar (slats)
H	2	1¹⁄₁₆ x 1¾ x 16" cedar (cleats)
I	6	¾ x 2½ x 15" cedar (slats)
J	4	¾ x 3 x 37¹¹⁄₁₆" cedar (apron)
K	4	3 x 3 x 28¹⁵⁄₁₆" cedar (leg)
L	4	¹¹⁄₁₆ x 3 x 50" cedar (rail)
M	1	¹¹⁄₁₆ x 3 x 46½" cedar (rail)
N	4	⅞ x 1¼ x 3" cedar (block)
O	9	¹¹⁄₁₆ x 5¼ x 50¼" cedar (slat)

Misc.: 1⅝" and 2" galvanized deck screws; ⅜"-dia. wood plugs; No. 20 biscuits; glue; 2 sheets ¾ x 4 x 8' MDF; clear decking stain.

Fig. 3 *Use ¾-in.-thick spacers between the bending form pieces. Clamp the form pieces together and fasten the alignment strips.*

Fig. 4 *Resaw the ⅛-in.-thick apron laminate strips on the band saw with a tall rip fence in place. Use a pushstick at the end of the cut.*

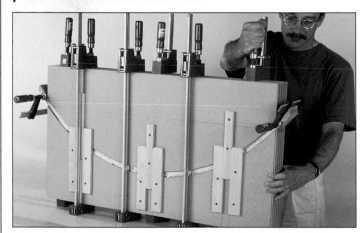

Fig. 5 *Clamp the laminate strips at either end to keep them from shifting. Apply pressure with equally spaced bar clamps.*

Each routed piece becomes the pattern. To prevent glue from sticking to the form, apply a coat of varnish to it. Then wax it after the varnish dries.

Next, place ¾-in.-thick blocks between the bending forms, and temporarily clamp the forms together. Fasten alignment strips to the surfaces of the forms (**Fig. 3**).

Set up the band saw with a tall rip fence and a ½-in.-wide, four-tooth-per-inch blade. Rip ⅛-in.-thick, 48-in.-long cedar strips (**Fig. 4**).

Spread glue on the strips, and place the six strips stacked in the form. Clamp the form together (**Fig. 5**). When all the apron blanks have been glued up, plane a square, straight edge on each blank, then rip the apron blanks to finished dimension.

Next, make a plywood cradle with a radius that matches the apron's finished outside length. Clamp the cradle to a long auxiliary fence attached to the table saw's miter gauge. The first cut removes one rough end from the apron (**Fig. 6**). Turn the apron around and crosscut the apron to finished length.

Use the cradle again to hold the apron as you cut the biscuit slot in each end (**Fig. 7**). Assemble the apron. Then apply glue to the apron ends, the biscuit slots, and the biscuits.

Use a band clamp to apply clamping pressure (**Fig. 8**). Check the apron diameter for distortion and adjust it if necessary. Rip, joint, and crosscut the leg stock to finished dimension. To cut the curved notch in the leg, first make a 90° cut and then use a sharp chisel to pare the curve.

Rip, crosscut, and notch the table rails and chamfer the edges. Spread glue on the notches and clamp the pieces together (**Fig. 9**). Position a table leg between a pair of rails and counterbore the screw holes. Fasten the legs and rails with galvanized deck screws.

Center a leg over each apron joint. Countersink the screw holes, and drive screws into each leg (**Fig. 10**). Now cut the

Fig. 6 *Make a cradle. Then crosscut the apron blank to finished length. The apron length and the cradle arc length are equal.*

Fig. 7 *Transfer the cradle to a sturdy bench, and use the cradle to hold the apron section in place while cutting the biscuit slots.*

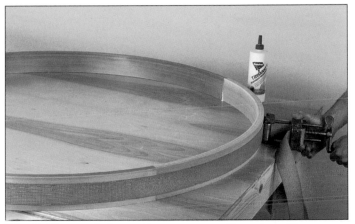

Fig. 8 *Glue and clamp the apron sections together using a strap clamp. Check its diameter at several points to ensure true round.*

crossrail to size. Place the crossrail into the leg assembly, and cut the glue blocks to fit at its ends. Glue the blocks in place.

Rip and crosscut the top slats to size. Use a rounding-over bit in the router to ease the slat edges. Clamp the center slat in position, bore its pilot holes, and fasten it to the apron. Fasten the remaining slats to the center rail spaced ⅜ in. from each other. Mark out the top's diameter and cut it to shape with a sabre saw (**Fig.11**). Sand the slat ends smooth, then use the router and rounding-over bit to ease their edges.

Use a plug cutter in your drill press to make the plugs to cover the screw holes. Glue the plugs over the screw heads, and use a chisel to pare the plugs smooth. Sand the table smooth with 120-grit sandpaper.

Chair Construction

The first step in chair construction is to make a thin plywood template for the rear leg. Rip and crosscut the rear leg blanks,

Fig. 9 *Glue and clamp together the half-lapped rail assembly. Carefully check that the parts are square to one another.*

SHOP*Helper*

Thread Lube
Driving screws is always easier if you lubricate the threads. A common material for this is bar soap, but soap can retain moisture causing rust, and a bar of soap is not the easiest thing to deal with when trying to quickly drive a few screws. Car wax is more convenient, with dip-and-go ease of use. You can also recycle kitchen bacon grease for this purpose. If no other lubricant is handy, coat the threads with the tip of a pencil to mimic the effect of graphite lubricant.

Fig. 10 *Position the apron so that each of its joints is centered on a leg. Use four screws at each joint to attach the apron to the legs.*

Fig. 11 *Space the boards equally, and screw them to the crossrail. Draw the outline of the top on the boards so that you can cut the diameter with a sabre saw.*

Fig. 12 *The first step in building each cedar chair is to make a precise template for the rear leg, and trace the shape on the leg blanks.*

Fig. 13 *Cut the outside curve on the leg. Then securely clamp it to the bench, and smooth the curve with a block plane.*

then trace around the pattern onto the leg (**Fig. 12**). Cut the outside of the leg to shape, and smooth its outline with a block plane (**Fig. 13**). Cut its inside surface to shape, and smooth it with a spokeshave.

The other chair components are ripped, crosscut, and planed to final dimension. Lay out the mortises and tenons on these pieces. The mortises are most easily cut with a router and a spiral up-cutting bit (**Fig. 14**). This will require that you cut the ends of the mortises square with a sharp chisel. However, this process will not work on the inside surfaces of the rear leg because the router fence does not have a straight edge to bear against.

Cut these mortises by laying the leg against a fence on a drill press table. Bore a series of overlapping holes (**Fig. 15**). Then cut the mortises square with a chisel.

Cut the tenons on the back slats, rails, and stretchers using a dado blade installed in the table saw (**Fig. 16**). On the rails and stretchers, be careful to keep track of which face of the component you are working on because the tenon is not centrally positioned on these pieces. Adjust the height of the dado blade accordingly. Also, note that the tenon that joins the side stretcher to the rear leg has an angled shoulder. Cut this by hand using a dovetail saw or backsaw.

Begin the final assembly by gluing and clamping together the side stretchers and the cross stretcher (**Fig. 17**). Measure diagonally from both corners of the assembly to check it for square. Next, glue and clamp together the rear legs, slats, and rail (**Fig. 18**). Glue and clamp the front legs and rail. Then glue and clamp together all the subassemblies (**Fig. 19**). Cut and install the cleats and the seat slats.

To finish the construction, install the wood plugs. Then finish the chairs and table with a clear coat of decking stain, or leave the pieces unfinished if you prefer the classic weathered gray finish that the wood takes on when unprotected from the elements.

Fig. 14 *Use a plunge router with its fence positioned on the leg's straight face. Cut the side rail and stretcher mortises.*

Fig. 15 *Remove the bulk of the material from the side rail mortises on the drill press. Chisel the mortise sides and ends square.*

Fig. 16 *Clamp a stop to the miter gauge fence. Use a dado blade to cut the tenons on the rails, stretchers, and back slats.*

Fig. 17 *Glue and clamp together two side stretchers with a cross stretcher. Measure diagonally to check the assembly for square.*

Fig. 18 *Clamp together the rear legs, a rear rail, and four back slats to make a chair-back assembly. Use one clamp at each joint location.*

TECH Tips

The Right Partner
When cutting and paring multiple sets of mortise and tenons, and paring down a particular tenon to a given mortise, you should mark the pieces so that they don't get mixed up during assembly. Use a gouge-numbering system—gouge small marks with a knife or chisel on faces that will be concealed after the piece is assembled. Be sure to mark the surfaces where they mate, so that you will correctly orient the pieces during final construction.

Fig. 19 *Glue and clamp together the rear leg subassembly, the front legs, and the stretcher subassembly.*

Swing Time

Nothing like an old-fashioned porch swing for some authentic summer relaxation.

The porch swing occupies a unique place in American culture. Think of all the movie scenes where the hero or heroine retreats to the porch swing to ponder the vagaries of life or cool off after a fiery family confrontation. It's probably not difficult for most of us to picture in our mind's eye the sight of teenagers or young adults sitting stiffly on the porch swing, working up the nerve for that first kiss. You might instead picture an older married couple, gently rocking, holding hands, and reflecting on the memories of their life together. Whatever your vision, this swing will bring it to life.

*Key*POINTS

TIME
Prep Time	2 hours
Shop Time	14 hours
Assembly Time	10 hours

EFFORT
Skill Level	intermediate
Maintenance	light
Assistance	one (for hanging)

COST / BENEFITS
Expense: moderate
- Exterior **home improvement** that can add value and charm to your home.
- Truly **relaxing** piece of outdoor furniture that can be used in all weather.

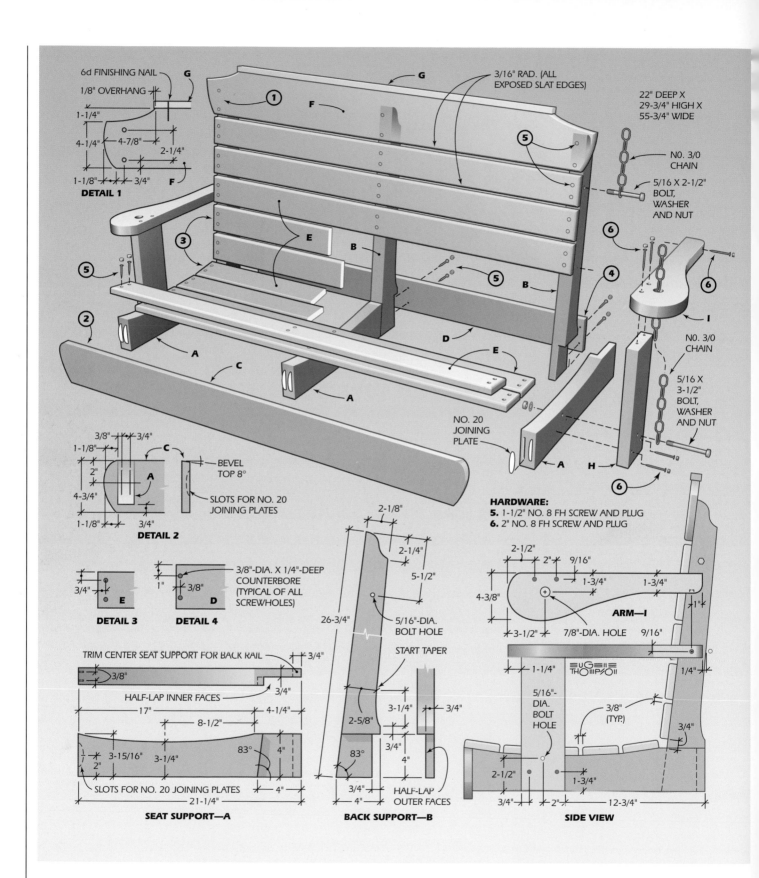

6d FINISHING NAIL
1/8" OVERHANG
G

1-1/4"
4-1/4"
4-7/8"
2-1/4"
1-1/8"
3/4"
F
DETAIL 1

3/16" RAD. (ALL EXPOSED SLAT EDGES)

22" DEEP X
29-3/4" HIGH X
55-3/4" WIDE

NO. 3/0 CHAIN

5/16 X 2-1/2" BOLT, WASHER AND NUT

1
F
5
5
6
4
B
B
E
3
5
2
A
C
D
E
A
H
A
6

NO. 20 JOINING PLATE

NO. 3/0 CHAIN

5/16 X 3-1/2" BOLT, WASHER AND NUT

3/8" 3/4"
1-1/8"
2"
4-3/4"
1-1/8" 3/4"
C
A
BEVEL TOP 8°
SLOTS FOR NO. 20 JOINING PLATES
DETAIL 2

3/4" E
1" 3/8" D
3/8"-DIA. X 1/4"-DEEP COUNTERBORE (TYPICAL OF ALL SCREWHOLES)
DETAIL 3   **DETAIL 4**

2-1/8"
2-1/4"
5-1/2"
26-3/4"
5/16"-DIA. BOLT HOLE
START TAPER
3-1/4" 3/4"
2-5/8"
3/4"
83°
83°
4"
3/4"
4"
HALF-LAP OUTER FACES
BACK SUPPORT—B

HARDWARE:
5. 1-1/2" NO. 8 FH SCREW AND PLUG
6. 2" NO. 8 FH SCREW AND PLUG

2-1/2" 2" 9/16"
1-3/4" 1-3/4"
4-3/8"
3-1/2" 7/8"-DIA. HOLE 9/16"
ARM—I
1"

TRIM CENTER SEAT SUPPORT FOR BACK RAIL
3/4"
3/8"
3/4"
HALF-LAP INNER FACES
17" 4-1/4"
8-1/2"
3-15/16" 3-1/4"
2" 83° 4"
SLOTS FOR NO. 20 JOINING PLATES 4"
21-1/4"
SEAT SUPPORT—A

1-1/4"
5/16"-DIA. BOLT HOLE
1/4"
3/8" (TYP.)
3/4"
2-1/2"
3/4" 2" 12-3/4"
1-3/4"
SIDE VIEW

EUGENE THOMPSON

There is good reason for this simple structure to hold such a particular place in our collective memory. The porch is unique in that it is connected to the home, yet slightly distant. It is protected but still part of the outdoors—a place where you can watch a storm and still stay dry. The swing provides the perfect comfortable spot. Like a rocking chair, its simple, swaying motion is restful and thought-provoking—and it has the wonderful capability of providing a seat for two.

Our porch swing is a relatively simple project. It's built from pine lumber that is readily available in home centers and lumberyards. Its parts are joined together with joining plates (biscuits) and wood screws. You can substitute dowels if you don't own a plate joiner. Using either dowels or joining plates, you should be able to complete this project in a couple of pleasant weekends in the home shop.

Building the Frame

To construct 1½-in.-thick blanks for the seat supports, glue and clamp together two pieces of ¾-in.-thick lumber. First, crosscut each piece 1 or 2 in. longer and wider than the finished part. Then spread glue on the mating surfaces of the pieces using a foam paint roller. Clamp the boards together until the glue sets.

First plane one edge of each blank straight and square, and then crosscut the blank to length. Next, lay out the curved seat cut on the top edge of each workpiece.

Cut a strip of wood ⅛ in. thick x 3⁄16 in. wide, and then bend this strip between two clamps attached to the workpiece. Run a pencil along the strip to trace the seat curve (**Fig. 1**). Use a sabre saw to cut the curve (**Fig. 2**).

Rip, crosscut, and glue together the pieces for the back support in the same manner as the seat supports. Use the plans to draw the finished shape on each back support, and cut the pieces to shape using a sabre saw. Keep the saw to the waste side of the line.

Next, clamp each back support and seat support in a vise, and then smooth their curved surfaces using a spokeshave (**Fig. 3**). Use a block plane on the straight surfaces.

Fig. 1 *To mark the curve for the seat supports, bend a thin strip between two clamps, and mark along the strip with a pencil.*

Fig. 2 *Clamp a seat support blank in a vise and cut the curved edge using a sabre saw. Keep the saw just to the outside of the line.*

Materials List

Key	No.	Size and description (use)
A	3	1½ x 4 x 21¼" pine (seat support)
B	3	1½ x 4 x 26¾" pine (back support)
C	1	¾ x 4¾ x 49¼" pine (front rail)
D	1	¾ x 4 x 45½" pine (back rail)
E	10	¾ x 3¼ x 47" pine (slats)
F	1	¾ x 5½ x 49¼" pine (top slat)
G	1	⅝ x 1 x 39¾" pine (top cap)
H	2	1⅛ x 4 x 12¼" pine (support)
I	2	1⅛ x 4⅜ x 17¾" pine (armrest)

Misc.: No. 20 joining plates; 2" No. 8 fh galvanized wood screws; 1½" No. 8 galvanized wood screws; 3" hexhead bolts, washers, and nuts; 2" hexhead bolts, washers, and nuts; 6d finishing nails; ⅜"-dia. wood plugs; 120- and 220-grit sandpaper; 3/0 chain as required.

When you're finished, take a sharp pencil and mark out the half-lap joints on the back and seat supports. Note that the half-lap joints on the left and right ends of the swing are mirror images of one another, and that the joint at the center seat support has ¾ in. removed (see the drawing marked Seat Support—A) to allow room for the rear rail to fit against it.

To cut the half-lap joints in the supports, install a dado blade in the table saw, and adjust the blade height to ¾ in. Guide each workpiece over the blade using a sliding miter gauge equipped with an auxiliary fence (**Fig. 4**).

Remember, you will need to readjust the angle on the miter gauge to cut the joints on different pieces. Be sure to keep the straight edge of the workpiece against the miter gauge when making the cuts.

Thoroughly spread glue on the half-lap joints, being careful not to get any on your hands or the worksurface. Assemble the parts, and clamp them together until the glue sets (**Fig. 5**).

Fig. 3 *Clamp the seat supports and the back supports in a sturdy vise, and smooth out the sawn surfaces using a spokeshave.*

Fig. 4 *Install an auxiliary fence on the miter gauge and hold each workpiece to it. Make several passes to cut the half-lap.*

Use two clamps on each joint to ensure that the pressure is evenly applied.

Rip and crosscut the front rail, and then use the table saw to cut a bevel on its top edge. Next, draw the outline of the curved ends, and cut the curve using a sabre saw. Smooth the curve with sandpaper and a spokeshave.

Lay out the locations of the joining plate slots for the joints between the front rail and the seat supports. Use the plate joiner to cut the slots.

To do this on the front rail, clamp an edge guide across the rail to help position the plate joiner (**Fig. 6**). To cut the joining plate slots in the seat support ends, clamp the supports to the workbench and use the benchtop as the registration surface (**Fig. 7**). Cut one slot, and then turn the seat support over to cut the second slot.

Apply glue to the slots and joining plates, and then clamp together the front rail and seat supports (**Fig. 8**). Check the assembly to be sure that all workpieces are square to one another, and let the glue set.

Rip and crosscut the rear rail, bore and counterbore pilot holes in it, and clamp it in position. Bore pilot holes into the seatback support assembly, and attach the rear rail with galvanized screws (**Fig. 9**).

Slats, Armrests, and Assembly

Rip and crosscut the seat and back slats. Install a ³⁄₁₆-in.-rad. rounding-over bit in the router table, and use it to shape the slat edges (**Fig. 10**).

Next, bore and counterbore pilot holes in the ends and center of each slat. Install the first slat flush with the front rail, and install the remaining slats with temporary ³⁄₈-in.-thick spacer blocks between them (**Fig. 11**). Install the back slats in the same manner. Note that the position of the first back slat is ¾ in. above the seat support.

Draw the curved ends on the top back slat, and cut the

Fig. 5 *Glue and clamp together the seat support and back support. The end pieces have a rabbet that receives the back rail.*

SHOP*Helper*

Shop Setup

The positioning of your power tools will not only make your woodworking easier, it will make the tools safer to use, and ensure their longevity. These guidelines are best-case rules. But even if you are trying to fit your tools into a confined space, you may want to modify the space to fit the rules listed below, rather than the other way around. Remember—safety is a key consideration in these guidelines:

Lathe: One of the most space-efficient tools, a lathe can actually be kept in a small, fairly cramped space. The construction of lathes ensures that good top-side air circulation will keep the moving parts fairly cool, and all you need is space enough to comfortably stand in front of the machine. However, the lathe needs extra space on the sides, a good thing to keep in mind in a small, odd-shaped workshop.

Table Saw: In contrast to the lathe, the table saw is one of the big space hogs in the workshop. It requires enough space for you to walk freely around the entire unit. Give yourself as much extra room as possible, because you don't want to be feeding stock through the saw while you are off balance or forced to lean precariously over the turning blade. Leave good air circulation space in front and back, and enough room on the sides to feed long and unwieldy boards safely.

Scroll Saw: You can butt this right up against the wall, but be sure to leave enough room so that you can comfortably move around the saw. Although you may think you'll only stand in front of the saw, when dealing with tight cuts, it is often easier to move your body than it is to move the workpiece.

Drill Press: Another tool that can safely be placed up against a wall, but you should leave a few feet on the sides to allow for long boards.

Band Saw: You need to allow room all around this tool, enough so that you can easily maneuver on any side.

Fig. 6 Clamp the front rail to the workbench, and then clamp a guide piece across it. Cut the slots in its back using a plate joiner.

Fig. 7 Cut the matching slots in the ends of each seat support by sliding the plate joiner on the surface of the workbench.

Fig. 8 Spread glue on the joining plates and their slots, and install them in the front rail. Then clamp the rail to the seat supports.

Safety Sense

ELECTRICAL ALERTNESS

Any well-equipped and well-used workshop has two things that can be very dangerous in close proximity—lots of flammable materials and a wealth of electrical equipment. A simple lapse in attention can result in a great loss of property ... or worse. That's why it's essential that you follow these safety precautions:

Regularly check your power cords for fraying and mispositioning. Make sure that rolling cabinets or power table tools have not crimped or frayed the cords. Avoid routing power cords around sharp corners, such as metal worktable legs, or stretching cords to their limit.

Never modify the prongs on a plug—it's an invitation to disaster. On a similar note, never use an extension cord that won't fit all the prongs of the plug.

To avoid circuit overload, use the shortest extension cord possible. (Longer cords need to be lower gauge to accommodate the load.) This is especially important with higher amperage tools (4 amps and higher) to prevent the cord from overheating or burning out the tool.

Be sure that the circuitry in your workshop supports your tools. This is especially important when you have a home workshop or when you buy new, large-amp power tools. Check the ratings on your circuits (you can usually find these on your junction box).

Don't replace fuses with any but a fuse that is the exact same rating. You could blow the fuse again or wind up with tool damage.

Keep the area around cords and outlets clear of any sawdust or wood debris. Good shop hygiene is your best defense against fire.

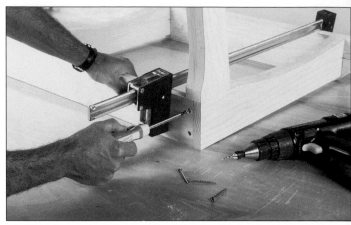

Fig. 9 *Clamp the rear rail to the seat supports, and bore pilot holes into each support. Fasten the rail with galvanized screws.*

Fig. 10 *Round the edges of each slat on the router table. Use a pushstick and a featherboard to ensure that you do this safely.*

Fig. 11 *Fasten each slat in place with a pair of screws at regular intervals at each end. Use temporary blocks to maintain consistent spacing.*

curve using a sabre saw. Rip and crosscut the top cap, and then attach it to the top slat with glue and 6d finishing nails. Set the nail heads, and then fill the holes with an exterior-grade wood filler. After the filler is dry, sand it smooth, and install the top slat and cap.

Rip and crosscut the armrest supports. Bore and counterbore the pilot holes in the supports, glue and clamp them in position, and drive in the galvanized screws (Fig. 12).

Use a sabre saw to cut the armrests to shape, and smooth the cut surfaces using a spokeshave. Bore and counterbore the pilot holes to attach each armrest to the supports.

Next, bore the chain clearance hole in each armrest (Fig. 13). Screw the armrests to their front supports, and then glue and screw the armrests to the back supports (Fig. 14).

Install a ⅜-in.-dia. plug cutter in the drill press, and cut the plugs that cover the screw heads.

Glue the plugs over each screw head so that the plug's grain is aligned with the grain of the surrounding wood surface. After you are sure that the glue has set, use a sharp chisel to pare the plugs flush (Fig. 15). For the cleanest look, and easiest time doing this, take the time to be sure that the chisel you use is extremely sharp.

Once all the plugs are cut flush, completely sand the swing with 120- and 220-grit sandpaper.

Bore the holes for the bolts that attach the chain to the swing sides, and install the bolts and chain after the swing has been primed and painted with an exterior-grade paint.

The swing should be hung from heavy ⁵⁄₁₆-in. eyehooks installed in the porch or house's framing, not just the beaded ceiling board or trim. If in doubt, position the eyehook and suspend a heavy weight from it. Adjust the chain lengths so the swing hangs with a level seat or tipped back a few degrees. Fasten the lengths of chain together using S hooks. The swing can be used as it is or you can buy a seat cushion.

Fig. 12 *Clamp each arm support in place, and bore pilot holes through it. Next, fasten the workpiece with galvanized screws.*

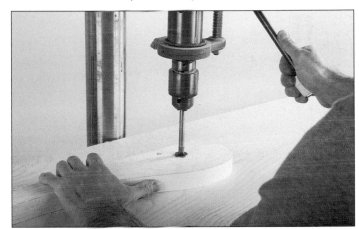

Fig. 13 *Bore the chain clearance hole in each armrest before fastening this piece to the back support and armrest support.*

Fig. 14 *Bore pilot holes through the edge of each armrest and its top. Fasten it to the armrest support first, then the back support.*

Fig. 15 *Gently push a glue-covered wood plug into each counterbored hole. When the glue has set, pare the plug flush with a chisel.*

Porch Classic

This piece of porch furniture makes life outside a little more comfortable and a little less hectic.

There are few things in life more restful than sitting in a well-designed rocking chair, passing the time on a front or back porch. It's hard to say whether the relaxation comes from the rocking motion or the gentle, rhythmic squeak of the floorboards. Maybe the enjoyment comes from knowing, as you rock, that you have put business aside for a while and can just watch the world go by in the calm of your yard or garden. These days, when most of us have so many demands pulling us in all directions, it's a great pleasure to have an outdoor spot dedicated to relaxation.

*Key*POINTS

TIME
Prep Time . . . . 2 hours
Shop Time . . . . 20 hours
Assembly Time . . . . 10 hours

EFFORT
Skill Level . . . . advanced
Maintenance . . . . light
Assistance . . . . none

COST / BENEFITS
Expense: inexpensive
• **Movable classic** that can be used on a porch, patio, or deck—even inside.
• Traditional durability of this piece makes it a **natural heirloom** hand-me-down.

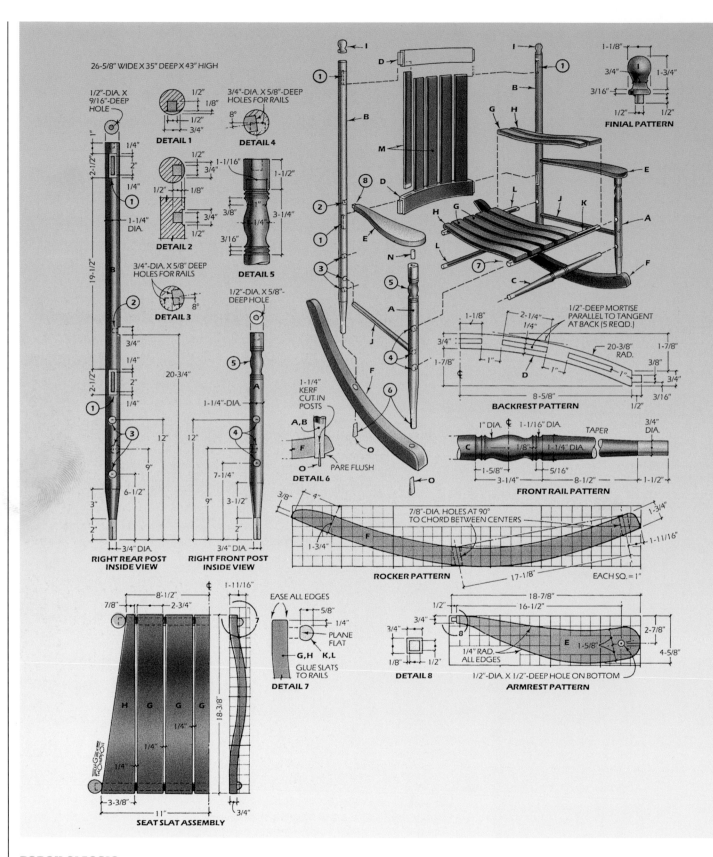

26-5/8" WIDE X 35" DEEP X 43" HIGH

1/2"-DIA. X 9/16"-DEEP HOLE

3/4"-DIA. X 5/8"-DEEP HOLES FOR RAILS

DETAIL 1

DETAIL 2

DETAIL 3

DETAIL 4

DETAIL 5

3/4"-DIA. X 5/8" DEEP HOLES FOR RAILS

1/2"-DIA. X 5/8"-DEEP HOLE

1-1/4" DIA.

19-1/2"

20-3/4"

12"

9"

6-1/2"

3"

2"

3/4" DIA.

RIGHT REAR POST INSIDE VIEW

1-1/4"-DIA.

12"

7-1/4"

9"

3-1/2"

2"

3/4" DIA.

RIGHT FRONT POST INSIDE VIEW

1-1/4" KERF CUT IN POSTS

A,B

PARE FLUSH

DETAIL 6

FINIAL PATTERN

1/2"-DEEP MORTISE PARALLEL TO TANGENT AT BACK (5 REQD.)

20-3/8" RAD.

8-5/8"

BACKREST PATTERN

1" DIA.   1-1/16" DIA.   TAPER   3/4" DIA.

1-1/4" DIA.

1-5/8"   5/16"   8-1/2"   1-1/2"

3-1/4"

FRONT RAIL PATTERN

7/8"-DIA. HOLES AT 90° TO CHORD BETWEEN CENTERS

ROCKER PATTERN

17-1/8"   EACH SQ. = 1"

8-1/2"

2-3/4"

7/8"

1-11/16"

7

EASE ALL EDGES

5/8"

1/4"

PLANE FLAT

G,H   K,L

GLUE SLATS TO RAILS

DETAIL 7

18-3/8"

H   G   G   G

1/4"

1/4"

1/4"

3-3/8"

11"

3/4"

SEAT SLAT ASSEMBLY

DETAIL 8

3/4"

1/8"   1/2"

18-7/8"

16-1/2"

1/2"

3/4"   3/4"

8

1/4" RAD. ALL EDGES

E   1-5/8"

2-7/8"

4-5/8"

1/2"-DIA. X 1/2"-DEEP HOLE ON BOTTOM

ARMREST PATTERN

This chair is built of solid birch and its construction is a relatively straightforward affair. Because the round back posts are longer than the distance between centers on most home lathes, we shaped the posts using a router table. The front- and back-seat support rails, as well as the side rails, are cut from ¾-in.-dia. dowels, available at any lumberyard. We chose to paint our rocker, but it would look just as good if it were simply stained and varnished. Finish it to match the color scheme of your porch or your home.

Making Posts

Begin the project by making two full-size drawings: one of the front-post profiles, and another showing how the posts and the rails intersect. The second drawing should include the rail centerlines.

Cut the blanks for the four posts, but leave the front posts ½ in. long so that they can be turned on the lathe. Then mark centerlines across the post tops and bore the ½-in.-dia. holes for the finials and dowels.

Next, lay out the mortises for the backrests and the front and back rails. Clamp the posts to the workbench, and cut the backrest mortises with a plunge router. Square the mortise ends with a chisel, then move the posts to the drill press (**Fig. 1**). Using an auxiliary fence, bore the front- and back-rail mortises with the posts clamped to the fence.

Round the four posts in four passes using a ⅝-in.-dia. rounding-over bit in the router table (**Fig. 2**). Use a pushstick toward the end of each pass to stay clear of the cutter, and work slowly to prevent injury.

Next, make a template of the bulb on the front posts.

Mount a front post on the lathe with a live center in the dowel hole. Transfer the layout from the template to the post (**Fig. 3**), and cut the bulb. Mark the top limit of the ¾-in.-long tenon, and cut the tenon as well as the tapered section above it.

The back posts are too long for the lathe, so shape their tenons and tapers by hand. Mark a ¾-in.-dia. circle on the bottom of each post (**Fig. 4**). Then mark the tenon length, and

Fig. 1 *Cut the backrest mortises in the back posts with a plunge router, and then use a chisel to chop the ends of the mortises square.*

Fig. 2 *Carefully shape the chair posts on the router table using a large rounding-over bit. Work slowly and make four passes per post.*

Materials List

Key	No.	Size and description (use)
A	2	1¼"-dia. x 20¾" birch (post)
B	2	1¼"-dia. x 41¼" birch (back post)
C	1	1¼"-dia. x 23¼" birch (rail)
D	2	2½ x 2⅝ x 18¼" birch (backrest)
E	2	¾ x 4¾ x 18⅞" birch (armrest)
F	2	1½ x 6 x 35" birch (rocker)
G	5	1¹¹⁄₁₆ x 2¾ x 18⅜" birch (slat)
H	2	1¹¹⁄₁₆ x 3⅜ x 18⅜" birch (slat)
I	2	1⅛"-dia. x 2⁷⁄₁₆" birch (finial)
J	2	¾"-dia. x 17⅛" birch (side rail)
K	1	¾"-dia. x 23¼" birch (seat support)
L	2	¾"-dia. x 18¼" birch (back rail)
M	5	¼ x 2¼ x 20½" birch (back slat)
N	2	½"-dia. x 1" birch (post dowel)
O	4	⅛ x ¾ x 2" birch (wedge)

Misc.: Sandpaper; glue; exterior-grade alkyd primer and enamel.

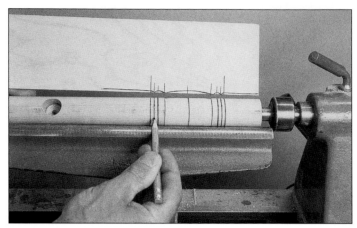

Fig. 3 *Make a detailed template of the decorative bulb. Transfer the shape to the post with a pencil while it spins on the lathe.*

Fig. 4 *The back posts are too long to fit on the lathe, so shape their tenons by hand. Begin by marking the tenon diameter.*

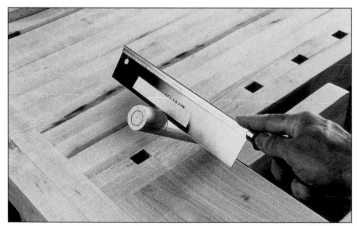

Fig. 5 *Mark the length of the tenon, and then saw on the line. Mark the depth of cut on the saw with a piece of masking tape.*

cut on this line using masking tape on the dovetail saw to mark the depth of cut (**Fig. 5**). Carve the tenon to rough size with a knife. Then smooth it to final diameter with a rasp (**Fig. 6**). Test fit the tenon using a block with a hole bored in it. Then use a spokeshave to shape the taper above the tenon (**Fig. 7**). Turn the post as you work to achieve a uniform taper.

Stand the front posts on the drawing of the posts and rails. Position the posts so that their front-rail holes are aligned with the centerlines for the front rails.

Now mark the position of the side rails using these centerlines (**Fig. 8**). Stand the back posts on the drawing, and repeat this procedure. Extend these marks along the posts, and then mark across the posts to establish the center of the side-rail mortises. Bore the rail mortises with the posts clamped to the fence on the drill press table. Also bore the mortise for the armrests.

Making Rails, Slats, and Rockers

Rip and crosscut the blank for the front tapered rail about 1 in. too long. Turn the blank to size, and cut the decorative center portion to shape.

Cut the taper on each side of the center. Because the rail is thin and long, use a steady rest for the lathe when cutting the taper to prevent the workpiece from chattering (**Fig. 9**). Sand the rail on the lathe and crosscut it on the table saw using a miter gauge.

Rip and crosscut a blank that is wide enough to make the top and bottom backrests. Next, lay out the curve on the edge of the backrest, and use the table saw and miter gauge to cut the tenons on the blank (**Fig. 10**).

Cut the outside curve of the backrest on the band saw. Then remove the saw marks, and refine the shape using a plane and scraper (**Fig. 11 and 12**). Cut the inside curve and

SHOP*Helper*

Hanging Out
You never seem to have enough hands when you want to check plans or a magazine article while you're working on the project. If tacking the pages to a wall isn't convenient, here's a handy shortcut to keep you working while you refer to your plan sheets. Run a clothesline across the inside of your workshop (a retractable type is best, so that it can be stored out of the way when you don't need it). Then clip the pages to the clothesline with clothespins and you'll have an eye-level reading holder that makes reference as easy as looking up.

Fig. 6 *Carefully carve the posts to rough diameter with a knife. Then bring the posts to final diameter with a rasp or plane.*

Fig. 7 *Cut the taper on the back posts using a spokeshave. Turn the post as you work to keep the taper uniform.*

Fig. 8 *Carefully mark the position of the side rails on the front and back posts using a full-size drawing as a reference.*

Fig. 9 *The bottom rail is too thin to turn without support. Use a steady rest in the lathe to keep it stable as it is shaped.*

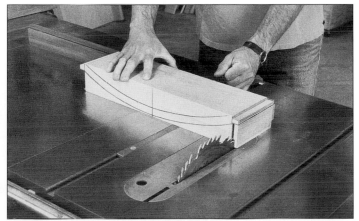

Fig. 10 *Cut the tenons on the backrests using the table saw and miter gauge. Make several clean passes for each face.*

Fig. 11 *Cut the backrests to shape on the band saw. Stay just to the waste side of the line, and feed the workpiece slowly.*

Fig. 12 *Completely remove the saw marks from the outside of the backrest using a block plane and a scraper.*

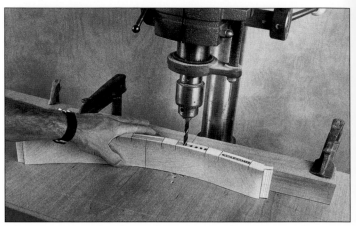

Fig. 13 *Rip the backrest blank in half. Mark the slat mortises on the backrest edge and bore them on the drill press.*

use a spokeshave and scraper to smooth it.

Rip the blank into two backrests, and lay out the back-slat mortises. Remove the bulk of each mortise by boring them on the drill press (**Fig. 13**). Then use a sharp chisel to pare the mortise walls parallel and the ends square.

Mark the tenon shoulders at the top and bottom edge of each backrest, and cut the shoulders with a dovetail saw. Then dry-fit the backrests to the posts, and trace around each backrest on the post.

Using this outline as a guide, chisel a flat surface around the rail mortise (**Fig. 14 and 15**).

Trace the armrest shapes onto blanks of ¾-in.-thick stock. Then use the table saw and miter gauge to cut three sides of each tenon before cutting out the armrest (**Fig. 16**). Cut out the armrests on the band saw. Smooth the armrest edges with a plane and a spokeshave. Then shape the corners with a ¼-in.-rad. rounding-over bit in the router.

Dry-fit the armrest to the back posts and trace the armrest ends on the posts. Cut a flat surface around the post as you did earlier. Then cut the rockers from a 1¾-in.-thick blank using the band saw, and smooth the cut edges with a plane, spokeshave, and scraper.

TECH *Tips*

Band Saw Blade Basics
There's a lot to know when it comes to choosing a band saw blade, and experts recommend looking at all factors of blade design before choosing one: thickness, width, the shape of the teeth and the space of the gullet between them (known as tooth form—there are three types: standard, hook, and skip), the set of the teeth (that is the way the teeth are bent or set to one side of the blade), and even the metal of which the blade is made. Read the manufacturer's information carefully when selecting a blade. Also keep in mind that a range of factors influence the blade performance: whether you are cutting hardwood or softwood, the wood thickness, and whether you are cutting with the grain, across the grain, or through the grain. No single blade will make all cuts well.

A couple of things to keep in mind when choosing a blade:

Blade Width: For curved cuts, use a narrower blade for tighter radii: a ¹⁄₁₆-in. blade can cut a minimum radius of about ⅛ in., a ⅛-in. blade can cut a ¼-in. radius, a ¼-in.-wide blade can cut a ½-in. radius, a ⅜-in. blade can cut a 1-in. radius, a ½-in. blade can cut a 1¼ in. radius, and a ¾-in. blade can cut a 1¾ in. radius.

Tooth Form: Blades with a standard form leave a finer finish. Hook tooth blades leave a coarser finish. Where speed is more important than finish, use a hook tooth blade. When you want to do straight line sawing but will be cutting some curves, use a skip tooth blade.

Fig. 14 *Press the backrest tenon into the post mortise and trace around it with a knife or sharp pencil to mark the flat.*

Fig. 15 *Pare the shallow flat around the mortise using a chisel. This is not difficult, but it does require a sharp chisel.*

Fig. 16 *Using the table saw, cut the tenon on the armrest. Hold the workpiece on edge against the miter-gauge fence.*

Fig. 17 *Prior to boring post holes, mark the post positions on the rockers using a piece of wood and a square.*

Fig. 18 *Bore the post holes in a rocker on the drill press. Support the rocker securely by placing a curved wedge underneath it.*

Note that the holes in the rockers that accept the post tenons are perpendicular to a chord that runs between the hole centers.

To mark the proper angle for the holes, cut a block to 17⅛ in. long (the distance between these centers). Place the block from center to center, and use a square to mark the angle along the side of the rocker (**Fig. 17**).

After you've done that, cut scrap blocks to support the rocker on the drill press table at the proper angle, then bore the holes (**Fig. 18**). Different blocks will be required for front and back holes.

Rip and crosscut the chair-seat blanks, and then cut their edge and face profiles on the band saw. Smooth the slat surfaces with a spokeshave and scraper, and ease the slat corners with a rasp and sandpaper.

Cut the wedge kerfs in the bottom of each post and turn the decorative finials for the top of the back posts. Most of the turning can be done with the finial between centers.

To complete the finial, mount it in a "pot" chuck. This device is formed by boring a hole in the center of a wood block mounted on the lathe faceplate (**Fig. 19**). The turned dowel on the finial's end makes a friction fit in this hole while the top is completed. Glue the finials to the post tops.

Cut the remaining rails from dowels and plane a flat face on the front and back seat support rails (**Fig. 20**). Rip and crosscut the backrest slats, then thoroughly presand all parts before beginning assembly. Make sure that you remove all dust from the pieces.

Assembly

Glue and clamp the front rails to the front posts and check the diagonal measurements of the assembly (**Fig. 21**). Then slide the back slats into the backrests and glue and clamp the back posts to the backrest assembly (**Fig. 22**).

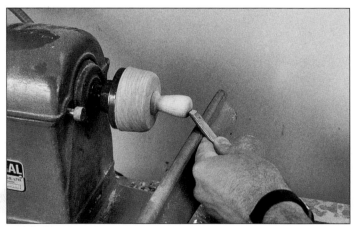

Fig. 19 *Fit the finial's dowel through a block of wood secured to a faceplate. Turn the finial to final shape using a handrest.*

Fig. 20 *The seat support rails are made from birch dowels. Clamp a rail to the bench and place a flat on one face.*

Fig. 21 *Glue and clamp together the front posts spanned by the rails. Check diagonal measurements and let the glue set.*

TECH

Tool Organizer
There are lots of ways to keep frequently used tools close at hand. Drill bits can be stored in holes they make. A block of wood with different diameter holes will work for both drill bits and screwdrivers. Use a spade bit to bore a hole large enough for a chisel. You can also mount a magnetic tool tray or mat above your bench— they are the same type that auto mechanics use and are sold in hardware stores, specialty tool catalogs, and woodworking tool catalogs.

Next, glue and clamp the side rails to join the front and back subassemblies. Then carefully install the short dowels to the tops of the front posts, and glue and clamp the armrests in place (**Fig. 23**).

Turn the chair upside down, and apply glue to the rocker mortises, post tenons, and the kerfs in the tenon ends. Slide the rockers over the tenons, apply glue to the wedges, and tap the wedges in place. After the glue sets, cut the tenons and wedges close to the rocker bottoms. Then trim them flush with a sharp chisel.

Glue and clamp the seat slats to the seat support rails using a scrap piece of plywood between the slats to ensure even spacing (**Fig. 24**).

Because the pieces have already been presanded, just go over the chair looking for rough spots and blemishes and sand as necessary in preparation for applying the finish. Finish the chair by applying a good-quality exterior primer, and then lightly sanding in any place where the grain is raised. Finally, apply the final coat of enamel following the can directions.

Fig. 22 *Glue and clamp together two back posts spanned by the backrests with slats, and the two back rails.*

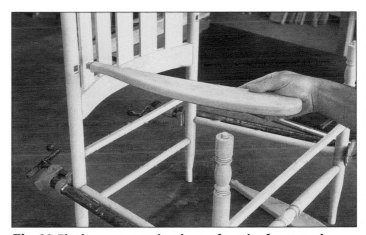

Fig. 23 *Fit the armrests in place after the front and back subassemblies have been glued and clamped together.*

Fig. 24 *Finish up construction by gluing and clamping the seat slats to the rails. Use alignment spacers between the slats.*

SHOP*Helper*

Extinguishing Worries

If you don't have a fire extinguisher in your workshop, you need one. But just picking up whatever's in the sale bin at the local home center isn't good enough—you need the right fire extinguisher for your circumstances. Fortunately, extinguishers are required by law to be rated for use, making shopping for one an easy exercise. The three ratings are A, B, and C, and will be clearly marked on the extinguisher. An "A" rating is put on extinguishers that are meant to be used on ordinary combustible fires, such as burning wood, fabric, or plastics. Extinguishers rated "B" are meant to be used on fires caused by flammable liquids, such as solvents you might use around the workshop. "C" class is put on those units to be used for electrical fires. Fortunately, for those of us who want to cover all our bases, there are multipurpose "ABC" extinguishers that can be used on any fire, regardless of the cause. Lastly, always be sure to read the simple, but extremely important instructions printed clearly on the fire extinguisher body. In the midst of a fire emergency is not the time to be figuring out how your extinguisher works.

Garden Grace

Stately elegance and comfort are the hallmarks of this inviting garden bench.

If the only thing you do in your yard is mow the lawn or occasionally trim the bushes, maybe it's time to add some creature comfort to your outdoor space. Our stately cedar bench is ideal for relaxing in the fresh air, enjoying the greenery, and just getting away from it all. And, it's more than just a great place to sit. Featuring a design influenced by the Arts & Crafts style, this piece will bring an upscale look to any yard. Best of all, the construction details are solid and simple, giving you a long-lasting piece of outdoor furniture that's relatively easy to build.

*Key*POINTS

TIME
Prep Time .... 8 hours
Shop Time .... 10 hours
Assembly Time .... 10 hours

EFFORT
Skill Level .... basic
Maintenance .... none
Assistance .... none

COST / BENEFITS
Expense: inexpensive
• A piece of outdoor furniture you can really enjoy.
• Elegant, adaptable style that will complement any type of garden or yard.

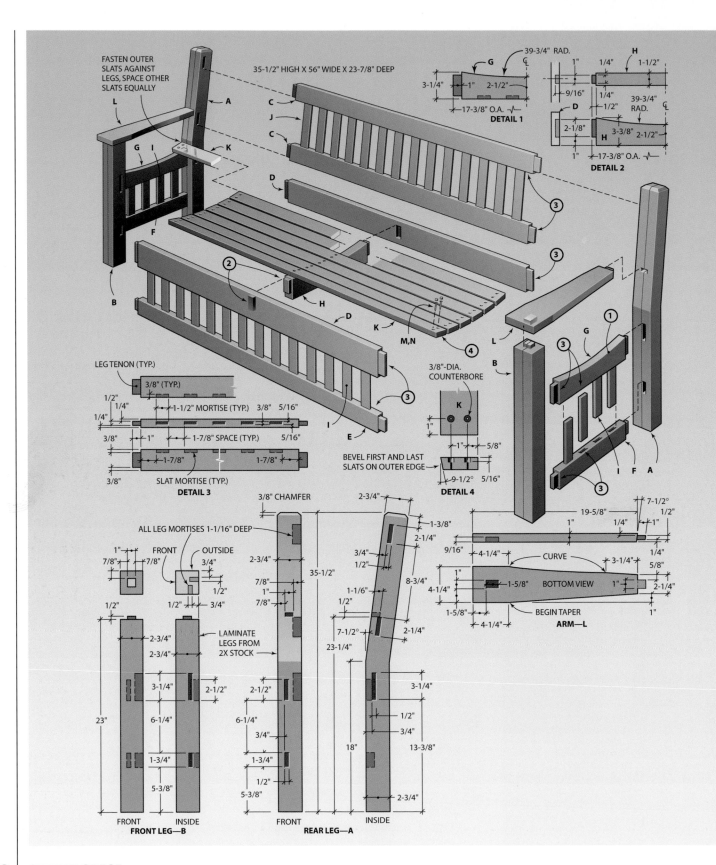

FASTEN OUTER SLATS AGAINST LEGS, SPACE OTHER SLATS EQUALLY

35-1/2" HIGH X 56" WIDE X 23-7/8" DEEP

39-3/4" RAD.

DETAIL 1

DETAIL 2

3/8"-DIA. COUNTERBORE

BEVEL FIRST AND LAST SLATS ON OUTER EDGE

DETAIL 4

LEG TENON (TYP.)

3/8" (TYP.)

1-1/2" MORTISE (TYP.)

1-7/8" SPACE (TYP.)

SLAT MORTISE (TYP.)

DETAIL 3

3/8" CHAMFER

ALL LEG MORTISES 1-1/16" DEEP

FRONT   OUTSIDE

LAMINATE LEGS FROM 2X STOCK

FRONT   INSIDE

FRONT LEG—B

FRONT   INSIDE

REAR LEG—A

CURVE

BOTTOM VIEW

BEGIN TAPER

ARM—L

We used red cedar for the bench—a material that's generally available at lumberyards and home centers. Because cedar is widely used for outdoor decking and trim, it's usually not kiln-dried and is often sold with a high moisture content. For the best results, buy the material a few weeks before beginning construction. Stack it in a dry location with spacers between the boards, allowing for good air circulation so the material will thoroughly dry.

Preparing the Legs

The 2¾-in.-thick legs are made by gluing together thinner stock. To make each rear leg, crosscut two 2x6 cedar pieces to 40 in. Use a roller to put glue on the mating surfaces (**Fig. 1**) and clamp the pairs together to form the leg blanks. For the front legs, follow the same procedure with 30-in.-long 2x4 stock. When the glue dries, rip the rear blanks to a width of 5 in., and use a band saw to trim them to 2¾ in. thick. Then saw the front legs to 2¾ in. square. Plane the cut surfaces smooth and crosscut the front legs to finished length.

Lay out the side profile of the rear legs on the cedar blanks (**Fig. 2**) and cut to the waste side of the lines with a band saw (**Fig. 3**). Then plane the sawn surfaces (**Fig. 4**). Use a sanding block or scraper to smooth the inside corner of each leg where the plane won't reach. Use a plunge router with a spiral up-cutting bit and an edge guide to remove most of the waste in each mortise (**Fig. 5**). Square the mortise ends with a sharp chisel. The arm mortises in the rear legs are cut at a 7½° angle to allow the arms to be level. To start the angled mortises, clamp a block with a square end to the vertical face of a leg and use it as a guide to drill out most of the waste (**Fig. 6**). Then use a sharp chisel to finish each mortise. Crosscut the top end of each rear leg so that it's square to the angled face of the leg. Chamfer the ends with a block plane (**Fig. 7**).

Bench Rails

Rip and crosscut 1-in.-thick stock for the rails. Also, cut a piece of 2x4 stock to size for the center seat-support rail. Use

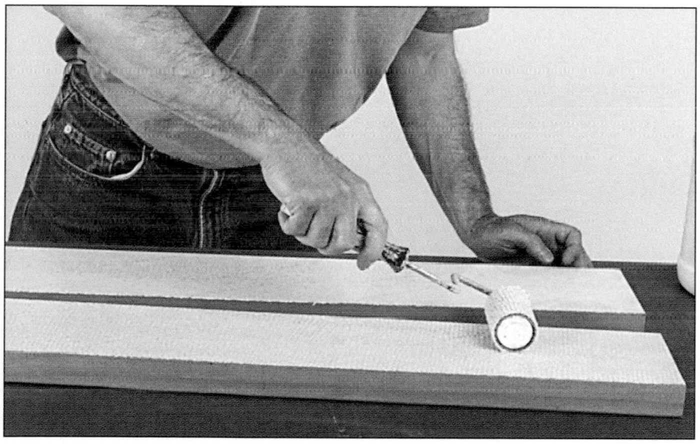

Fig. 1 ***Apply glue to pairs of 2x6s, and then clamp them together to form the rear leg blanks. Use 2x4s for the front legs.***

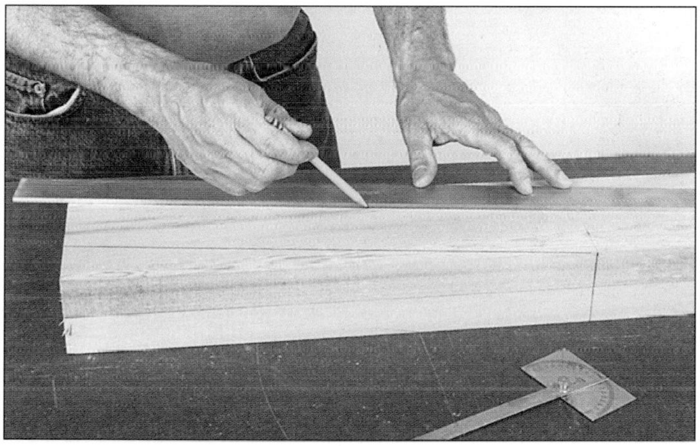

Fig. 2 ***Band saw the rear leg blanks to 5 in. wide and 2¾ in. thick. Plane the leg blanks smooth and lay out the side profile.***

Materials List

Key	No.	Size and description (use)
A	2	2¾ x 5 x 35½" cedar (rear leg)
B	2	2¾ x 2¾ x 23½" cedar (front leg)
C	2	1 x 3 x 51" cedar (back rail)
D	2	1 x 4 x 51" cedar (seat rail)
E	1	1 x 2½ x 51" cedar (front rail)
F	2	1 x 2½ x 17⅜" cedar (side rail)
G	2	1 x 3¼ x 17⅜" cedar (side rail)
H	1	1½ x 3⅜ x 17⅜" cedar (center rail)
I	22	⅜ x 1½ x 6¼" cedar (bottom slat)
J	14	⅜ x 1½ x 8¾" cedar (back slat)
K	6	¾ x 2¼ x 54½" cedar (seat slat)
L	2	1 x 4¼ x 20⅝" cedar (arm)
M	36	1½" No. 8 fh wood screw
N	36	⅜"-dia. cedar plug

Misc.: Exterior glue; 120-grit sandpaper; clear decking stain.

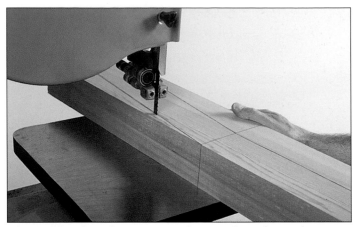

Fig. 3 *Use a band saw to cut the rear legs from the blanks. Be sure to keep the saw kerf on the waste side of the layout line.*

Fig. 4 *Use a sharp plane to smooth the sawn surfaces. Switch to sandpaper, spokeshave, or a scraper at the back inside corner.*

Fig. 5 *Mark the mortise locations on the front and rear legs, and use a plunge router and edge guide to make the cuts.*

Fig. 6 *To cut the angled arm mortises, clamp a board to the leg to act as a guide. Bore the holes, then finish them with a chisel.*

Fig. 7 *Crosscut the leg top so that it's square to the angled face of the leg. Use a chisel or block plane to chamfer the end.*

Fig. 8 *Use a dado blade in the table saw to cut the rail tenons. The rip fence acts as a stop to ensure tenons of equal length.*

a scrap stick as a beam compass to mark the 39¾-in. radius on the top side rails and center rail, but don't cut the curves at this point.

Install a dado blade in the table saw and cut the tenons on the ends of the side, front, and back rails (**Fig. 8**). Use the table saw rip fence as a stop to ensure that the tenons are of equal length. Readjust the blade height to cut the shoulder at the top and bottom edge of each tenon.

Clamp a scrap fence to the table saw fence and position it so that only ½ in. of the dado blade will be exposed. Turn on the saw and raise the blade to a height of ⅞ in., and cut the tenons on the top ends of the front legs (**Fig. 9**).

Readjust the saw again to cut the tenons on the ends of the center seat-support rail.

Next, mark the precise locations of the slat mortises in the side, front, and back rails and use a plunge router to quickly cut the mortises (**Fig. 10**).

Because the rails are somewhat narrow, clamp a second board to the workpiece to help support the router base. Square the mortise ends with a sharp chisel. Work carefully when making these cuts, as there are no shoulders on the slats to hide oversize mortises.

Lay out the mortises for the center seat-support rail in the front and back rails. Use a Forstner bit in a drill press to remove most of the waste (**Fig. 11**), and square with a chisel. Then cut the curved profiles on the side and center support rails, and rip and crosscut the bench slats to finished size.

Assembly

Begin assembly by joining a set of slats to the side rails (**Fig. 12**). It isn't necessary to glue the slats in place because they will be held captive between the rails. But if they fit too loosely, you can place a spot of glue in the mortises to prevent them from rattling.

Spread exterior glue in the leg mortises and on the side rail tenons, assemble one of the bench sides, and clamp until the glue sets (**Fig. 13**).

Repeat the process for the other side. Join the slats to the front rails. If necessary, use three or four clamps to press the slats all the way into the joints (**Fig. 14**). Then spread glue in the front and back rail mortises and on the center rail tenons, and join the parts (**Fig. 15**).

Use a clamp to pull the joints tight, and set the assembly aside to let the glue dry (**Fig. 16**).

Assemble the back rails and slats and join this subassembly to one of the bench sides (**Fig. 17**). When the glue cures, join the front and back seat rail assembly to the same side. Complete the bench frame by joining the opposite side to the rail ends.

Rip and crosscut ¾-in. stock to size for the seat slats. Adjust the table saw blade angle to 9½° and bevel one edge of the front and back slats. Leave the rest of the slat edges square.

Use a combination bit to bore screw pilot holes and

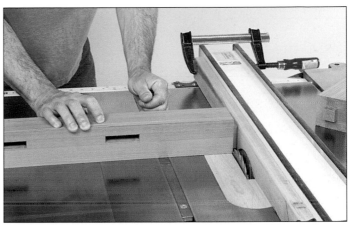

Fig. 9 *To cut the tenons on top of the legs, raise the dado blade into a scrap fence to yield a ¹/₂-in.-wide x ⁷/₈-in.-high cut.*

Fig. 10 *Rout the slat mortises in the bench rails. Clamp a second board to the workpiece to help support the router base.*

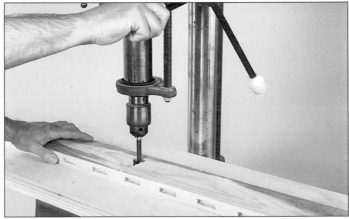

Fig. 11 *Mark the mortise locations for the center seat-support rail. Use a Forstner bit to remove most of the waste.*

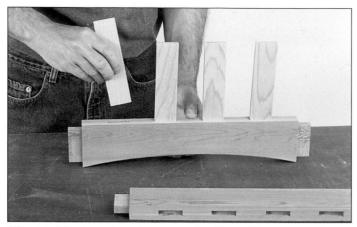

Fig. 12 *After cutting the curved rail profiles, press the side slats firmly into their mortises. It's not necessary to use glue.*

⅜-in.-dia. x ⁵⁄₁₆-in.-deep counterbores in the seat slats. Then fasten the slats with galvanized deck screws.

Maintain an equal space between the slats. Use a ⅜-in. plug cutter in your drill press to cut screw plugs out of a cedar board (**Fig. 18**). Then spread glue in the screw holes and on the plugs, and insert a plug into each hole (**Fig. 19**). When the glue dries, pare each plug flush.

Rip blanks to 4¼ in. wide for the arms, and crosscut them a few inches longer than finished length. Use a dado blade in your table saw to cut a square shoulder tenon on the end of each blank.

Then lay out the angled shoulder and cut the finished tenon with a sharp backsaw (**Fig. 20**). Refine the cuts with a sharp chisel where necessary. With the tenons done, crosscut the arms to finished length.

Mark the location of the mortise on the underside of each bench arm, and use your drill press with a Forstner bit to bore

Fig. 13 *Spread glue in the leg mortises and side rail tenons, and assemble one of the bench sides. Clamp until the glue sets.*

Fig. 14 *Use three or four clamps to squeeze the front rail assembly tight, pressing the slats to the bottom of the mortises.*

Fig. 15 *Spread glue in the shallow center rail mortises and on the seat-support rail tenons. Then go ahead and join the parts.*

Fig. 16 *Use a bar clamp to securely pull the front rail and back rail assembly tight to the center seat-support rail.*

overlapping holes that remove most of the waste.

Then use a sharp chisel to square the mortise walls. Note that the arm mortise is elongated so that the tenon at the opposite end of the arm will easily slide into the leg mortise. Lay out the finished shape of the arms on the blanks and cut to the lines with a band saw.

After smoothing the sawn edges, join the arms to the bench using two clamps to ensure that the pressure is applied to both joints while the glue sets (**Fig. 21**).

Finishing

Sand the bench with 120-grit sandpaper. Brush off all sanding dust before applying a finish. We applied a coat of clear decking stain to our bench. This finish is easy to apply and provides good protection for outdoor pieces. Brush on a liberal coat and allow it to dry for at least 24 hours before using the bench.

Fig. 17 *Join the back to one of the bench sides. When the glue cures, add the front and back seat rail assembly to the same side.*

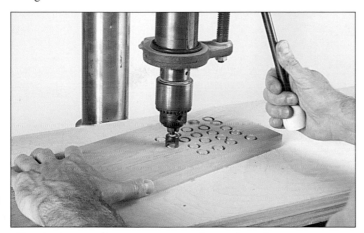

Fig. 18 *Use a plug cutter to make cedar plugs to cover the seat screws. Pop the plugs free with a flat-tip screwdriver.*

Fig. 19 *Spread glue in the holes and on the plugs and place a plug into each hole. Pare each one flush with a sharp chisel.*

Fig. 20 *After cutting square tenons at the arm ends, use a backsaw to cut the angled shoulders. Refine the tenons with a chisel.*

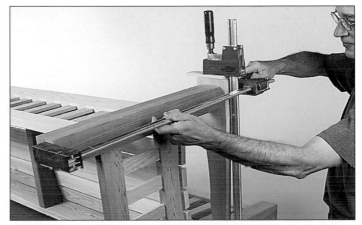

Fig. 21 *Join the arms to the bench using two clamps so that the pressure is applied to both joints while the glue sets.*

Fencing and Accessories

Screen Gem

Add character and a little mystery to your backyard or garden with our cedar privacy screen.

Whether you have a small garden in town or an expansive country estate, there's nothing like relaxing totally at ease in your own backyard. When the weather's fine, it's the ideal place to shed that cooped up feeling—without leaving home. Sometimes, though, your personal wide-open spaces might be a little too wide-open for that quiet lunch with a good book. Or maybe your yard needs a little dividing to increase the visual interest of the space. What you need to do is define the area without limiting it. And one great way to do this is with a privacy screen.

*Key*POINTS

TIME

Prep Time	5 hours
Shop Time	8 hours
Assembly Time	12 hours

EFFORT

Skill Level	intermediate
Maintenance	light
Assistance	none

COST / BENEFITS

Expense: moderate

• Can be used as both functional screen and as a yard or garden **design element**.

• Simply multiply instructions and materials to **customize** length.

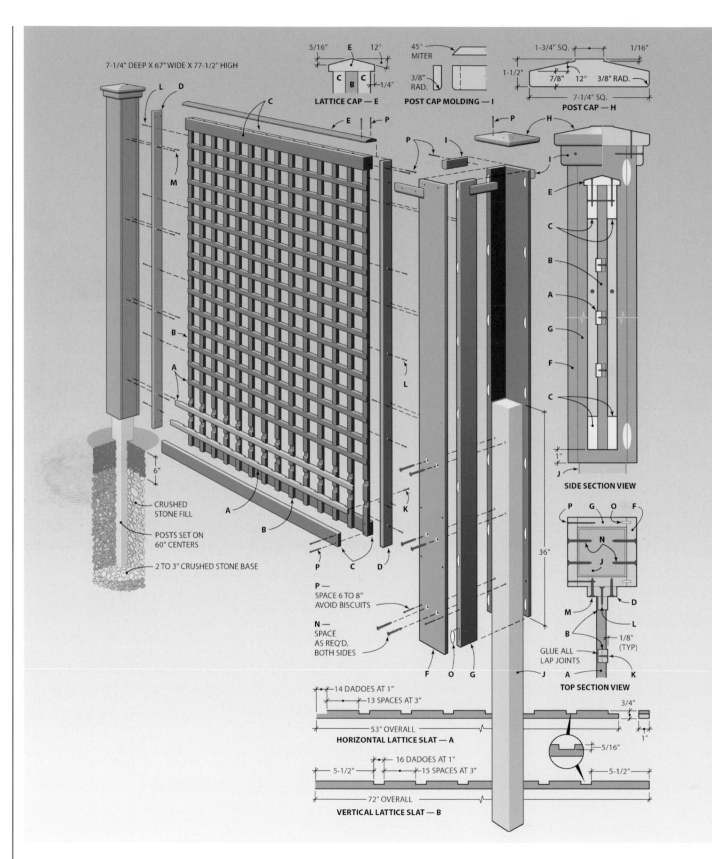

7-1/4" DEEP X 67" WIDE X 77-1/2" HIGH

LATTICE CAP — E
5/16"
E
12°
C B C
1/4"

POST CAP MOLDING — I
45° MITER
3/8" RAD.

POST CAP — H
1-3/4" SQ.
1/16"
1-1/2"
7/8"   12°   3/8" RAD.
7-1/4" SQ.

6"

CRUSHED STONE FILL

POSTS SET ON 60" CENTERS

2 TO 3" CRUSHED STONE BASE

P — SPACE 6 TO 8" AVOID BISCUITS

N — SPACE AS REQ'D, BOTH SIDES

36"

SIDE SECTION VIEW
1"
J

TOP SECTION VIEW
P   G   O   F
N
J
M
B
D
L
1/8" (TYP)
GLUE ALL LAP JOINTS
A   K

14 DADOES AT 1"
13 SPACES AT 3"
53" OVERALL
HORIZONTAL LATTICE SLAT — A

16 DADOES AT 1"
5-1/2"
15 SPACES AT 3"
72" OVERALL
VERTICAL LATTICE SLAT — B

3/4"
1"
5/16"
5-1/2"

Our screen is essentially a short fence with large lattice panels that provide a sense of intimacy, but are open enough to allow for a view. We built it out of red cedar, a good wood for exterior projects. To get the most out of your lumber, buy 1x6 stock for the post faces, rails, caps, and end strips, 1x8 stock for the lattice slats and post sides, and 2x8 stock for the post caps.

Making the Lattice

First, crosscut 1x8 stock to length for the vertical and horizontal lattice members. Clamp each set of blanks in a stack with the ends flush, and mark the locations of the half-lap joints on the stock edges.

Use a dado blade to cut ⁵⁄₁₆-in.-deep notches at the half-lap joint marks (**Fig. 1**). Make two passes to complete each notch. Then rip the lattice slats from the wide stock (**Fig. 2**).

To assemble a lattice panel, first lay out the horizontal slats with a 3-in. space between each. Spread glue in the notches of a vertical slat and in the mating notches on the horizontal slats. Firmly seat the joints, and drive a ¾-in. No. 4 brass screw at each intersection (**Fig. 3**). Install the remaining vertical slats in the same way. Rip and crosscut the top and bottom rails to size, and fasten them to each side of the lattice with 6d galvanized finishing nails (**Fig. 4**). Cut the vertical end strips to size, and nail them to the ends of the top and bottom rails. Attach the end strips to the end vertical lattice slats with screws placed in between the horizontal slats (**Fig. 5**).

Rip and crosscut blanks for the lattice panel cap. Then tilt your table saw blade to 12° and cut the top bevels. Completely smooth the cut surfaces with 120-grit sandpaper, and use galvanized finishing nails to fasten the cap to the top rails and end strips (**Fig. 6**).

Fig. 1 *After cutting the 1x8 lattice stock to length, lay out the half-lap joint notches and cut them with a dado blade in the table saw.*

Fig. 2 *After the notches are cut, rip the 1-in.-wide horizontal and vertical lattice strips from the 1x8 blanks.*

Materials List

Key	No.*	Size and description (use)
A	16	¾ x 1 x 53" cedar (horizontal slat)
B	14	¾ x 1 x 72" cedar (vertical slat)
C	4	¾ x 2½ x 53" cedar (rail)
D	2	¾ x 2¼ x 72" cedar (lattice end)
E	1	¾ x 2¾ x 54½" cedar (top cap)
F	4	¾ x 5¼ x 76" cedar (post face)
G	4	¾ x 3¾ x 76" cedar (post side)
H	2	1½ x 7¼ x 7¼" cedar (post cap)
I	8	½ x 1½ x 6¼" cedar (molding)
J	2	6'-long 4x4 pressure-treated post

Key	No.*	Size and description (use)
K	224	¾" No. 4 fh brass wood screw
L	10	1½" No. 8 fh brass wood screw
M	16	1½" No. 10 fh brass wood screw
N	24	2" No. 10 fh brass wood screw
O	56	No. 0 plate
P	as reqd.	6d galvanized finishing nail

Misc.: 120-grit sandpaper; white penetrating alkyd primer; acrylic house and trim paint.

*Quantities based on one lattice panel and two posts.

Fig. 3 *Apply glue to the half-lap joints and press the lattice strips together. Reinforce each joint with a single screw.*

Fig. 4 *Position the top and bottom rails along each side of the lattice panel, and secure them with galvanized finishing nails.*

The Posts

Rip and crosscut the post faces and sides to finished size. Although it's not necessary to use fasteners other than nails, post assembly is easier if you use joining plates to help position the parts. Clamp a fence to the worktable and cut plate-joint slots in the post faces. Then cut the corresponding slots in the edges of the post sides. Install the joining plates in the faces. Because the plates are only positioning aids, it's not necessary to use glue. Position the side pieces over one face, add the opposite face, and secure with 6d galvanized finishing nails. Take care not to nail through the joining plates (**Fig. 7**).

Cut 2x8 stock into 7¼-in. squares for the post caps, and set up the table saw to make the angled cuts on the caps. Begin by clamping a tall guide to the table saw fence. Tilt the saw blade to 12° and raise it so that the top of the blade is 2¾ in. above the table. Adjust the fence so that it's ⅞ in. from the blade at the table.

Securely clamp one edge of a cap block to a 2 x 6 x 12 in. backer board. Then turn on the saw and cut one of the angled faces (**Fig. 8**).

When the blade enters the backer board, shut off the saw, wait until the blade completely stops moving, and then remove the assembly. Then proceed to make the remaining cuts in the same way.

If using the raised fence, backer board, and clamps seems too complicated for your level of comfort, simply shape the cap bevels with a hand plane. This may take longer, but it's a more relaxed procedure.

Mount a ⅜-in.-radius, quarter-round bit in your router table and shape the bottom edges of the post caps. Sand the caps and nail them to the post tops (**Fig. 9**).

Then use the same bit to round one edge of ½ x 1½ in. stock for the cap molding. Cut the molding pieces to length

with a miter saw, and nail the mitered pieces under the post caps (**Fig. 10**).

Assembly and Finishing

Bore screw holes in the lattice panel side strips, position a panel on one of the posts, and secure with screws. Repeat the procedure for each lattice/post joint.

Cut pressure-treated 4x4s to 6-ft. lengths. Slide one of these pieces into the bottom end of each post so that 30 to 36 in. protrudes. Notice that the post cavity is ¼ in. wider than the 4x4, to make installation easier. Drive two screws through the post into the 4x4 to temporarily hold it in place. After you install the screen, you can remove the screws to adjust the relative heights of the posts.

Set all nail holes, then prime the screen with a quality exterior-grade primer. Fill all nail holes with glazing compound or painter's putty, then apply a coat of a 100 percent acrylic topcoat. To install the screen, mark the post centers on the ground, and use a post hole digger or shovel to dig holes at least 30 in. deep. Place a few inches of crushed stone or gravel in the bottom of each hole.

Bring the screen to the site and reassemble it. Tip the 4x4 post ends into the holes, and brace the screen so that the posts are plumb. Fill the holes with more crushed stone to within 6 in. of the surface, tamping it down to provide a solid base. Then top off the holes with topsoil.

Check that the bottom rail of the screen is level. If necessary, remove the screws that hold the posts to the 4x4s and adjust the height of the screen as required. Install more screws to hold the posts to the 4x4s, then fill the holes over the screw heads and touch up the paint. This system will work for locations where the ground slopes no more than 2 in. from one end of the screen to the other. For dramatically sloped yards, you'll need to construct posts that accommodate the difference in grade.

Fig. 5 *Nail the vertical end strips to the top and bottom rails, and add screws between the horizontal lattice members.*

Fig. 6 *After ripping the angles on the top of the lattice cap, fasten the cap to the rails and end strips with finishing nails.*

Fig. 7 *Assemble the box posts with plates but no glue. Then use galvanized finishing nails to fasten the pieces together.*

Fig. 8 *Use a tall auxiliary fence when cutting the post cap angles. Clamp the stock to a backer board to support the cut.*

Fig. 9 *Position the cap so that it overhangs the post uniformly. Then fasten it to the top of the post with galvanized finishing nails.*

Fig. 10 *Miter the ends of the cap molding pieces. Fit each piece under a cap and secure it with galvanized finishing nails.*

Fantastic Fences

Build our board-and-lattice fence with fanciful moon gate and you'll actually get three fences in one!

Take a stroll through most residential neighborhoods and you'll discover that fences are no longer being used strictly to separate one piece of property from another. Fences, depending on the design, provide varying degrees of privacy and protection. They help to control roaming children and pets and establish boundaries for gardens, work, and play areas. But an attractive, well-designed fence will do all these things while enhancing the beauty of—and adding value to—your home. Conversely, an ill-considered fence, installed with no thought to its surroundings, will detract from your property.

*Key*POINTS

TIME
Prep Time	5-8 hours
Shop Time	8-14 hours
Assembly Time	10-14 hours

EFFORT
Skill Level	moderate
Maintenance	light
Assistance	one-two

COST / BENEFITS
Expense: moderate
- Use the variations in the fence design for **differing levels of privacy**.
- **Moon gate provides unusual and unique design element**.

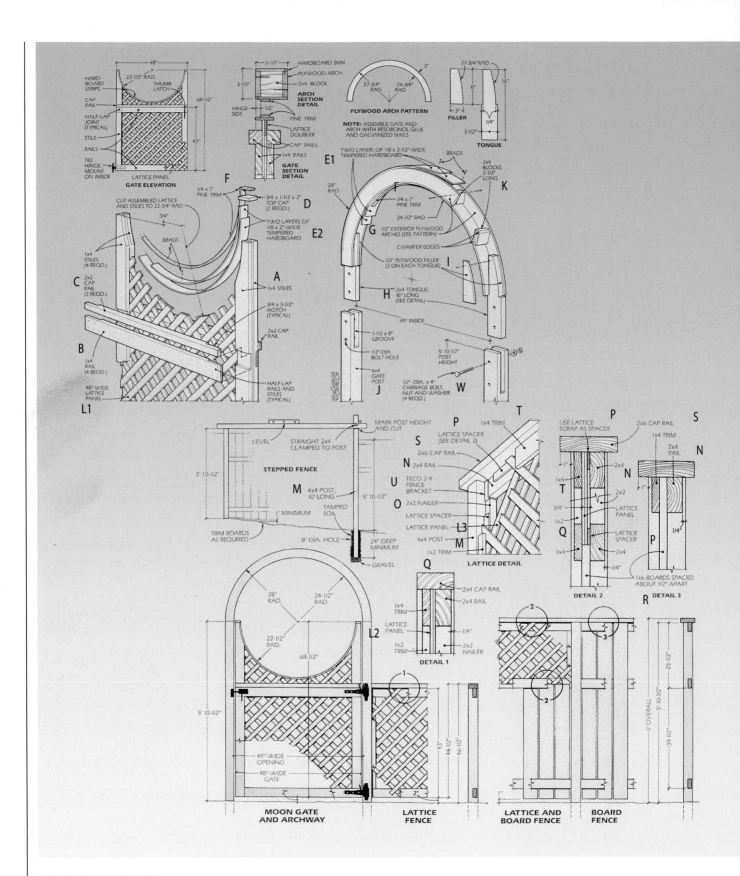

Our objective with this fence project was to design a highly attractive fence "system" that would provide varying degrees of privacy. Consequently, we essentially built three types of fences that, although interlinked, serve different purposes. On the side of the house, dividing the front lawn from the backyard, we constructed a 4-ft.-high lattice fence that incorporates a lovely round-top moon gate. Perpendicular to the lattice fence, separating the property from the neighbor's, is a 6-ft.-high fence constructed of vertical 1x6 boards topped with 2 ft. of lattice. This design offers slightly more privacy while maintaining an open, airy feeling. To provide maximum privacy for the backyard, we installed a 6-ft.-high fence constructed of just vertical 1x6 boards.

Materials List

Key	No.	Size and description (use)
A	4	1 x 4 x 68½" pressure-treated pine (gate stiles)
B	4	1 x 4 x 48" pressure-treated pine (gate rails)
C	2	2 x 2 x 48" pressure-treated pine (gate cap rail)
D	2	¾ x 1½ x 2" pressure-treated pine (gate top cap)
E1	4	⅛ x 3½ x 96" tempered hardboard (top arch strip)
E2	2	⅛ x 2 x 96" tempered hardboard (bottom arch strip)
F	2	¼ x 1 x 22½" pine (gate arch trim)
G*	2	½" exterior-grade plywood (exterior arch strip)
H	2	1½ x 3½ x 16" pressure-treated pine (arch connecting tongue)
I	4	½ x 3 x 8" exterior-grade plywood (tongue filler)
J	2	4 x 4 x 68½" pressure-treated pine (gate post)
K	5	2 x 4 x 2½" pressure-treated pine (arch blocks)
L1*	1	48 x 68½" pressure-treated pine (gate lattice)
L2**	as reqd.	43" pressure-treated pine (lattice fence panel)
L3**	as reqd.	25½" pressure-treated pine (lattice top section for board fence)
M	as reqd.	4 x 4 x 120" pressure-treated pine (fence post)
N**	as reqd.	2 x 4" pressure-treated pine (fence rail)
O	as reqd.	2 x 2 x 25½" pressure-treated pine (fence nailer)
P	as reqd.	lattice spacer
Q	as reqd.	1 x 2 x 25½" pressure-treated pine (trim)
R	as reqd.	1 x 6 x 69½" pressure-treated pine (fence boards)
S**	as reqd.	2 x 6" pressure-treated pine (cap rail)
T**	as reqd.	1 x 4" pressure-treated pine (trim)
U	as reqd.	2 x 4 fence bracket
V	2	Metal tee hinges
W	4	½"-dia. carriage bolt, nut, and washer

Misc.: 20d galvanized nails; 2" galvanized wood screws; 1½" galvanized wood screws; 4d galvanized finishing nails; resorcinol glue; gravel for post holes; ⅝" brads; thumb latch or gate handle.

*Cut to pattern shape and size.
**Length determined by fence panel length.

Material Selection

The fences shown are built of pressure-treated pine. Redwood or cedar could also be used. The framework of the fences is constructed with common-size stock including 1x4, 2x2, 2x4, and 2x6. Use 4x4 stock for the posts.

The pressure-treated lattice comes in 4x8-ft. sheets. Each lattice strip measures ¼ in. thick x 1½ in. wide. Make the curved arch above the moon gate out of ½-in. exterior-grade plywood and ⅛-in. tempered hardboard. To help resist corrosion, use hot-dipped galvanized nails and screws. Metal fence brackets are used to install the 2x4 rails to the fence posts (**Fig. 5 and 6**).

Use two-part waterproof resorcinol glue to laminate together the hardboard strips that form the curved arch.

We decided not to finish the fence, but rather, allow it to weather naturally to a silvery gray. If you decide to apply paint or stain, you must wait three to six months for the pressure-treated wood to dry out. If the wood was wet during construction, you may need to wait up to one year; even longer in rainy regions.

Because of the various chemicals used in pressure-treated wood, there are certain health precautions that you should follow stringently. Always were a dust mask and goggles when

Fig. 1 Dig the fence post holes to about 30 in. deep with a post hole digger. This hand tool is available from most rental equipment dealers.

Fig. 2 *Support the post in the hole with two diagonal braces clamped to stakes driven in the ground. Use a level to plumb the post.*

Fig. 3 *Backfill around the post and tamp the soil with a spare 2x4 rail. Continue to add soil and tamp until it's level with the surrounding ground.*

Fig. 4 *Mark the position of the metal fence brackets on the 4x4 posts. The galvanized brackets are used to join the 2x4 rails to the posts.*

sawing, boring, and planning pressure-treated wood. Dispose of short cutoffs and scrap in the garbage, not compost piles, and never burn pressure-treated wood. Also, after handling pressure-treated wood, be sure to wash your hands thoroughly before eating or drinking.

The first step before starting construction is to find out exactly where your property line is. A copy of your house survey will help to determine this. If you can't find one in your files, get one from your local building department.

Plan to erect the fence about 6 in. inside the property line, or in accordance with your local building codes. Then draw a rough sketch of the fence layout to help estimate materials and total cost.

Setting the Posts

Begin by stretching a string between two stakes along the proposed fence run to determine the fence posts' locations. Use 6-ft.-long 4x4 posts for the 4-ft.-high lattice fence, and 8-ft. posts for the 6-ft.-high fences.

Also, use two 8-ft. posts to support the arch. Each post hole must be about 30 in. deep. Add 6 in. of gravel to each hole to provide a solid foundation and adequate drainage.

Start by digging holes for the two gate posts. Be sure the inside dimension between the posts is 49 in. to provide clearance for the 48-in.-wide gate. Dig the holes about 8 in. square using a post hole digger (available at rental equipment dealers) and a shovel (**Fig. 1**). After adding a base of gravel to each hole, be sure that the gate posts stand up out of the ground 5 ft., 10½ in.

Next, cut a 1½-in.-wide x 8-in. groove in the top end of each gate post to accept the 2x4 tongues of the arch. To form the grooves, first bore a 1½-in.-dia. hole through each post to establish the bottom of the grooves. Then use a portable circular saw or handsaw to cut away the waste. Square up each groove bottom with a chisel.

Place one of the posts in a hole and support it temporarily with two diagonal braces (**Fig. 2**). Check it for plumb with a level, and then backfill around the post with soil. Install the

Fig. 5 *Mount the brackets to the posts with 1¼-in galvanized screws. An electric screw gun provides a no-sweat way to drive screws.*

Fig. 6 *Place a 2x4 rail in the bracket and bore pilot holes to prevent splitting. Then fasten the rail with 1½-in. galvanized screws.*

Fig. 7 *Fasten 1x6 fence boards to the 2x4 rails with 1½-in. screws. To keep the boards even, butt them against a cleat clamped in place.*

Fig. 8 *Attach 2x2 nailer strips to the fence posts with 2½-in. screws. The strips provide a solid surface for fastening the lattice.*

second gate post and support it with two 2x4 braces clamped to the first post. Plumb the second post and backfill around it. Now use a 2x4 to firmly tamp the soil around each post (**Fig. 3**). Add more soil as needed and compact it again. Leave the 2x4 braces clamped to the posts to maintain the 49-in. dimension until the arch is installed.

Next, starting from one of the gate posts, lay out and dig post holes for a run of lattice fence. Use 6-ft.-long posts spaced 96 in. apart (inside dimension) to accommodate an 8-ft. lattice sheet. Here's how to level the tops of the fence posts. Mark a line on the gate post 45 in. above the ground. Then, using a line level, stretch a level string from this mark along the proposed fence run.

Now install the posts at the same height as the line. If the property runs up or downhill severely, install a stepped fence, as shown in the drawing detail.

Construct the lattice fence using the drawing as a guide. Note that the lattice, ripped to 43 in. wide, is sandwiched between 2x4 rails and 1x4 trim (see exploded diagram Detail 1). Mark the metal fence bracket positions (**Fig. 4**) and mount the brackets with galvanized screws (**Fig. 5**). Join the rails to the posts with fence brackets (**Fig. 6**). Top off the fence with a 2x4 cap rail.

Arch and Gate Construction

Refer to the arch pattern drawing and cut two arches of ½-in. exterior-grade plywood. Next, from 2x4 stock, cut two 16-in.-long tongues that will fit in the grooves in the gate posts.

Also, cut four ½ x 3 x 8-in.-long plywood fillers, and five 2½-in.-long blocks from 2x4 stock. Glue and nail one filler to each side of both tongues. Then glue and nail the tongues to one of the plywood arches.

Be sure the tongues are exactly parallel and 49 in. apart (inside dimension). Glue and nail the 2½-in.-long blocks to the arch at a slight angle so that the corners of each block

Fig. 9 *Bore pilot holes to prevent splitting the lattice. Then attach the lattice to the rails and 2x2 nailers with 4d galvanized finishing nails.*

Fig. 10 *Use 1x4 trim to conceal the joint where the lattice meets the 1x6 boards. Fasten 1x4 trim with 2½-in. galvanized screws.*

Fig. 11 *Attach vertical 1x2 trim at the ends of the lattice panels with 2-in. screws. Bore pilot holes first to avoid splitting the trim.*

Fig. 12 *Top off the fence with a 2x6 cap rail. Fasten the rail with 20d (4-in.) galvanized nails. Space the nails about 24 in. apart.*

MATERIAL *Matters*

Lattice Wisdom
If you are buying your lattice from a large home center or lumberyard (where you'll find the best prices), you're likely to come across two types—a flimsier garden lattice, and the more solid fencing lattice that we use here. The choice is clear.

Garden lattice is cheaper, but it is stapled, where fencing lattice is nailed. In addition, most fencing lattice is pressure-treated and thicker, making it much more durable for long-term fencing use.

However, if you are planning on painting the entire fence white, or if the fence you build will be exposed to severe elements, you may want to consider plastic lattice as an alternative to wood types. Although the plastic variety is a little more difficult to cut and work with than wood lattice, the plastic lasts a very long time, does not require repainting or any other maintenance, and is usually less expensive than wood types. And with today's plastic lattice, it's often hard to tell the difference.

extend beyond the arch ¼ in. Now glue and nail the second arch to the assembly. Use a plane to chamfer the 2x4 block corners flush with the plywood arches. This creates solid nailing surfaces for attaching the hardboard skin.

Rip four 3½-in.-wide x 8-ft.-long strips of ⅛-in. tempered hardboard. Glue and nail one strip to the top edge of the arch assembly using ⅜-in. brads and resorcinol glue. Then glue and nail a second strip over the first strip.

Use a backsaw to trim the overhanging strips to length. Attach the two remaining hardboard strips to the inside curve of the arch using the procedure described above. Also, attach a ¼ x 1-in.-wide pine strip to the inside curve of the arch ½ in. from the edge (see arch section exploded diagram detail). Now attach the assembled arch to the gate posts by inserting the tongues into the grooves in the posts. Secure the arch with four carriage bolts, as shown.

Next, build the gate using the drawing as a guide. Cut four 1x4 stiles 67¾ in. long and four 1x4 rails 48 in. long. Also, cut two 2x2 rails 48 in. long.

These members form the frame around an 8-in.-wide x 67¾-in. lattice panel. Cut half-lap joints as shown, and assemble the gate with glue and nails. Be sure the gate is square.

Then use a string and pencil to mark a 22¾-in. radius on the stiles and lattice. Cut the radius with a sabre saw. Glue small lattice strips to the lattice section above the 2x2 rails. This double-thick lattice provides a solid surface for attaching the hardboard skin.

Glue and nail two layers of 2-in.-wide hardboard to the gate radius. Attach a ¾ x 1½ x 2-in. top cap to each stile. Then add ¼ x 1-in.-wide trim to the hardboard to align with the trim on the arch.

Hang the gate with a pair of tee hinges. Fasten the hinges to the gate with carriage bolts and to the post with screws. Install a thumb latch, or similar hardware, to hold the gate closed.

Six-Foot Fences

Construction of the two 6-ft.-high fences is virtually identical except that one is topped with 2 ft. of lattice. Set 8-ft.-long posts 8 ft. apart. Leave 5 ft., 10½ in. of the first post out of the ground. Stretch a level string from the top of the first post and set the remaining posts to the line.

Next, attach metal fence brackets to the fence posts and install 8-ft.-long 2x4 rails (**Fig. 5 and 6**). Each 8-ft. fence section requires three 2x4 rails.

Then attach 1x6 fence boards to the rails with 1½-in. galvanized screws (**Fig. 7**). Space the boards approximately ½ in. apart.

Now screw 2x2 nailer strips between the upper and middle rails to support the half-sheet lattice panels (**Fig. 8**). Attach the lattice to the fence with 4d galvanized finishing nails (**Fig. 9**). The all-board fence doesn't require 2x2 nailers.

Simply screw 5-ft., 9½-in. long 1x6 boards to the 2x4 rails.

Attach three 1x4 rails to each 8-ft. fence section with 2½-in. galvanized screws (**Fig. 10**). Attach 1x2 trim to the ends of the lattice panels with 2-in. screws (**Fig. 11**). Position the 1x4s opposite the 2x4 rails (see exploded diagram Details 2 and 3).

Finally, install a 2x6 cap rail to the top of the fence using 20d galvanized nails (**Fig. 12**). Bore pilot holes first and space the nails approximately 24 in. apart. Finally, prime and paint—or stain—the gate arch to match the rest of the fence.

Safety Sense

Uplifting Insight

We all know the simple basics of lifting heavy timber … so why do we all seem to ignore those same basics when we're in the heat of a project? It pays to pay attention to little things that will prevent lifting injuries, and keep your dream project from turning into a nightmare.

DO:

Wear gloves. Always put on a good pair of gloves before lifting heavy pieces of lumber. The gloves will prevent slipping on wet spots and will provide a better grip. As a bonus, you'll spare yourself splinters.

Bend properly. That means from the knees, keeping your back straight. This is especially important on the first thing you lift—the muscles in your back are cold—and the last thing you lift, when fatigue can make you sloppy.

DON'T:

Lift without a helper. Research shows that seven out of 10 average men on the street will misjudge how much they can dead lift.
Avoid this mistake, and the pain it can lead to, by asking a friend to help out with the lifting phase of the project.

Lift on slippery surfaces. Falls lead to breaks, especially when the heavy piece of wood you're carrying lands on top of you. If the path you're using to carry the wood is wet, lay down sawdust, gravel, or other material that will allow you to gain good traction.

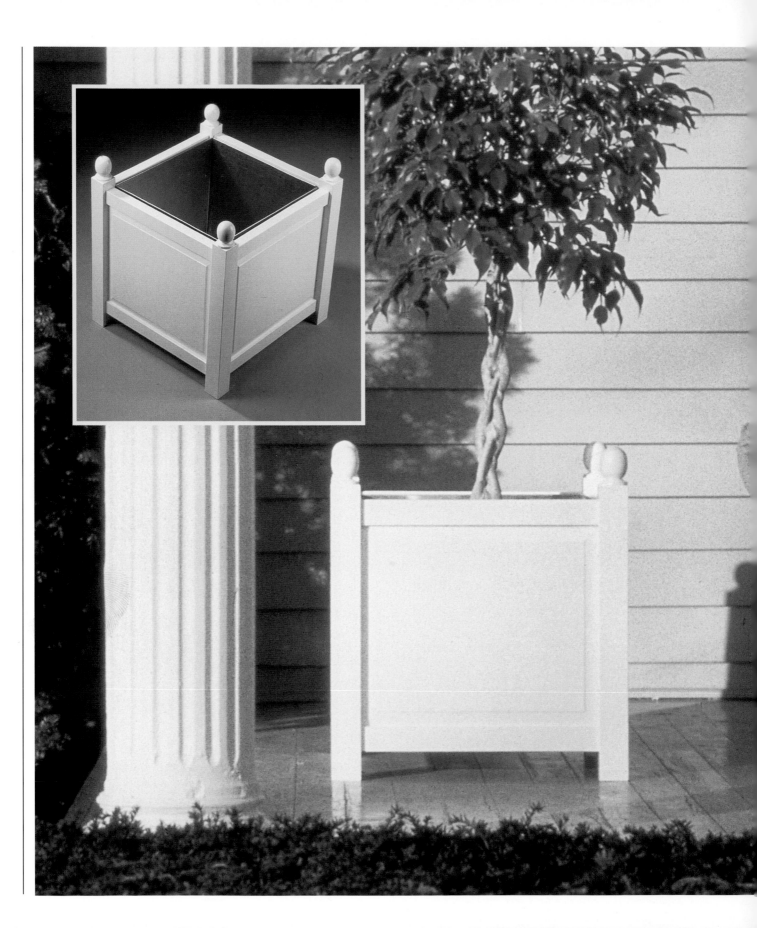

Pretty Planter

Build this planter for your porch, deck, or patio, and give a blooming plant a sturdy, beautiful home.

Using trees, flowers, and shrubs to decorate your home is a great way to add color and warmth. The containers that most plants come in, however, leave much to be desired. Terra cotta pots tend to look bland, and more colorful versions tend to the garish, or are so ornate as to be a complete mismatch to your home and yard. The best solution to the problem is to make your own wooden planter boxes. Our version is designed for use indoors or out, on any surface. With its galvanized liner it can handle direct planting. Or leave out the liner and use the unit to hold a potted plant.

*Key*POINTS

TIME
Prep Time . . . . **2 hours**
Shop Time . . . . **6 hours**
Assembly Time . . . . **3 hours**

EFFORT
Skill Level . . . . **intermediate**
Maintenance . . . . **none to light**
Assistance . . . . **none**

COST / BENEFITS
Expense: **low**
• Lightweight planter is **inexpensive**, but a classic design.
• Replace finial with another to **suit the style of your home** or outdoor space.

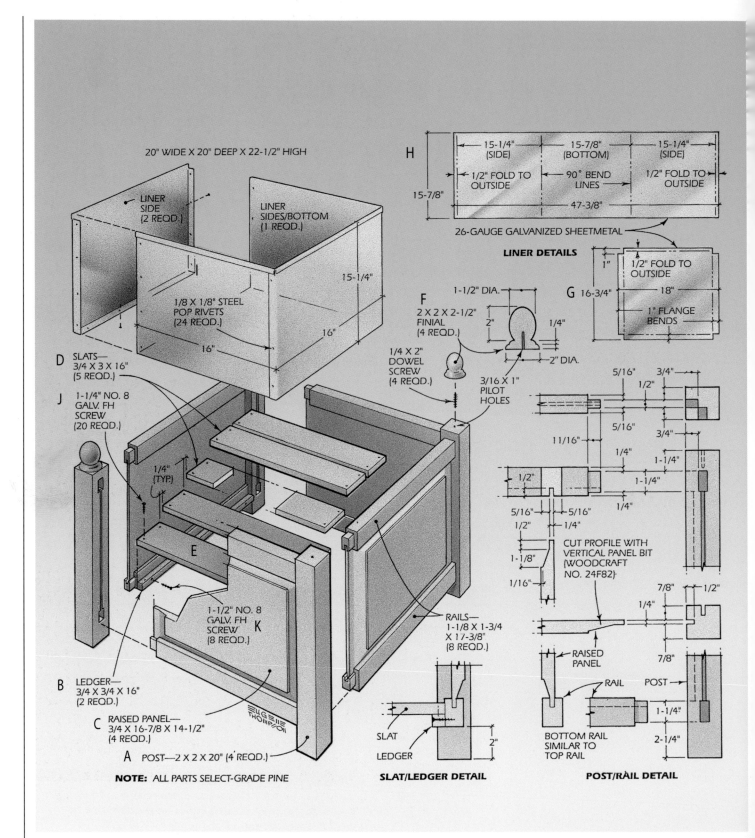

20" WIDE X 20" DEEP X 22-1/2" HIGH

LINER SIDE (2 REQD.)

LINER SIDES/BOTTOM (1 REQD.)

1/8 X 1/8" STEEL POP RIVETS (24 REQD.)

15-1/4"

16"

16"

D SLATS— 3/4 X 3 X 16" (5 REQD.)

J 1-1/4" NO. 8 GALV. FH SCREW (20 REQD.)

1/4" (TYP.)

E

K 1-1/2" NO. 8 GALV. FH SCREW (8 REQD.)

B LEDGER— 3/4 X 3/4 X 16" (2 REQD.)

C RAISED PANEL— 3/4 X 16-7/8 X 14-1/2" (4 REQD.)

A POST—2 X 2 X 20" (4 REQD.)

RAILS— 1-1/8 X 1-3/4 X 17-3/8" (8 REQD.)

NOTE: ALL PARTS SELECT-GRADE PINE

H

15-1/4" (SIDE)   15-7/8" (BOTTOM)   15-1/4" (SIDE)

1/2" FOLD TO OUTSIDE   90° BEND LINES   1/2" FOLD TO OUTSIDE

15-7/8"

47-3/8"

26-GAUGE GALVANIZED SHEETMETAL

LINER DETAILS

1"   1/2" FOLD TO OUTSIDE

G 16-3/4"   18"

1" FLANGE BENDS

F 1-1/2" DIA.

2 X 2 X 2-1/2" FINIAL (4 REQD.)

2"   1/4"

1/4 X 2" DOWEL SCREW (4 REQD.)

2" DIA.

3/16 X 1" PILOT HOLES

5/16"   3/4"

1/2"

5/16"

11/16"   3/4"

1/4"   1-1/4"

1/2"   1-1/4"

5/16"   5/16"   1/4"

1/2"   1/4"

1-1/8"

1/16"

CUT PROFILE WITH VERTICAL PANEL BIT (WOODCRAFT NO. 24F82)

7/8"   1/2"

1/4"

RAISED PANEL

7/8"

RAIL   POST

1-1/4"

2-1/4"

BOTTOM RAIL SIMILAR TO TOP RAIL

SLAT

LEDGER

2"

SLAT/LEDGER DETAIL

POST/RAIL DETAIL

We used select-grade pine for our planter. This sturdy wood is readily available and takes a nice painted finish. If you want an unpainted look, cedar, cypress, or redwood would be suitable.

Preparing the Pieces

First, cut 12 pieces of $\frac{3}{4}$-in. stock to $2\frac{1}{4}$ in. wide and 24 in. long. Then, using waterproof glue, laminate sets of three pieces face to face to produce four $2\frac{1}{4}$-in. sq. x 24-in.-long blanks. Crosscut the blanks to 20 in. and set aside the cutoffs to use for the finials. Use a jointer or hand plane to true and square two adjacent sides on each post blank, then use the table saw to rip the posts to the 2-in. finished dimension. Sand the newly cut edges to remove the saw marks.

Lay out the locations of the mortises in the posts and cut these with a plunge router and edge guide. It's best to use a spiral up-cutting bit, as this type draws the chips out of the cut and plunges easily without burning. Square the mortise ends with a chisel (**Fig. 1**). Next, switch to a $\frac{1}{4}$-in. bit and rout the grooves that hold the edges of the raised panels.

Rip and crosscut 5/4 stock to size on the ends. Use a dado blade in the table saw to cut the tenons (**Fig. 2**). Then readjust the blade height to cut the tenon shoulders. It's best to cut the tenons slightly oversize and pare them to finished dimension. Then reset the dado blade and cut the panel grooves in the rail edges (**Fig. 3**).

Glue together $4\frac{3}{4}$-in. stock for the raised panels, trim them to final dimensions when the glue is dry, and then sand, scrape, or plane them smooth. Use a plate joiner to aid in aligning the panel boards (**Fig. 4**). Cut the raised panel profile on the router table using a vertical panel-raising bit (**Fig. 5**). Use a tall router-table fence to support the workpiece. Make

Materials List

Key	No.	Size and description (use)
A	4	2 x 2 x 20" pine (post)
B	2	$\frac{3}{4}$ x $\frac{3}{4}$ x 16" pine (ledger)
C	4	$\frac{3}{4}$ x $16\frac{7}{8}$ x $14\frac{1}{2}$" pine (raised panel)
D	5	$\frac{3}{4}$ x 3 x 16" pine (slats)
E	8	$1\frac{1}{8}$ x $1\frac{3}{4}$ x $17\frac{3}{8}$" pine (rails)
F	4	2 x 2 x $2\frac{3}{4}$" pine (finial)
G*	2	$15\frac{1}{4}$ x 16" sheet metal (liner side)
H*	1	$47\frac{3}{8}$ x $15\frac{7}{8}$" sheet metal (liner side/bottom)
I	24	$\frac{1}{8}$ x $\frac{1}{8}$" steel pop rivets
J	20	$1\frac{1}{4}$" No. 8 galvanized fh screw
K	8	$1\frac{1}{2}$" No. 8 galvanized fh screw

*Liner box constructed of 26-gauge galvanized sheet metal.

Fig. 1 ***After cutting the leg mortises with a plunge router and guide fence, trim the ends square with a sharp chisel.***

Fig. 2 ***Cut the rail tenons with a dado blade. A stop block clamped to a miter gauge extension ensures accurate repetitive cuts.***

Fig. 3 ***Reset the dado blade and make the $\frac{1}{4}$-in.-wide x $\frac{1}{2}$-in.-deep grooves in each rail. Use a pushstick to move the work safely.***

Fig. 4 *Make the side panels by gluing the narrower stock pieces together. Use a plate joiner to ensure good alignment of the pieces.*

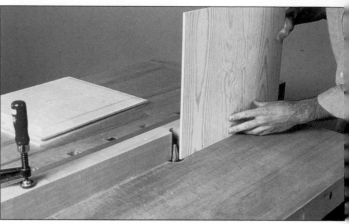

Fig. 5 *After trimming the panel to exact size, cut the raised panel profile on a router table with a vertical panel-raising bit.*

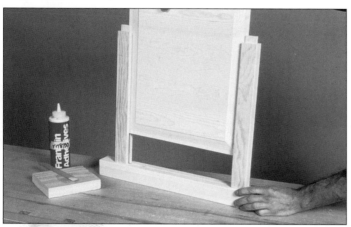

Fig. 6 *Begin assembly by gluing two rails to one post. Then slide the panel into the grooves, add the opposite post, and clamp the joints tight.*

Fig. 7 *Check that the assembly is square by measuring opposite diagonals. If necessary, loosen the clamps and adjust the entire piece to square.*

Fig. 8 *Install the ledgers to two opposite lower rails with screws and glue. Countersink pilot holes for flathead screws.*

Fig. 9 *Use a template as a guide to shape the finials. Leave a stub at the top end and sand while it's in the lathe. Then sand the stub smooth.*

the cuts in several stages, moving the fence back slightly after each cut. Cut the endgrain edges on all panels first. Thoroughly sand the panels with a small sanding block and 120-, 180-, and 220-grit sandpaper. Bore pilot holes in the post tops for securing the finials. Use a doweling jig to position the holes and to keep them square to the post end.

Assembly

Apply glue to the mortises and tenons for one side of the planter. Insert the rails into their mortises in one post, and slide the panel into position (**Fig. 6**). Avoid getting glue in the panel groove. Put the second post in place and clamp. Compare diagonals to make sure that the assembly is square, and adjust if necessary (**Fig. 7**). Assemble the opposite side in the same way. Join the two sides and the remaining rails and panels on a flat surface to avoid a twist in the planter frame.

Cut the ledger strips and slats to size. Bore and countersink pilot holes in the strips and slats. Install the strips to opposite bottom rails using screws and glue (**Fig. 8**). Then install the slats with screws only.

Mount one of the finial blanks in the lathe, and use a gouge to turn it to a 2-in.-dia. cylinder. Make a template of the finial profile and transfer the critical transition points of the finial design onto the cylinder. Shape the finial leaving only a small attachment at the top end to hold the work in the lathe (**Fig. 9**). Sand the piece while in the lathe, then remove, cut off the top stub, and sand it smooth.

Bore pilot holes in the finials and use locking pliers to thread a steel dowel screw in each. Then install the finials on the corner posts and sand the planter. Apply a coat of exterior primer and three coats of exterior latex enamel.

Making the Liner

Begin by drawing the pieces on 26-gauge sheet metal. Use a felt-tipped pen to mark the metal and make the cuts with a pair of heavy-duty shears (**Fig. 10**).

Mark the bend lines as shown on the drawing. Then clamp two ¾-in.-thick hardwood strips on either side of a sheet at a bend line at the top edge of the liner. Use the wooden strips as a lever to bend the metal 90° (**Fig. 11**). Then use sheet metal pliers to tightly fold over this top edge and complete the remaining top edges in the same way.

Next, make the two 90° bends in the long strip of metal that forms the bottom and two sides. Finally, make the bends in the two remaining sides to form the tabs that join these sides to the rest of the liner.

Join the pieces together with ⅛ x ⅛-in. steel pop rivets. Use locking pliers or clamps to hold the pieces together while you drill ⅛-in. pilot holes. Then install the pop rivets to assemble the liner (**Fig. 12**).

For a truly waterproof liner, apply silicone caulk to all interior seams and rivets. Let the caulk cure for 24 hours before filling the liner with soil.

Fig. 10 *Use a felt marker and straightedge to lay out, cut, and bend lines on the sheet metal. Make the cuts with heavy-duty shears.*

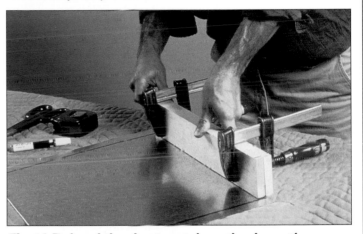

Fig. 11 *To bend the sheet metal neatly, clamp the hardwood strips at the bend line. Then use the strips to bend the metal to a 90° turn.*

Fig. 12 *To assemble the liner, first bore ⅛-in. holes, then install pop rivets. Use silicone caulk to make the seams watertight.*

Fencing Lessons

A fence may be a practical addition to your yard, but that doesn't mean that it can't be beautiful as well.

Homeowners build fences for a lot of different reasons. Some want total backyard privacy while others can live with a partial screen—enough to peek at the neighbors without feeling on display. And then there are the practical types who lean toward chain link for keeping the kids in and the neighbor's dog out. The fact is, a well-designed fence is one of the best ways to add personality to your home. If it also defines your space in a useful way—so much the better. This lovely classic picket fence does all that with style. This fence is not only a divider of space, it's also a wonderful yard decoration.

*Key*POINTS

TIME
Prep Time	8-12 hours
Shop Time	15-25 hours
Assembly Time	7-13 hours

EFFORT
Skill Level	intermediate
Maintenance	light
Assistance	none

COST / BENEFITS
Expense: moderate
• Can be designed to **fit your yard**, and works with other fences.
• **Flexible design** allows you to customize the fence for your own needs.

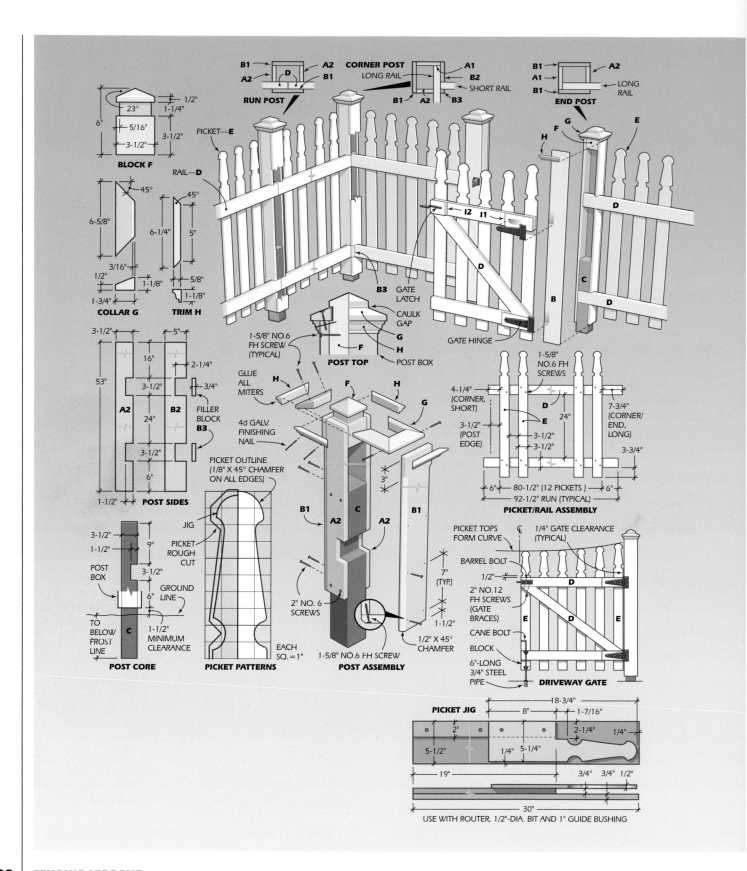

BLOCK F
1/2"
23°
6"
5/16"
1-1/4"
3-1/2"
3-1/2"

RUN POST
B1
A2
D
A2
B1

CORNER POST
A1
B2
LONG RAIL
SHORT RAIL
B1
A2
B3

END POST
B1
A2
A1
B1
LONG RAIL

PICKET—E
RAIL—D

COLLAR G
45°
6-5/8"
3/16"
1/2"
1-3/4"

TRIM H
45°
6-1/4"
5"
5/8"
1-1/8"
1-1/8"

POST SIDES
3-1/2"
5"
53"
16"
2-1/4"
3/4"
3-1/2"
A2
B2
FILLER BLOCK
B3
24"
3-1/2"
6"
1-1/2"

POST CORE
3-1/2"
1-1/2"
9"
POST BOX
3-1/2"
6"
GROUND LINE
TO BELOW FROST LINE
C
1-1/2" MINIMUM CLEARANCE

PICKET PATTERNS
JIG
PICKET ROUGH CUT
PICKET OUTLINE (1/8" X 45° CHAMFER ON ALL EDGES)
EACH SQ. = 1"

1-5/8" NO.6 FH SCREW (TYPICAL)

POST TOP
CAULK GAP
G
H
POST BOX
F
B3
GATE LATCH

GLUE ALL MITERS
4d GALV. FINISHING NAIL
H
F
H
G

POST ASSEMBLY
B1
A2
C
A2
B1
2" NO. 6 SCREWS
1-5/8" NO.6 FH SCREW
3"
7" (TYP.)
1-1/2"
1/2" X 45° CHAMFER

GATE HINGE
B
G
E
H
F
D
C
D

PICKET/RAIL ASSEMBLY
1-5/8" NO.6 FH SCREWS
4-1/4" (CORNER, SHORT)
3-1/2" (POST EDGE)
D
E
24"
3-1/2"
3-1/2"
7-3/4" (CORNER/ END, LONG)
3-3/4"
6"
80-1/2" (12 PICKETS)
6"
92-1/2" RUN (TYPICAL)

DRIVEWAY GATE
PICKET TOPS FORM CURVE
1/4" GATE CLEARANCE (TYPICAL)
BARREL BOLT
1/2"
2" NO.12 FH SCREWS (GATE BRACES)
CANE BOLT
BLOCK
6"-LONG 3/4" STEEL PIPE
D
E
D
E

PICKET JIG
18-3/4"
8"
1-7/16"
2"
2-1/4"
1/4"
5-1/2"
1/4"
5-1/4"
19"
3/4" 3/4" 1/2"
30"
USE WITH ROUTER, 1/2"-DIA. BIT AND 1" GUIDE BUSHING

I2 I1

The partial screen of a picket fence adds an element of friendly privacy to the landscape—you're not shutting the world out, you're just organizing it.

Our fence is made up of 1x4 pickets screwed to 2x4 rails. Although the picket/rail assembly is conventional, our post design has several unique features. First, the posts are boxed—¾-in.-thick pine encases a pressure-treated 4x4 core. Then, instead of full-length 4x4s, ours extend from below the frost line to about 20 in. above grade. This stub post negates the effect of excessive twist common in longer lengths of 4x4 stock. The box-post design also makes it easy to notch in the rails and completely enclose the rail ends. At the top, our post has a 4x4 core block with a pyramid-shaped upper end. Surrounding the block and recessed into it is a sloped collar that seals out the weather. Decorative trim completes the top.

Ground Work

This fence is designed for a relatively level site. If your site has minor elevation variations, plan for the tops of the pickets and posts and the top rails to be level. Cut the bottoms of the pickets and posts to suit the grade and adjust the bottom-rail position accordingly. We preassembled the picket/rail sections in modular lengths of 12 pickets (about 8 ft.), and built shorter, custom sections where necessary. Note that rail lengths change depending on whether the picket/rail assembly is in the middle of a straight run of posts, at a corner, or at an end or terminating post.

Materials List

Key	Size and description (use)
A1, A2	¾ x 3½ x 53" pine (post side)
B1, B2	¾ x 5 x 53" pine (post side)
B3	¾ x ¾ x 1½" pine (filler block)
C*	3½ x 3½" pressure-treated pine (post core)
D*	1½ x 3½" spruce (rail)
E	¾ x 3½ x 48" pine (picket)
F	3½ x 3½ x 6" cedar (post block)
G	1⅛ x 1¾ x 6⅝" pine (post collar)
H	⅝ x 1⅛ x 6¼" pine (post trim)
I1	¾ x 3½ x 8" pine (hinge block)
I2	¾ x 3½ x 4" pine (latch block)

Misc.: Tee hinges; gate latch; cane bolt; barrel bolt; 1⅝" No. 8 galvanized fh wood screws; 2" No. 8 galvanized fh wood screws; 2" No. 12 galvanized fh wood screws (hinges); 4d galvanized finishing nails; exterior glue and filler; latex primer and semi-gloss paint; ogee bit.
*Cut length to suit.
Note: Quantities to suit your own fence plan.

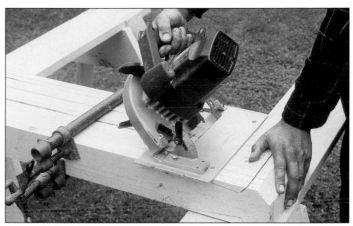

Fig. 1 *Gang together the picket blanks and use a circular saw set at a 45° angle to make most of the cuts for the rough picket shape.*

Carefully lay out the post hole positions and dig the holes below the frost line. Keep the removed soil covered on a tarp or plywood panel until it's time to backfill the holes.

The Pickets and Rails

We used a router to shape the pickets. To reduce the load on the router, first rough out the shape of each picket with straight cuts. Make a template of the rough picket profile as shown in the drawing and use this to mark your work. Gang a number of pickets together, make sure they're aligned, and hold them in place with a pipe clamp. Then make the 45° cuts with your circular saw (**Fig. 1**). Use a sabre saw to make final cuts on the sides of the individual pickets (**Fig. 2**).

Build the jig shown in the drawing to hold each picket while the final shape is routed. Clamp each picket in the jig and use a ½-in. straight bit and 1-in. guide bushing to make the cuts (**Fig. 3**). Use a router table and piloted chamfer bit to

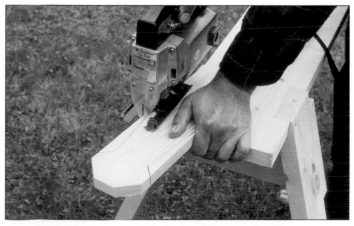

Fig. 2 *Finish the rough picket outline by making the longer side cuts on individual pickets with a sabre saw. Cut one picket at a time.*

Fig. 3 *Use a router with a ½-in. bit, 1-in. guide bushing, and a picket jig to trim the rough pickets to the finished shape.*

Fig. 4 *Build an assembly table with stops to position the rails. Use spacers to locate the pickets and attach them with two screws per rail.*

Fig. 7 *Slide the three-sided collar around the block from the open side of the post. Secure it with screws and attach the remaining side with glue and screws.*

shape a ⅛-in. bevel around the top and sides of each picket.

Cut the rails to length based on your plan. Note that the distances from the outer pickets of each section to the rail ends vary depending on the type of post. At an end post the rails extend through the inside of the box. At a corner, the rails of one section run long while the rails of the adjacent section are short and butt against the longer rails. In a continuous run of fence, the rails meet at the post centerlines.

Preassemble the rail and picket sections, securing each picket with two screws at each rail (**Fig. 4**). Use a piece of plywood with stops attached to locate the rails. Then use spacer blocks to position the remaining pickets.

The Posts

Rip 1x6 pine to 5 in. wide for the wider post faces. Cut two 5-in.-wide pieces and two 1x4 pieces to length for each post. Use the chamfer bit and router table to shape the stopped chamfer on the wider pieces as shown. Then cut the rail notches with a sabre saw. Screw two 1x4 pieces to a 5 in. piece to make three-sided posts (**Fig. 5**). Bore angled screw pilot holes so that the screw heads miss the chamfers. Countersink the holes slightly.

Cut the top 4x4 blocks to length and shape the ends with a miter saw. We used cedar for the top blocks because it was dry and dimensionally stable. If you use pressure-treated stock, you may need to trim the 4x4s with a power plane or hand plane so that the blocks fit the 3½-in.-sq. box openings. Build a jig to rout the recess around each block as shown. Attach each top block to a post with screws driven through on two adjacent sides (**Fig. 6**).

Make the collar stock by ripping 5/4 pine to the angle shown. Miter each collar piece to length and assemble three-sided collars with screws and exterior glue. Slide each partial collar in place from the open side of the post, align it, and secure one side with screws (**Fig. 7**). Then add the fourth

collar piece on each post and screw the collar to the box sides.

Use an ogee bit to rout the post cap trim in 5/4 pine, miter the trim, and install three sides around the box post.

Cut the 4x4 core posts to length, check that they will fit in the box cavities, and plane the faces if necessary. Place each in its hole and use a line level to locate the notch positions. Cut the notches by making a series of cuts with a circular saw and removing the waste with a chisel (**Fig. 8**). Check that the bottom of each box post will end at the correct height above the ground, and trim if necessary. Secure the posts to the 4x4 cores with four screws on two adjacent sides.

Installation and Finish

After priming the posts, place them in their holes with open sides facing the inside of the fence. Then clamp a picket/rail assembly to each pair of posts. Screw the bottom rail of each section to the notch in the 4x4 core post (**Fig. 9**).

Fig. 5 *Assemble the three-sided post boxes. Bore screw pilot holes and drive the screws at a slight angle so that the heads miss the post chamfers.*

Fig. 6 *After routing the recess around each block, install the three-sided posts and secure them with a screw on two adjacent sides.*

Fig. 8 *Cut the 4x4 post notches by making a series of kerfs with a circular saw. Then remove the waste with a sharp chisel.*

Fig. 9 *With the posts resting in their holes, install the picket/rail assemblies. Screw the bottom rails to the 4x4 posts, then plumb and align the fence.*

Use braces screwed to stakes to hold the posts upright in the holes. Plumb each post and sight down the fence to make sure they're aligned. Backfill the holes, tamping down the soil.

Install the remaining post sides with screws driven into the existing post boxes, post cores, top blocks, and upper rails. Cover all screw heads with exterior-grade wood filler, and nail the remaining piece of trim at the top. Build each gate as a typical fence section, except with end pickets flush with each pair of rail ends. Position the picket tops to create a concave curve and screw them to the rails. Cut a diagonal brace to fit, secure it to the rails with 2-in. No. 12 screws, and screw the pickets to the brace. Apply a bead of paintable silicone caulk to the gap around the post collar and along all mitered seams. Attach the gates with heavy-duty tee hinges, using 2-in. screws where the hinge screw holes are over the fence rails (**Fig. 10**). Fill and sand all remaining holes. We finished our fence with an acrylic primer followed by semi-gloss acrylic white paint.

Fig. 10 *Clamp support sticks to the gate to help align it with the fence. Use 2-in. screws to secure the hinges to the fence rails.*

Garden Helper

You'll roll right through the toughest jobs in your yard with this handy garden cart.

Any gardener knows what a chore it can be to haul materials around the yard. Whether you're moving plants, bags of fertilizer and seed, or tools, it is a relief to have a convenient way to move materials. Now you do, with this sturdy garden cart. In designing our cart, we combined utility with good looks. We built it out of mahogany marine plywood, finished with a tough exterior polyurethane to resist moisture. And we fastened the plywood panels using aluminum channel, so it would be lightweight. But don't be fooled: It's built to take whatever punishment you want to deal out.

*Key*POINTS

TIME
Prep Time	4 hours
Shop Time	6 hours
Assembly Time	6 hours

EFFORT
Skill Level	basic
Maintenance	none
Assistance	none

COST / BENEFITS
Expense: moderate
- Handy garden helper that will **pay for itself** in use.
- **Rugged construction** ensures many years of faithful use.

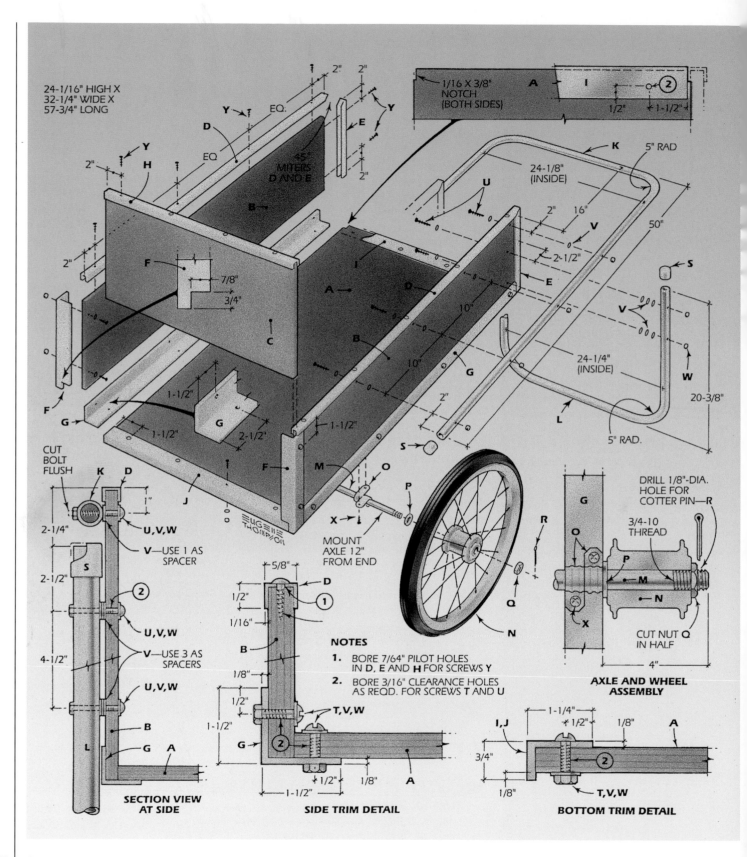

24-1/16" HIGH X
32-1/4" WIDE X
57-3/4" LONG

1/16 X 3/8"
NOTCH
(BOTH SIDES)

A I ②
1/2" 1-1/2"

Y 2" 2"
EQ.
D
Y E
EQ.
45°
MITERS
D AND E
B
H
2"
2"
F
7/8"
3/4"
C
F
G
1-1/2"
G
1-1/2" 2-1/2"

K
5" RAD
24-1/8"
(INSIDE)
U
2" 16"
V
2-1/2"
E
S
V
W
24-1/4"
(INSIDE)
10"
G
L
5" RAD.
20-3/8"

A
I
B
D
G
10"
2"
1-1/2"
F
M
O
X
MOUNT
AXLE 12"
FROM END
P
S
N
R
Q

CUT
BOLT
FLUSH
K D
1"
2-1/4"
S
②
2-1/2"
U,V,W
V—USE 1 AS
SPACER
U,V,W
V—USE 3 AS
SPACERS
4-1/2"
U,V,W
B
G A
L

**SECTION VIEW
AT SIDE**

5/8"
D
1/2"
①
1/16"
B
1/8"
1/2"
1-1/2"
G
②
T,V,W
1/2" 1/8"
1-1/2"
A

NOTES
1. BORE 7/64" PILOT HOLES
   IN D, E AND H FOR SCREWS Y
2. BORE 3/16" CLEARANCE HOLES
   AS REQD. FOR SCREWS T AND U

SIDE TRIM DETAIL

G
O
P
M
N
X
DRILL 1/8"-DIA.
HOLE FOR
COTTER PIN—R
3/4-10
THREAD
CUT NUT Q
IN HALF
4"

**AXLE AND WHEEL
ASSEMBLY**

1-1/4"
I,J
1/2"
1/8"
A
3/4"
②
1/8"
T,V,W

BOTTOM TRIM DETAIL

The cart's woodworking is not difficult. The wooden parts are cut to size and then fastened with aluminum angle stock. The metalwork is also straightforward. The cart has two panels—front and back—that slide in and out to make use more convenient.

Building the Cart Body

Although we built the cart body from mahogany marine plywood, you can use marine fir plywood or pressure-treated plywood. Begin construction by laying out the cart pieces on the plywood sheet. Support the plywood on a sawhorse, and clamp a straightedge to the panel to guide the saw when cutting the panels to size (**Fig. 1**).

Next, smooth the ends of the plywood panels using a belt sander or a sanding block and 120- and 220-grit sandpaper. Apply the finish to the plywood panels before the cart is assembled, so that even the covered areas will be protected. Drive finish nails into the panel ends and suspend the panels between sawhorses (**Fig. 2**). Apply the finish.

Next, cut the 1½ x 1½-in. angle stock. Because it's hard to see a layout mark on the aluminum surface, put a piece of masking tape over the angle stock, and mark your cutlines on the tape with a pen. Clamp the angle firmly in a vise, and

make the cut (**Fig. 3**). Cut just to the waste side of the line and then remove burrs and square the cut if necessary using a file. Cut the notches in the front piece of the angle stock.

Put another piece of tape along the angle stock, and mark for the pilot holes along the length of the workpiece. Bolt a fence to the drill-press table, and then clamp the angle stock to the fence to support it while drilling the holes (**Fig. 4**).

Cut the ½-in. channel stock to length for the top and edge of the side panels. Next, cut the miters on the pieces by laying them in a miter box supported on a piece of ½-in.-thick scrap (**Fig. 5**). File off any burrs after the miters are cut.

Drill the pilot holes in the ½-in. channel stock in the same

Materials List

Key	No.	Size and description (use)
A	1	½ x 23 x 41½" mahogany plywood (bottom)
B	2	½ x 12 x 41¹/₁₆" mahogany plywood (side)
C	1	½ x 13½ x 23¹⁵/₁₆" mahogany plywood (end)
D	2	½ x 41⅛" aluminum channel (side top trim)
E	2	½ x 12¹³/₁₆" aluminum channel (side end trim)
F	2	1½ x 1½ x 11¹¹/₁₆" aluminum angle (corner trim)
G	2	1½ x 1½ x 39¾" aluminum angle (side bottom trim)
H	1	½ x 23¹⁵/₁₆" aluminum channel (end trim)
I	1	¾ x 1¼ x 22⅞" aluminum angle (bottom trim)
J	1	¾ x 1¼ x 23" aluminum angle (bottom trim)
K	1	¾"-dia. x 120" metallic tubing (handle)
L	1	¾"-dia. x 120" metallic tubing (leg)
M	1	¾"-dia. x 32¼" cold-rolled steel bar stock (axle)
N	2	1¾ x 20"-dia. wheel
O	4	1"-dia. conduit strap
P	2	¾"-inside-dia. washer
Q	2	¾" 10 hexnut
R	2	⅛ x 1¼" cotter pin
S	4	1"-inside-dia. plastic cap
T	28	¾" x 10-32 rh machine screw
U	12	2" x 10-32 rh machine screw
V	60	No. 10 washer
W	40	No. 10-32 hexnut
X	4	½" No. 8 self-tapping screw
Y	16	¾" No. 6 self-tapping screw

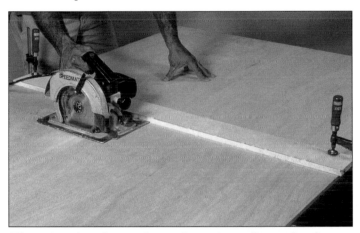

Fig. 1 *Cut the plywood panels to size using a circular saw. Carefully clamp a guide to the panel and run the saw along it.*

Fig. 2 *Suspend the plywood panels between sawhorses. Apply the exterior polyurethane finish on the panels' faces and edges.*

Fig. 3 *Apply tape to the angle stock and mark the cutline on the tape. Clamp the angle stock firmly in a vise while cutting it.*

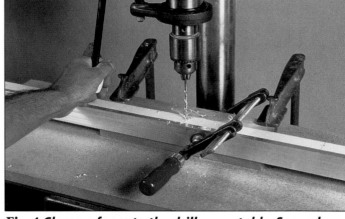

Fig. 4 *Clamp a fence to the drill-press table. Securely clamp the angle stock to the fence to support the stock while drilling.*

Fig. 5 *Cut miters on the ends of the channel stock using a miter box and hacksaw. Support the channel walls with a scrap block.*

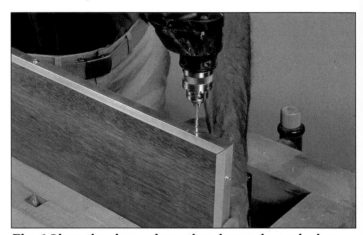

Fig. 6 *Place the channels on the plywood panel edges. Bore the pilot holes for the screws that will hold the channels in place.*

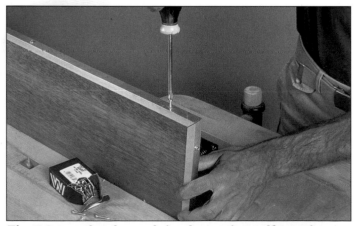

Fig. 7 *Screw the channels in place using self-tapping roundhead screws. These screws will hold firmly in marine plywood.*

Fig. 8 *File a small bevel on the miter corners where the channels meet. If you don't have a fine file, use a sanding block.*

manner as with the angle stock. Next, install the channel stock on the top and back edges of the side panels. Bore ⁷⁄₆₄-in.-dia. holes into the panel before driving the screws (**Fig. 6**). Fasten the channel to the panel using ¾-in. No. 6 roundhead self-tapping screws (**Fig. 7**). Remove the sharp corner where the channel is mitered using a file (**Fig. 8**). If you lack a fine file, use a sanding block and fine abrasive paper.

Place a bottom angle in position on a side panel, and clamp it in place with a scrap block behind it. Use the angle as a template to bore pilot holes in the panel (**Fig. 9**). Fasten the angle stock to the panel using machine screws, so that the screw heads are on the panel's inside (**Fig. 10**).

Cut a piece of ¾ x 1¼-in. angle stock to length for the front end of the cart bottom. Drill the pilot holes through both the angle and bottom panel, and install it with the screw heads on the inside of the panel and the washers and nuts on the bottom. Lay the bottom panel upside down on the workbench, and place one of the sides in position (**Fig. 11**). Bore pilot holes through the bottom. Again, use a backer block to prevent splitting out the veneer where the bit exits the hole. Screw the bottom and side together.

Cut the remaining piece of ¾ x 1¼-in. angle stock to length for the open side of the cart. Drill the pilot holes through it, and fasten it in place. Test fit the sliding plywood panel (**Fig. 12**). If the panel binds slightly, apply a bit of wax or Teflon spray to both panel ends and the angle stock that forms the track. Cut and apply the ½-in. channel stock along the top edge of the sliding panel.

Wheels, Axle, Handle, and Stand

The axle is made from a piece of ¾-in.-dia. cold-rolled bar steel. You can cut it to length with a hacksaw, but it's easier to specify the length and have the material supplier cut it.

Cut the threads on the axle using a ¾-in.-10 die (¾ in. dia., 10 threads per inch) held in a die stock. Clamp the axle upright in a vise and position the die over the end of the axle. Apply some cutting oil to the bar, and slowly advance the die about one-eighth of a turn. Then reverse direction to clear the chips from the die's cutting edges. Proceed until you have threaded 1 in. of the axle (**Fig. 13**). Repeat this procedure on the other end. If you don't have a tap-and-die set or don't feel comfortable doing this, most hardware stores and large home centers will cut the threads for a nominal fee.

Position the axle on the cart bottom, and fasten it in place using two conduit straps at each end of the axle. Drill pilot holes through the angle stock, and attach the straps using ½-in. No. 8 screws (**Fig. 14**).

We used heavy-duty spoked wheels. Slide a ¾-in. washer over each end of the axle, and slide the wheel against the washer. The wheels are held in place by a ¾-in. nut, but because the nut is too thick for this application, you must cut it in half. Clamp the nut in a vise, and cut it in half with a hacksaw (**Fig. 15**). Use a file to clean up the cut surface and

Fig. 9 *Clamp a scrap block and an angle to a side panel. Bore pilot holes through the panel, the angle stock, and the channel.*

Fig. 10 *Attach the angle stock to both cart sides and the bottom with machine screws. The screw heads go inside the cart.*

Fig. 11 *Lay the bottom panel upside down on the bench. Then position the side panels, and bore the screw pilot holes.*

Fig. 12 *Test fit the sliding plywood panel. If it sticks a little, apply lubricant such as Teflon spray to the panel edges and to the channels.*

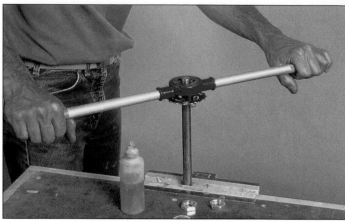

Fig. 13 *Cut the threads on the axle with a tap and die. Take small turns, back off, and then cut some more. Use plenty of cutting oil.*

Fig. 14 *Attach the axle to the cart bottom using electrical conduit straps and screws. Use two straps at each axle end.*

Fig. 15 *Clamp the nut in a vise and then slowly saw it in half. Clean up the saw marks with a fine file or a sanding block.*

Fig. 16 *Temporarily install the wheels and nuts. Dimple the axle using a centerpunch to mark the location of the cotter pin hole.*

Fig. 17 *Clamp the axle and support block to the drill-press table. Use a good deal of cutting oil when drilling the cotter pin hole.*

remove any rough edges. Tighten the nut until the wheel is held in place without any side-to-side play.

Next, install a cotter pin through the axle to hold the nut in place. To mark the pin hole, dimple the axle with a centerpunch (**Fig. 16**). Remove the nuts, wheels, and axle. Place the axle on a support block. This block is just a piece of scrap with a shallow ¾-in.-wide channel cut into it. Clamp the block and the axle to the drill-press table. Set the drill press to its slowest speed, apply plenty of machine oil to the bar stock, and drill the hole (**Fig. 17**).

The drill bit will probably leave a burr where it exits the bar stock. Do not use a file to remove this burr as it will damage the axle threads. Instead, clamp the axle in a vise and use the die, with plenty of cutting oil, to remove the burrs. Reinstall the axle on the cart. Install the cotter pins through the axle. Bend the legs of the cotter pin to the side with a pair of pliers (**Fig. 18**). Make the leg and handle from ¾-in. electrical conduit. This material is quite a bit easier to bend without kinks than aluminum tubing. The conduit is bent using a jig made from scrap plywood. If you don't want to make the jig, you can rent a conduit bender to do the job.

To make the jig, trace the desired radius on two pieces of panel stock. Cut the radius using a sabre saw, then use a router to cut a ½-in.-rad. cove along the shaped edge. Screw the two pieces of panel stock together so that the coves oppose each other. This makes a bending form with a 1-in.-dia. cove along its edge. Mark the beginning and end of the bend on the form. Use the marks and the dimensions in the plan to make the bend in the tubing at the correct place. Mark the tubing with a pencil and align the tubing with the marks on the form. In bending the handle, the entire 10-ft. length of tubing is used. The leg, however, is bent to shape, and the excess material is cut off. You should bend the leg and then cut it to length. Bending the tubing at full length allows you to take advantage of the leverage the tubing provides (**Fig. 19**). With both the leg and the handle, the form is clamped securely to the bench and the tubing is clamped to the form.

Press the plastic furniture caps on the ends of the leg and the handle. We bought these caps at the local hardware store. If the caps are difficult to press into place, soak them in hot water for a few minutes to soften and expand them. Next, drill pilot holes through the leg and handle for mounting screws. Clamp them on the cart and use the holes in the leg and handle as a guide when boring the pilot holes into the cart body. Use scrap blocks to prevent the drill bit from splintering the plywood as it exits.

Use 2-in. No. 10-32 screws (32 threads per inch) to install the legs and handle on the cart (**Fig. 20**). Use three washers between the leg and cart sides, and use one washer between the handle and cart side to maintain proper spacing. The 2-in. screws are longer than necessary for this job, so cut off the excess screw with a hacksaw. Use a file to smooth the cut end of each screw.

Fig. 18 *Clean off the burrs on the axle. Install the axle, washer, wheel, nut, and pin. Use a pair of pliers to bend the legs of the cotter pin.*

Fig. 19 *Align the marks on the tubing with those on the jig, and clamp the bending jig securely to the workbench.*

Fig. 20 *Cover tubing ends with furniture caps. Use three washers between the leg and the sides. Cut off the excess screw shaft, and file it smooth.*

Glossary

A

Actual Dimension:
The true dimension of a stock piece of lumber after it has been cut, smoothed, and dried. Usually less than the stock or rough measurements.

Air-Dried:
The process of drying wood naturally, either outside or in a controlled environment inside, as opposed to kiln drying.

Annual Growth Rings:
The rings of new tissue accumulated as a tree ages, and that show as semicircles in the endgrain of a board.

Arbor:
An outdoor structure with two sides and an overhead support, usually with lattice or other open-pattern construction. Used as a decorative garden structure, and to support climbing plants.

Auger:
A power tool used to dig post holes quickly and efficiently.

Apron:
The top frame under a tabletop, to which the legs are fastened.

B

Backsaw:
A handy tool with a metal bracket that holds a blade with very fine teeth. This saw is generally used for fine finishing work.

Bead:
The term used for quarter-round molding, but also for the decorative edge that is sometimes routed along a workpiece or board.

Beam:
The piece of lumber that supports joists, as with decks.

Bird's Mouth:
The specialized cut that allows a rafter to sit securely on a cap plate.

Bench Dog:
A post that is made of metal or wood and sits in any of several holes in a workbench to secure a workpiece. Bench dogs are often just simple pegs, or can be more complex, with spring mechanisms to help hold them in place.

Biscuit:
Also called a plate, this is a thin oval wood disc used to join workpieces together.

Block Plane:
A useful, smaller plane used for taking boards down along the endgrain.

C

Box Joint:
A type of corner construction where the two joining pieces are attached by overlapping, long, thin tongues in the ends of each board.

Brad:
Any headless finishing nail less than 1 in. long.

Butt Joint:
A very simple corner construction, in which two boards abut each other at a right angle.

Caliper:
A measuring device that allows you to re-create sections of a pattern or template along a lathe-turned leg or other workpiece.

Cap Plate:
A 2x4 or other board used as an additional layer on top of the top plate of a wall.

Case-Hardening:
Condition in which the outside of the wood dries much quicker than the inside, leading to defects in the finished boards.

Caul:
A flat surface, such as a pad, used between clamp jaws and the workpiece, both to distribute the force of the clamp evenly over the surface, and to protect the surface from marring.

Chalkline:
A retractable string coated with chalk that is used to precisely mark a line along a surface for cutting or alignment of other workpieces.

Chord:
A roof member that connects and supports opposing rafters.

Closed Coat:
Abrasive covering all of the sheet, so that it sands efficiently but can clog easily. Closed coat papers are used for finish sanding.

Compass:
A device for marking circles on a surface; can be a manufactured tool with adjustable legs joined at a pivot point, or a shopmade unit consisting of a board and drawing point that are rotated around a central pivot point.

Compass

Crook:
A defect in a board in which the ends fold up.

Crosscut:
Cut that is sawn across the board.

Cupping:
A defect in a board in which the edges pull toward each other.

D

Deck Height:
The measurement from the top of the decking to grade.

Deflection:
The sag or general bending in a support member, such as a joist, when it is placed under a weight load.

Dowel Center:
A round metal marker with a point, placed in a dowel hole to position the companion hole in the workpiece to be joined.

Dressed Size:
The measurement of a board after it has been planed.

E

Edge Guide:
A metal guide on a power tool, such as a power saw or lathe, used to guide the workpiece.

Endgrain:
The rough, ringed pattern end of a board.

F

Fascia:
Boards used to cover the ends of the rafters at the eaves.

Featherboard:
A board with extensions, used to hold another board in position while it is being cut, routed, or joined.

Flatsawn:
A type of lumber cut in which the board is cut at less than a 45° angle to the annual growth rings. You can determine flatsawn boards by looking at the endgrain—if the rings are parallel to the edges, the board is flatsawn. Flatsawn boards are considered inferior to quartersawn, and are consequently less expensive.

Forstner Bit:
Special drill bit that makes an extremely clean hole with a cleared-out bottom.

Footing:
Solid base of concrete or packed gravel that forms the foundation for posts, or under steps.

Free Water:
Moisture in a board that will escape while drying.

Frost Line:
The lowest level at which the soil in your area freezes.

G

Gable:
Triangular construction at the end of a pitched roof.

Gazebo:
Usually an octagonal structure, with a roof, open sides, and floor set high up to offer the best view all around.

Glue Joint:
A joint created by grooving the end of one board so that it can be glued securely to the edge of another board.

Green Wood:
Freshly cut boards that have not completely dried yet.

Gum or Pitch Pocket:
A small area of concentrated sap resin in a piece of lumber.

H

Heartwood:
Good wood found in a log between the soft pith center and the outer sapwood. Generally considered desirable for its concentrations of resins, which make it more rot- and insect-resistant.

Hip Rafter:
Rafters placed diagonally from the roof ridge to a corner of a building.

Hurricane Ties:
A method of using connectors to tie rafters to top or cap plates.

J

Jig:
A form that holds a workpiece in place for modification or assembly.

Joiner:
The table-mounted power tool that removes wood from boards to true them.

Joists:
The framing members that are aligned on a beam or wall to create the support structure for a floor or roof.

Joists

K

Kerf:
The cut channel left behind by a saw blade.

Key Block:
A block of wood situated at the intersection of the rafters in a gazebo.

Kickback:
The dangerous reaction when a saw binds on a piece of wood and flexes it back toward the in-feed.

Kick Pad:
A piece of wood or metal used across the bottom of the door, to protect the door from boots or other damage.

Kiln Dried:
The process of artificially drying lumber in ovens under controlled condition, to speed the drying process.

L

Lagbolt:
An oversized bolt used to secure one large structural framing piece against another.

Lagscrew:
The screw equivalent of a lag bolt, often used for affixing a header against a solid piece, such as house framing.

M

Medium Density Fiberboard (MDF):
A type of tempered hardboard, made with a smooth finish so that it can be used in fine applications, such as cabinet making.

Mortise:
Shaped hole cut in one piece of wood to accept a mating "tenon" shaped on another piece of wood.

N

Nominal Size:
The standard size a piece of lumber is referred to as, such as 2x4, but that usually does not reflect it's finished size (see Actual Size).

O

On Center:
The measurement from the center of a board as placed, to the center of the next board as placed.

Open Coat:
A type of abrasive sheet in which coverage is less than 70%, allowing the sanding of large, loose particles, such as paint, because the paper is less likely to clog.

Out-Feed:
The side on which the board exits a power tool, such as a table saw or planer.

P

Particleboard:
A heavy, dense type of plywood usually used for internal purposes, such as walls or countertops.

Pitch:
Sticky resinous sap; also used to describe the number of teeth per inch of a saw blade.

Pilot Bit:
A special router bit that is constructed with a piece at the end of the cutting blade, which follows the edge of the workpiece to guide the cut.

Pith:
The center section of a tree, which is very soft wood.

Plainsawn:
See Flatsawn.

Plumb:
Quality of being perfectly perpendicular to level ground.

Plate:
Another term for a biscuit (see Biscuit).

Plunge Router:
A special router with a frame that allows the router head to be pushed straight down into the workpiece.

Plunge Router

Proud:
Sitting just above a surface.

Push Stick:
A scrap piece of wood or board used to push a workpiece through a power saw or other power tool where safety is an issue.

Q

Quartersawn:
The process of cutting boards perpendicular to the annual growth ring, making these boards higher quality than flatsawn boards.

R

Rabbet:
Similar to a dado—a channel cut in the edge of a board.

Rail:
The horizontal board used between the stiles or other vertical pieces of a door frame.

Rafter:
The vertical member that runs from the ridge of a building to the cap or top plate to create the support structure for the roof.

Rafter Tail:
The end length of the rafter beyond the wall of the structure.

Ready Mix:
Concrete mixed in a truck and run out in bulk, used to lay large foundations or footings, or entire patios.

Ridge:
The top peak of a roof.

Rim Joist:
The joist that is placed on the outside perimeter of a project, such as a deck.

Rip:
A type of cut that runs the length of a board.

Rise:
The distance from the top of the wall to the top of the roof.

S

Sapwood:
The live wood from the outside of the log, usually lighter in color and containing more blemishes than heartwood.

Scarf Joint:
A joint that involves cutting two boards at an angle to allow them to be bonded together.

Seasoning:
The aging and drying of new lumber to improve its quality for woodworking purposes.

Slope:
The measurement of how far the roof rises in a foot of horizontal space.

Spading:
The practice of sticking a straight shovel or spade at an angle into newly laid concrete to remove air bubbles.

Starved Joint:
A joint that is weak because not enough glue was used in bonding it.

Stickers:
Strips of wood used to separate layers of drying wood.

Story Stick:
A rough measuring device, made of a stick or wood scrap, which is marked with measurements off of one workpiece, to be used on another workpiece.

Stile:
The board in a door frame attached to the horizontal rails.

Snipe:
An accidental blemish made at the end of a workpiece as it goes through a joiner.

Spline:
A piece of wood that is used in a grooved slot to create a joint.

Squeeze-Out:
Excess glue that is forced out between two pieces of wood being joined when they are clamped.

Surfacing:
The process of preparing a piece of lumber for sale. Surfaced lumber has been planed on most or all of its edges and faces.

T

Tearout:
Fraying or splintering of a board at the end of a crosscut.

Tempered Hardboard:
Special type of fiberboard that has been treated to make it more durable and moisture resistant, making it good for outbuildings and some other outdoor projects.

Template Guide:
A router jig that is mounted on the bottom of the router to allow it to follow a set profile.

Tenon:
A shaped tongue created on the edge or end of one piece of wood to mate with a companion hole, or mortise, on another piece of wood.

Tenons

Toenail:
To nail a board to a board at an angle.

V

Veneer-Core Plywood:
Plywood made of overlapping sheets of veneer, providing interesting and varying grain patterns.

W

Wane:
The term used to describe a lessening of material near the end of a board, or the presence of bark at that point.

Warp:
Any of a number of defects that cause the lumber to vary from straight and flat.

Wash Coat:
The preliminary coat of a finish, such as paint, used to prime the surface and seal the wood pores.

Picture Credits

GARDEN HIDEAWAY (Pg. 10):
Lead Photo: Neal Barrett;
Illustration: Eugene Thompson;
Step Photos: Neal Barrett.

SUPER SHED (Pg. 18):
Lead Photo: Neal Barrett;
Illustration: Eugene Thompson;
Step Photos: Neal Barrett.

PLANTER PLACE (Pg. 26):
Lead Photo: Carl Weese;
Illustration: Eugene Thompson;
Step Photos: Joseph Truini.

SHADY SHELTER (Pg. 34):
Lead Photo: Mark F. Molesky;
Illustration: Dyck Fledderus;
Step Photos: William Winans.

BACKYARD BARN (Pg. 42):
Lead Photo: Geoffrey Gross;
Illustration: Eugene Thompson;
Step Photos: Geoffrey Gross.

WASTE NOT (Pg. 52):
Lead Photo: Rosario Capotosto;
Illustration: Eugene Thompson;
Step Photos: Rosario Capotosto.

BASIC BEAUTY (Pg. 62):
Lead Photo: Merle Henkenius;
Illustration: Eugene Thompson;
Step Photos: Merle Henkenius.

GARAGE OVERFLOW (Pg. 70):
Lead Photo: Merle Henkenius;
Illustration: Eugene Thompson;
Step Photos: Merle Henkenius.

SMALL ADDITION (Pg. 78):
Lead Photo: Merle Henkenius;
Illustration: Eugene Thompson;
Step Photos: Merle Henkenius.

UNDER COVER (Pg. 88):
Lead Photo: Neal Barrett;
Illustration: Eugene Thompson;
Step Photos: Neal Barrett.

BENCH MARK (Pg. 98):
Lead Photo: Rosario Capotosto;
Illustration: Eugene Thompson;
Step Photos: Rosario Capotosto.

LAID BACK (Pg. 108):
Lead Photo: Neal Barrett;
Illustration: Eugene Thompson;
Step Photos: Neal Barrett.

DINING OUT (Pg. 116):
Lead Photo: J.R. Rost;
Illustration: Eugene Thompson;
Step Photos: Neal Barrett.

REFINED RECLINE (Pg. 124):
Lead Photo: John Griebsch;
Illustration: Eugene Thompson;
Step Photos: Neal Barrett.

SITTING AROUND (Pg. 130):
Lead Photo: Neal Barrett;
Illustration: Eugene Thompson;
Step Photos: Neal Barrett.

SWING TIME (Pg. 138):
Lead Photo: Neal Barrett;
Illustration: Eugene Thompson;
Step Photos: Neal Barrett.

PORCH CLASSIC (Pg. 146):
Lead Photo: J.R. Rost;
Illustration: Eugene Thompson;
Step Photos: Neal Barrett.

GARDEN GRACE (Pg. 156):
Lead Photo: Neal Barrett;
Illustration: Eugene Thompson;
Step Photos: Neal Barrett.

SCREEN GEM (Pg. 166):
Lead Photo: Neal Barrett;
Illustration: Eugene Thompson;
Step Photos: Neal Barrett.

FANTASTIC FENCES (Pg. 172):
Lead Photo: Peter Tenzer;
Illustration: Eugene Thompson;
Step Photos: Eugene Thompson.

PRETTY PLANTER (Pg. 180):
Lead Photo: John Griebsch;
Illustration: Eugene Thompson;
Step Photos: Neal Barrett.

FENCING LESSONS (Pg. 186):
Lead Photo: Thomas Klenck;
Illustration: Eugene Thompson;
Step Photos: Thomas Klenck.

GARDEN HELPER (Pg. 192):
Lead Photo: Neal Barrett;
Illustration: Eugene Thompson;
Step Photos: Neal Barrett.

Conversion Chart

US STANDARD TO METRIC

US Standard = Metric

Inches x 2.54   = centimeters

Feet x 30.48   = centimeters

Yards x .9144   = meters

Sq. in. x 6.452   = square cm

Sq. ft. x 929   = square cm

Sq. yd. x 8361   = square cm

Ounce x 28.85   = gram

Pound x .45   = kilogram

Common Approx. Conversions

$3/8$ in. = 1 cm

1 in.   = 2.5 cm

2 in.   = 5 cm

2 in.   = 6.5 cm

1 ft.   = 30 cm

Metric Conversion Tables

Metric Measurement	Imperial Equivalent	Imperial Measurement	Metric Equivalent
1mm	$1/32$ in.	$1/8$ in.	3.2mm
2mm	$1/16$ in.	$1/4$ in.	6.4mm
3mm	$1/8$ in.	$3/8$ in.	9.5mm
6mm	$1/4$ in.	$1/2$ in.	13mm
7mm	$9/32$ in. ($1/4$")	$5/8$ in.	16mm
10mm	$13/32$ in. ($3/8$")	$3/4$ in.	19mm
2cm (20mm)	$3/4$ in.	$7/8$ in.	2.2cm
3cm	$1^3/16$ in.	1 in.	2.5cm
4cm	$1^9/16$ in.	$1^1/4$ in.	3.2cm
5cm	2 in.	$1^1/2$ in.	3.8cm
6cm	$2^3/8$ in.	$1^3/4$ in.	4.4cm
7cm	$2^3/4$ in.	2 in.	5.1cm
8cm	$3^1/8$ in.	$1^1/4$ in.	5.7cm
9cm	$3^1/2$ in.	$2^1/2$ in.	6.4cm
10cm	$3^{15}/16$ in. (4")	$2^3/4$ in.	7.0cm
15cm	$5^7/8$ in.	3 in.	7.6cm
20cm	$7^7/8$ in.	$3^1/4$ in.	8.3cm
25cm	$9^{13}/16$ in.	$3^1/2$ in.	8.9cm
30cm	$11^{13}/16$ in.	$3^3/4$ in.	9.5cm
35cm	$13^3/4$ in.	4 in.	10.2cm
40cm	$15^5/8$ in.	$4^1/2$ in.	11.4cm
42cm	$16^1/2$ in.	5 in.	14.0cm

Index